CITY KIDS, CITY TEACHERS

City Kids, City Teachers

REPORTS FROM THE FRONT ROW

EDITED BY WILLIAM AYERS
AND PATRICIA FORD

THE NEW PRESS
New York

LIBRARY OF CONGRESS CATALOGING-IN-PUBLICATION DATA

Ayers, William, 1944–
    City kids, city teachers / William Ayers and Patricia Ford.
        p.   cm.
    Includes bibliographical references and index.
    ISBN 1-56584-328-2 (HC). ISBN 1-56584-051-8 (PB).
    1. Education, Urban—United States. 2. Socially handicapped children—Education—
        Social aspects—United States. 3. Cities and towns—United States—Social
        conditions.   I. Ford, Patricia.   II. Title.
LC5131.A94   1996
371.19'348'0973—dc20   95-40353
CIP

Published in the United States by THE NEW PRESS, NEW YORK
Distributed by W. W. NORTON & COMPANY, INC., NEW YORK

ESTABLISHED IN 1990 AS A MAJOR ALTERNATIVE TO THE LARGE, COMMERCIAL
PUBLISHING HOUSES, THE NEW PRESS IS A FULL-SCALE NONPROFIT AMERICAN BOOK
PUBLISHER OUTSIDE OF THE UNIVERSITY PRESSES. THE PRESS IS OPERATED
EDITORIALLY IN THE PUBLIC INTEREST, RATHER THAN FOR PRIVATE GAIN;
IT IS COMMITTED TO PUBLISHING IN INNOVATIVE WAYS WORKS OF EDUCATIONAL,
CULTURAL, AND COMMUNITY VALUE THAT, DESPITE THEIR INTELLECTUAL MERITS,
MIGHT NOT NORMALLY BE COMMERCIALLY VIABLE. THE NEW PRESS'S EDITORIAL
OFFICES ARE LOCATED AT THE CITY UNIVERSITY OF NEW YORK.

Book design by HALL SMYTH
Composition by DIX!
Production management by KIM WAYMER
Printed in the UNITED STATES OF AMERICA

97 98 99   9 8 7 6 5 4 3 2

This book is dedicated to five city kids:

—TIFFANY, STEPHANIE, CHESA, MALIK, AND ZAYD—

and to the memory of SARAH ELIZABETH FORD,
Pat's mother and first teacher, who touched those around her
with wisdom, strength, courage, and compassion.

LIFT EVERY VOICE AND SING

Lift every voice and sing
Till earth and heaven ring,
Ring with the harmonies of Liberty;
Let our rejoicing rise
High as the listening skies,
Let it resound loud as the rolling sea.
Sing a song full of the faith that the dark
past has taught us,
Sing a song full of the hope that the
present has brought us,
Facing the rising sun of our new day begun
Let us march on till victory is won.

Stony the road we trod,
Bitter the chastening rod,
Felt in the days when hope unborn
had died;
Yet with a steady beat,
Have not our weary feet
Come to the place for which our fathers
sighed?
We have come over a way that with tears
has been watered,
We have come, treading our path through
the blood of the slaughtered,
Out from the gloomy past,
Till now we stand at last
Where the white gleam of our bright star
is cast . . .

—*James Weldon Johnson*

CONTENTS

Contents

III. *City Teachers*

To read this book is to get a sense of siege—of children and of the cities in which they live under relentless attack. I feel the pain, and the anguish, and the fear, particularly in the words of the children. Yet, I also find consolation, as well as inspiration and determination. The schools of America are where much of the war to redeem America must and will be fought. It's good for the soldier to know where the battlefield is.

This book continually demonstrates that even in the welter of alarm and misjudgment, malice and racial spite, cultural obtuseness and official coldness of heart, all is not lost. The battle, though already joined, is far from over. There's a pressing need for troops and volunteers. We who care still have a chance to win, but to do that we must enlist now in the great cause. Hurry up, get smart, and get moving. This book gives invaluable information. It's intellectually handy, a knapsack companion. You can read it as you run.

The technology that was supposed to liberate us, has instead all but abandoned us, leaving behind empty promises stalled among our children like Trojan horses. Children, who should be our culture's most shining exemplars, are now consigned to benign neglect and flagrant inattention. If they are not rescued and defended, all will be lost.

The teacher's urgent mission now is to engage, with the help and inspiration of the very children they teach, in a tough and tender campaign toward not only survival but excellence. These are our marching orders: to save the future by saving those who must inhabit it. If we believe in children—as teachers must—then we must fight to give these children a chance to overcome. That must be our battle plan, our strategic objective.

As we all know, it is quite possible for us simultaneously to love and resent our children. Children, through no fault of their own, stand squarely in our way. Our precious darlings are not the enemy, of course, but an impediment, blocking our view, coming between us and our private yearnings toward prosperity, demanding time and attention we think we cannot spare. Their helplessness and vulnerability make them a burden. They get in the way of our other ambitions. "Where the hell are the teachers? Why haven't they cleaned up this mess?" we cry in pique and anger. In this relentless war of attrition, good teachers conspire always to be where they should be: on the side of the children.

Teaching children is certainly no casual thing. It's an overwhelming expenditure of time, and energy, and love. Teachers cannot invest so heavily and completely in the effort to mold the budding character of children, then walk away. Society will hold the teachers responsible. To preserve the children, teachers must be prepared to go to war, to learn the art of military dissembling. They must smile at what they hate in the bureaucratic outside world, keeping their minds stayed on the secret objective.

When war is declared and the battle is joined, good manners end and civility goes out the window. It is a war not of our choosing, but one we must win at all costs, defeat becomes unthinkable. The teacher who cares must become a soldier. True allies in this war are hard to come by: the families, the schools, religious congregations, the state, and anyone else willing to join the struggle. Most important, though, are the children themselves. Children are natural conspirators against the heartless rigors of the worlds in which they must live. There comes a time when we must forge an alliance with these heroes, enlisting their youth and enthusiasm, strength and glorious imagination. We teach them how to read and write, how to vote and hold a job, but more than that is required. We must teach them not only to think, but to criticize, to conspire—if need be—against stupidity and arrogance, and against the nondemocratic, inhuman ways our society sometimes governs. The students teachers train must be sent back into the world, not only to profit from it, but to improve it.

To wait for the rest of society to come to its senses is futile. Power concedes nothing without a demand, as Frederick Douglass said. Where there is no struggle there is no progress, and, in the case of education, no survival. This struggle may be a physical one, Douglass continued, or a moral one, or it may be both, but it must be a struggle. *City Kids, City Teachers* is, in its own way, a handbook of the principles of combat in that struggle. It calls itself "Reports From the Front Row"; "From the Front Line" would be equally apt. What is needed in this war is organization and determination, understanding and support, and a willingness to sacrifice much, if not all, for the good of the cause.

In this book, our cities' students and teachers share their problems, their prospects, and their plans. It is vital that all of us look deep into these pages, to listen and to learn. The enemies are arrogance, thoughtlessness, and selfishness on one side, hopelessness and helplessness on the other. There is fear and confusion in the ranks of those who want to do better by our children. But the war begins in the mind. Look to these pages for guidance and for light.

Ossie Davis
January 1996

ACKNOWLEDGMENTS

No worthwhile work is an autonomous accomplishment or act of splendid isolation. All human effort is in some sense an expression of our intense interconnectedness, our mutuality. This book is no exception.

We are grateful to be living in a time of upheaval and possibility, among a wide range of people of courage and hope. We are conscious that we stand on the shoulders of many others, known and not known; aware, as well, that we draw upon a collective consciousness only partially perceived. Thanks to all, including Joan Anderson, Terry Bailey, LaDonna Barron, Alice Ocrey Brent, Sarah Cohen, Linda Darling-Hammond, Greg Darnieder, Tamara Doig, Brenda Dukes, Norm Fruchter, Sharon Gallowayhall, Michelle Gauthier, Caroline Heller, Vance Henry, Cindy Hughes, Oscar Joseph, Joe Kahn, Mike Klonsky, Susan Klonsky, Herb Kohl, Jonathon Kozol, Rebbekah Levin, Charlie Matthews, Tammy Matthews, Bruce McPherson, Steve Mogge, Craig Nash, Roxanne Owens, Kate Power, Mike Rose, Mara Sapon-Shevin, William Schubert, Michelle Smith, Juanita White, and Tamara Witz.

Thanks to Marilyn Geron for her patience, her care and compassion, and her dedicated hard work.

Thanks to all the caring and thoughtful people at the New Press: Hall Smyth, Grace Farrell, André Schiffrin who pursued the idea for this book, and Ellen Reeves. More than an editor, she has been a teacher, a friend, a co-conspirator.

"What is it," we asked a huge gathering of urban school administrators, "about the presence of large numbers of poor, African-American, or Latino city kids in your schools that makes those places . . ." we paused dramatically, "Wonderful?"

There was a kind of stunned silence. Several looks of disbelief. Some nervous laughter. And then a forceful response: "Come on," said one older man from the front row, his voice ringing, almost angry: "Our jobs are hard enough without you ridiculing us."

The opening question was not meant to ridicule, but to disconnect an unexamined and glib fiction about city kids. It is true that the last word—"wonderful"—sounds a decidedly discordant note. Until then the question hums along quite comfortably, a familiar melody. But when the anticipated last bar—something like "terrible," or "difficult," or, at best, "challenging"—is not delivered, the whole thing sounds out of tune. It is within that jarring discrepancy that we want to begin to think about city kids and city teachers.

We are, each in our own way, city people ourselves. Born to privilege and a suburban family, Bill fled *to* Chicago in the mid-1960s, around the time Pat was born and her mother moved her young family into a rowhouse in the then-hopeful—now infamous—Chicago public housing project called Cabrini-Green. Pat's memories include a strong, nurturing mother, her loving aunt and cousins, a community that held her and helped her grow, a normal neighborhood before it was turned ugly by drugs; she maintains a close link to Cabrini today through family and friends and years of community organizing. (Our stories are told more fully in "Organizing and Teaching," p. 305.) Both of us find in the city real reasons for sadness and anger, but also sources of inspiration and hope. We see the problems, of course, but in the ordinary people we work with, we see the possibilities for transformation as well.

An assumption that sits heavy and dogmatic on most city schools is that there is nothing about the presence of African-American, Latino, or immigrant youngsters—especially in today's environment, black boys—that is deemed valuable, hopeful, or important. Their very presence in school is an encumbrance. They are an obstruction, a handicap, and a burden. If these youngsters are known at all, they are known exclusively by their deficits and their putative inadequacies. Schools tend to focus on the least interesting and simplest of questions. What don't these kids know? What can't they do? School becomes, then, entirely a matter of remediation and repair. Good intentions notwithstanding, feelings of hopelessness and despair define these places for kids and teachers alike.

We were asked recently to look at hundreds of applications filled out by city teachers who had been nominated for an "outstanding teacher" award. One question asked "What is the biggest obstacle in your teaching?" To our amazement nearly half of the respondents answered in one way or another that the *kids* were the biggest obstacle to their teaching. Not everyone just blurted it out—many said things like, "I used to be a better teacher, but kids today have so many problems." Some wrote, "If these kids could only speak English . . ." But it still added up to a powerful message that schools and classrooms would function much, much better if the kids would simply not show up. Picture the perfect city school: the classrooms are always quiet, the cafeteria calm, the hallways orderly. No fights, no hassles, no graffiti. Bells ring, mimeo machines hum, paychecks are delivered. The place is efficient, clean, peaceful. No kids? No problem. In this context even to raise the question of the *value* of city kids is to sound slightly mad.

And yet that is precisely where we begin—with the value of city kids. We reject the notion that city kids (or city teachers or the city itself for that matter) can best be understood as all deficit, all danger. We see, instead, a sense of life, energy, freedom, and hope in the city and in poor, immigrant, and African-American communities. It is our intention to point to possibility: to portray conflicts, contradictions, and complexities, to present the struggle for education in urban settings honestly and fully, and also to look toward an unmapped future whose core demand will be learning to live together, united yet diverse, something being rehearsed in our cities today.

Most city teachers struggle mightily to do a good job in spite of inadequate resources and difficult circumstances. But the structure of most city schools—the strict schedule, the division of knowledge, the press of time, the pretense toward rational efficiency, and the huge numbers of students—leads to a factory-like operation characterized by hierarchy, control, and anonymity which turns teachers into clerks and students into objects to fear and coerce. We do not contend that teaching in the city is *identical* to teaching anywhere (in wealthy suburbs, for example); city teaching is better in some ways, harder in others, interestingly similar and importantly unique.

Most powerful, hopeful learning projects begin with learners, and knowing city kids as learners, discovering them as three-dimensional beings, as fellow creatures, is an important place for teachers to begin. What experiences, knowledge, and skills do kids bring with them to school? What kinds of thought and intelligence is there to challenge and nurture? A sustained engagement with these questions is a basic starting point for city teachers. And it is followed closely by the demand to create an environment for learning that is wide enough and deep enough to nurture and challenge the huge range of students who actually walk through the classroom door (as opposed to the fantasy students, the stereotypes, ingrained in our consciousness from too many years of *Leave it to Beaver* or *Beverly Hills 90210*). This means there must be multiple entry points to learning, a variety of ways to begin, an assortment of pathways to success. And it points toward another complex teaching task: building bridges of understanding from the experience and knowledge youngsters bring with them into the classroom toward deeper and wider ways of knowing—an excruciatingly difficult goal. And this whole dynamic enterprise begins with knowing the student.

City Kids, City Teachers is a book that begins with students, with sketches of city kids in city schools, with portraits of intelligence and creativity enacted in extreme circumstances. The book contains a section of thoughtful commentary on some of the critical issues facing city teachers: language, race, class, culture, violence, and poverty. This section highlights what teachers need to know in order to be thoughtful, caring, and successful. And it circles back to classrooms, ending with city teachers teaching—accounts of classroom life told by teachers themselves in their own voices.

City Kids

PART I

Not that success, for him, is sure,
   infallible.
But never has he been afraid to reach.
His lesions are legion.
But reaching is his rule.
—GWENDOLYN BROOKS

Education is our passport to the future, for tomorrow belongs to the
people who prepare for it today.
—MALCOLM X

I am invisible, understand, simply because people refuse to see me.
—RALPH ELLISON

The impulse to dream had been slowly beaten out of me by experience.
Now it surged up again and I hungered for books, new ways of
looking and seeing.
—RICHARD WRIGHT

Me: A Name I Call Myself

Boyz 'N the Hood, John Singleton's stark portrait of growing up black in urban America, opens in death and school. Four youngsters detour from their regular morning route to visit the site of last night's slaying—up a street marked "ONE WAY," down an alley proclaiming "WRONG WAY," under the yellow police tape signalling the scene of the crime.

"What happened?" asks one of the kids, wide-eyed.

"Somebody got smoked, stupid."

"At least I know my times tables."

A precocious discussion follows concerning the separation of plasma from blood cells as the scene fades to the classroom. Black history and motivational posters share the walls with children's paintings: a casket, a police helicopter, an L.A. squad car. The teacher—white, well-meaning, a bit harried—is relating the Thanksgiving myth and the "unity of the Indians, excuse me, Native Americans, and the European settlers." She's modern, progressive. When Tre Styles interrupts her, she asks him if he'd like to come up and lead the class.

"Yeah, I can do that." Tre is confident; the teacher thinks him arrogant.

"Come on up," she urges. "Instruct us. What will be the basis of your lecture?" She drips sarcasm.

"Huh?"

"What will you tell us about?" Her look is pure patronization.

Tre teaches that Africa is the birthplace of humanity. One student cracks a joke about monkeys in the jungle, and within minutes they're trading blows. Tre is suspended. As he makes his way home, we hear the teacher lecturing his mother over the phone. Again the voice, patronizing, professional, slightly harassed: "He's highly intelligent; he has an enormous vocabulary. But he has a very bad temper that makes it very hard for him to interact with his peers." And then the inevitable questions: "Are there any problems at home?" "Are you employed?" "Then you are educated?" The mother is furious (though she's heard it all before), and the teacher is annoyed. They are speaking past each other, over a yawning chasm. And Tre, the object of their misunderstanding, is entirely overlooked.

Tre Styles lives in a single-parent, mother-headed household at the time of his suspension. Being kicked out of school is an indication of a more serious disengagement. Tre's neighborhood contains a high concentration of unemployment, street crime, and gang activity. And, of course, he is African-American and poor. In the popular rhetoric of the day, Tre Styles is "at risk."

But "at risk" of what? He is, first, "at risk" of having problems in school, but then, he's already having those difficulties. The future is now, and noting that Tre is having problems says nothing about cause, effect, responsibility, or judgment. It could be that he attends a terrible school; it could be that the teacher is cruel or oppressive or disrespectful or unresponsive; it could be that education has been structured for a particular child with a specific background and a stipulated set of experiences or attitudes and that when a kid like Tre shows up, the school simply malfunctions. Never mind. Tre is "at risk" for school failure.

He is "at risk," too, of living in a neighborhood where lots of other people are "at risk." Once again, this isn't something that *might* happen—this is in fact where he lives. He is "at risk" of living with a single-parent, "at-risk" of associating with gang members, "at risk" of being exposed to violence. But these things are already accomplished, already done. To posit them as possibilities or predictions is a logical sleight-of-hand: look what *might* happen to this child and presto, same-o—it has happened. The magic of social science produces a simple-minded redundancy.

"At risk" adds an authenticating medical dimension to a description and a prescription made before the investigation begins. We talk of cancer risks and the risk-factors for AIDS. Here social scientists—white coated and somber—attach that identical language to a specific group of children and their families. Society as we find it is assumed to be unquestionably healthy and well except for an invasion of "at risk" microorganisms; children carry the social disease; we must act boldly, scientifically, and in the best interest of the patient. Symptoms include a range of behaviors (teenage pregnancy, single-parent, mother-headed household) but the decisive indicators are being poor and black. Any of the other symptoms applied to a white, middle-class professional, for example, are seen as a choice, or a temporary aberration, or something other than justification for membership in the "at risk" group.

This is all something of a hoax, or perhaps a kind of voluntary group madness. If everyone sees evidence of witchcraft, there surely must be witches. In our society today, "at risk" functions as a kind of witch-hunting metaphor: void of any credible data, it is a label in search of content. It offers a thin surface of scholarship and pseudoscience to cover the thickest and most persistent stereotypes about poor and African-American people. After all, Tre is mostly "at risk" of being black and poor. And the label falls conveniently in step with contemporary political and policy priorities. It blames poor people for poverty and sanctions findings which locate character and behavioral defects inside individuals—without searching out or discovering any corresponding structural problems within the economic or social system.

Being "at risk" is a kind of pathology. To the liberals and the well-meaning, it is an unfortunate fate that simply befalls some people; to the mean-spirited, the bogeyman is black people themselves. While poverty was once an act of God and proof of a morally defective character (and this attitude persists), then an act of biology and proof of poor genes (this rationale is making a strong comeback), today the hip, sophisticated observer attributes the problem to "a culture of poverty." The ascendancy of mystifying, quack social science.

While everyone wants to "help" the children "at risk," that "help" breaks down into two large camps. One is a kind of entangling "help"—the more you get, the more you need and the more ensnared you become. The other is the kind of "help" meted out by an overly-zealous stern father—this beating will make you better. This help includes building ever-increasing numbers of prisons, sterilizing poor women or forcing them to wear birth control implants, and some forms of "workfare." Both camps think that they know best; neither would think to ask youngsters or their families to define their own situations or their own needs and experiences in their own ways. Being "at risk" disqualifies human beings from self-awareness or meaningful social commentary.

There is no end to the names and labels and identifiers assigned to the poor and to African-Americans: "culturally deprived," "minority," "underclass." It is doubtful that these names are satisfactory self-identifiers for anyone (Hi, My name is Rachel, I'm "at risk"), and unlikely that their logical opposites will ever catch on (the popularity of "underclass," for example, will not likely be matched by a corresponding "overclass"). "At risk" is not what young African-Americans call themselves. In fact, in all our years of working in oppressed communities, we've never heard a person call himself or herself "at risk." It's simply not anyone's self-definition. This is a broad hint of what can destroy good intentions.

In a beautiful poem about growing up poor in Chicago's South Side, Nikki Giovanni ends with this:

> . . . and I really hope no white person ever has cause
> to write about me
> because they will never understand
> Black love is Black wealth and they'll
> probably talk about my hard childhood
> and never understand that
> all the while I was quite happy.

There is, interestingly, an available literature that illuminates some of these questions of self-identification. It is a literature of childhood—autobiographical and recollected. Neither accusatory nor patronizing, this literature speaks of interior meaning-making against an external world that is seen as hard and often impenetrable. It is a literature largely ignored by scholars and policymakers precisely because it is self-authored. And yet it is ignored at our collective peril.

The reason this literature is of some urgency is because self-identity and meaning-making are causal for human beings—more important in shaping action and behavior than any conceivable cause and effect research design can grasp or contain. This is perhaps the most difficult idea to hold on to in the face of behaviorism—the pervasive and popular on-charging mock science. People, in the behaviorist view, are like billiard balls—strike them here, they go there. In reality, uniform behavioral response is an illusion and people are hardly predictable—ask the *aparachiks* and party officials from the east. More to the point, people *behave* and *act* on the basis of interpretation of other actions and other experiences. In other words, human beings construct meaning, and act on the basis of the meanings they make. Unlike a billiard ball, a direct hit on a human being can result in that person coming back at you at an even faster rate of speed.

For example, at the height of the civil rights movement in the South, the organized white supremacists circulated a photograph of Martin Luther King, Jr. attending a workshop at the Highlander Folk School seated next to the editor of the *Daily World*. With the caption, "Martin Luther King at Communist Training School," the White Citizen's Councils paid to make this photo into postcards, posters, and billboards which went up all over the South. To them, the discrediting meaning was clear and obvious. They intended to discourage wider participation in the movement.

One day Myles Horton, founder of Highlander, was driving a group of young people in a van to a civil rights demonstration, and they passed first one and then another of the billboards. As a third appeared in the distance, one of the youngsters turned to Myles and complained, "That is the stupidest advertisement I've ever seen. It doesn't even give you a phone number or a place to write for more information." Far from discrediting King, the racists would be stunned to know their ad campaign promoted communism—this child was ready to sign up.

Similarly, in the summer of 1964 the Ku Klux Klan murdered James Chaney, Mickey Schwerner, and Michael Goodman as a warning to civil rights volunteers gathered in Ohio and preparing to launch a massive voting rights campaign in Mississippi. Their message was, "Stay out of the South!" Their actions had the exact opposite effect—the ranks of the volunteers swelled as the message received was, "We must redouble our efforts to end segregation"—and Mississippi Freedom Summer became a massive success.

And so it goes. Joan of Arc. The execution of the Rosenbergs. Countless examples from each of our lives. The contradictory nature of human life, the illusion of uniformity, of cause and effect. The essential arrogance of mainline social science is the denial to others of that which we demand for ourselves: they marry because they share a socioeconomic background and a geographical space, whereas we marry for love; they neglect their kids and couldn't love them, whereas we are busy at work. If understanding is a goal, somewhere we must try to respect behavior as linked to the immediate and local meanings of actors. We then need to ask people what they mean.

This section seeks meaning from insiders, from those who live the lives described. There are echoes here of other insider accounts, reflections of other autobiographers. The quest in these works centers on being understood, being known, creating a name of one's own. One of the most powerful generators of this tradition is Malcolm X's searing life story, an account that has achieved epic status *(The Autobiography of Malcolm X,* Haley, A. and Malcolm X, 1964).

For Malcolm X, first memories of school are also the beginning of a lifelong struggle with issues of naming and self-identity:

> At five, I . . . began to go to school . . . The white kids didn't make any great thing about us . . . They called us "nigger" and "darkie" and "Rastus" so much that we thought those were our natural names . . . it was just the way they thought about us (pp. 8–9).

His name becomes a focal point in that struggle. In junior high, fellow students treated him as a novelty, popular and in demand, but somehow in their view lacking the same feelings and needs they attributed to themselves, and still a "nigger."

No one can see young Malcolm as he sees himself, a whole person with a full complement of human desires, needs, hopes, dreams, aspirations, and feelings. He is a thing to them, a one-dimensional object, stuck in their immutable expectations and their essentialist, entirely predetermined universe. He is, to them, lacking in some core moral or intellectual or spiritual element that would allow him full and complete membership into the human family. Nothing personal, nothing sensible, just business as usual. Malcolm is "nigger"—neither more nor less.

Malcolm's family is decimated after his father's death at the hands of white supremacists. Malcolm, his brothers, and his sisters all become "state children," wards of the court, and again the destruction is accomplished by "well-meaning" people acting on a convenient label—in this case "crazy" or mentally unstable—applied to Malcolm's mother.

Malcolm dropped out of school. He had succeeded in school in many ways—high marks, active in sports and clubs, class president. And yet he came to believe that school was not the path to a better life for him. He knew many people who had succeeded in school yet still had cramped, narrow, unhappy existences. He could not connect school success with happiness or broadening life chances. And so Malcolm became part of the massive, inarticulated school boycott movement known as drop-outs.

His struggle to name himself, to create a self-identity, to become educated and visible, to win full membership in the human family was only beginning. In Boston, where he had felt "a sense of being a real part of a mass of my own kind for the first time" (p. 35) he would become known as "Detroit Red," the flamboyant, zoot suit–wearing street hustler. In prison, where "you never heard your name, only your number—it grew stenciled on your brain" (p. 152) he was the incorrigible con, "Satan." Soon he became the redeemed Minister Malcolm X, converted by his brother and sisters to Islam.

Finally, shortly before his death, Malcolm X became El-Hajj Malik El-Shabazz, internationalist and revolutionary. Cut down at thirty-nine, Malcolm X's struggle for a full and powerful identity was partially realized, perhaps, in the space he created for others to name themselves with self-respect and strength. Ossie Davis, well-known actor and intellectual, said "Malcolm . . . was refreshing excitement . . . [he] knew that every white man in America profits directly or indirectly from his position vis-a-vis Negroes, profits from racism though he does not practice it or believe in it. He also knew that every Negro who did not challenge on the spot every instance of racism, overt or covert, committed against him and his people, who chose instead to swallow his spit and go on smiling, was an Uncle Tom and a traitor . . . He would make you angry as hell, but he would also make you proud." (p. 458). Ossie Davis gives him a new name to call himself: "a hero and a martyr in a noble cause" (p. 459).

The chapters that follow are in this tradition—they are voices of people struggling to be heard, striving to be seen, questing to be understood in a world bent on their silence, their acquiescence to their own subjugation.

1. Always Running

LUIS RODRIGUEZ

Our first exposure in America stays with me like a foul odor. It seemed a strange world, most of it spiteful to us, spitting and stepping on us, coughing us up, us immigrants, as if we were phlegm stuck in the collective throat of this country. My father was mostly out of work. When he did have a job it was in construction, in factories such as Sinclair Paints or Standard Brands Dog Food, or pushing doorbells selling insurance, Bibles, or pots and pans. My mother found work cleaning homes or in the garment industry. She knew the corner markets were ripping her off but she could only speak with her hands and in a choppy English.

Once my mother gathered up the children and we walked to Will Rogers Park. There were people everywhere. Mama looked around for a place we could rest. She spotted an empty spot on a park bench. But as soon as she sat down an American woman, with three kids of her own, came by.

"Hey, get out of there—that's our seat."

My mother understood but didn't know how to answer back in English. So she tried in Spanish.

"Look spic, you can't sit there!" the American woman yelled. "You don't belong here! Understand? This is not your country!"

Mama quietly got our things and walked away, but I knew frustration and anger bristled within her because she was unable to talk, and when she did, no one would listen.

We never stopped crossing borders. The Rio Grande (or *Rio Bravo*, which is what the Mexicans call it, giving the name a power "Rio Grande" just doesn't have) was only the first of countless barriers set in our path.

We kept jumping hurdles, kept breaking from the constraints, kept evading the border guards of every new trek. It was a metaphor to fill our lives—that river, that first crossing, the mother of all crossings. The Los Angeles River, for example, became a new barrier, keeping the Mexicans in their neighborhoods over on the vast east side of the city for years, except for forays downtown. Schools provided other restrictions: don't speak Spanish, don't be Mexican—you don't belong. Railroad tracks divided us from communities where white people lived, such as South Gate and Lynwood across from Watts. We were invisible people in a city which thrived on glitter, big screens, and big names, but this glamour contained none of our names, none of our faces.

The refrain "this is not your country" echoed for a lifetime.

First day of school.

I was six years old, never having gone to kindergarten because Mama wanted me to wait until La Pata became old enough to enter school. Mama filled out some papers. A school monitor directed us to a classroom where Mama dropped me off and left to join some parents who gathered in the main hall.

The first day of school said a lot about my scholastic life to come. I was taken to a teacher who didn't know what to do with me. She complained about not having any room, about kids who didn't even speak the language. And how was she supposed to teach anything under these conditions! Although I didn't speak English, I understood a large part of what she was saying. I knew I wasn't wanted. She put me in an old creaky chair near the door. As soon as I could, I sneaked out to find my mother.

I found Rano's class with the mentally disabled children instead and decided to stay there for a while. Actually it was fun; they treated me like I was everyone's little brother. But the teacher finally told a student to take me to the main hall.

After some more paperwork, I was taken to another class. This time the teacher appeared nicer, but distracted. She got the word about my language problem.

"Okay, why don't you sit here in the back of the class," she said. "Play with some blocks until we figure out how to get you more involved."

It took her most of that year to figure this out. I just stayed in the back of the class, building blocks. It got so every morning I would put my lunch and coat away, and walk to my corner where I stayed the whole day long. It forced me to be more withdrawn. It got so bad, I didn't even tell anybody when I had to go to the bathroom. I did it in my pants. Soon I stunk back there in the corner and the rest of the kids screamed out a chorus of "P.U.!" resulting in my being sent to the office or back home.

In those days there was no way to integrate the non-English-speaking children. So they just made it a crime to speak anything but English. If a Spanish word sneaked out in the playground, kids were often sent to the office to get swatted or to get detention. Teachers complained that maybe the children were saying bad things about them. An assumption of guilt was enough to get one punished.

A day came when I finally built up the courage to tell the teacher I had to go to the bathroom. I didn't quite say all the words, but she got the message and promptly excused me so I didn't do it while I was trying to explain. I ran to the bathroom and peed and felt good about not having that wetness trickle down my pants leg. But suddenly several bells went on and off. I hesitantly stepped out of the bathroom and saw throngs of children leave their classes. I had no idea what was happening. I went to my classroom and it stood empty. I looked into other classrooms and found nothing. Nobody. I didn't know what to do. I really thought everyone had gone home. I didn't bother to look at the playground where the whole school had been assembled for the fire drill. I just went home. It got to be a regular thing there for a while, me coming home early until I learned the ins and outs of school life.

Not speaking well makes for such embarrassing moments. I hardly asked questions. I just didn't want to be misunderstood. Many Spanish-speaking kids mangled things up; they would say things like "where the beer and cantaloupe roam" instead of "where the deer and antelope roam."

That's the way it was with me. I mixed up all the words. Screwed up all the songs.

"You can't be in a fire and not get burned."

This was my father's response when he heard of the trouble I was getting into at school. He was a philosopher. He didn't get angry or hit me. That he left to my mother. He had these lines, these cuts of wisdom, phrases and syllables, which swept through me, sometimes even making sense. I had to deal with him at that level, with my brains. I had to justify in words, with ideas, all my actions—no matter how insane. Most of the time I couldn't.

Mama was heat. Mama was turned-around leather belts and wailing choruses of Mary-Mother-of-Jesus. She was the penetrating emotion that came at you through her eyes, the mother-guilt, the one who birthed me, who suffered through the contractions and diaper changes and all my small hurts and fears. For her, dealing with school trouble or risking my life was nothing for discourse, nothing to debate. She went through all this hell and more to have me—I'd better do what she said!

Mama hated the *cholos*. They reminded her of the rowdies on the border who fought all the time, talked that *calo* slang, drank mescal, smoked marijuana, and left scores of women with babies bursting out of their bodies.

To see me become like them made her sick, made her cringe and cry and curse. Mama reminded us how she'd seen so much alcoholism, so much weed-madness, and she prohibited anything with alcohol in the house, even beer. I later learned this rage came from how Mama's father treated her siblings and her mother, how in drunken rages he'd hit her mom and drag her through the house by the hair.

The school informed my parents I had been wreaking havoc with a number of other young boys. I was to be part of a special class of troublemakers. We would be isolated from the rest of the school population and forced to pick up trash and clean graffiti during the rest of the school year.

"Mrs. Rodriguez, your son is too smart for this," the vice principal told Mama. "We think he's got a lot of potential. But his behavior is atrocious. There's no excuse. We're sad to inform you of our decision."

They also told her the next time I cut class or even made a feint toward trouble, I'd be expelled. After the phone call, my mom lay on her bed, shaking her head while sobbing in between bursts of how God had cursed her for some sin, how I was the devil incarnate, a plague, testing her in this brief tenure on earth.

My dad's solution was to keep me home after school. Grounded. Yeah, sure. I was thirteen years old already. Already tattooed. Already sexually involved. Already into drugs. In the middle of the night I snuck out through the window and worked my way to the Hills.

At sixteen years old, Rano turned out much better than me, much better than anyone could have envisioned during the time he was a foul-faced boy in Watts.

When we moved to South San Gabriel, a Mrs. Snelling took a liking to Rano. The teacher helped him skip grades to make up for the times he was pushed back in those classes with the retarded children.

Mrs. Snelling saw talent in Rano, a spark of actor during the school's thespian activities. She even had him play the lead in a class play. He also showed some facility with music. And he was good in sports.

He picked up the bass guitar and played for a number of garage bands. He was getting trophies in track-and-field events, in gymnastic meets, and later in karate tournaments.

So when I was at Garvey, he was in high school being the good kid, the Mexican exception, the barrio success story—my supposed model. Soon he stopped being Rano or even José. One day he became Joe.

My brother and I were moving away from each other. Our tastes, our friends, our interests, were miles apart. Yet there were a few outstanding incidents I fondly remember in relationship to my brother, incidents which despite their displays of closeness failed to breach the distance which would later lie between us.

When I was nine, for example, my brother was my protector. He took on all the big dudes, the bullies on corners, the ones who believed themselves better than us. Being a good fighter transformed him overnight. He was somebody who some feared, some looked up to. Then he developed skills for racing and high-jumping. This led to running track and he did well, dusting all the competition.

I didn't own any talents. I was lousy in sports. I couldn't catch baseballs or footballs. And I constantly tripped when I ran or jumped. When kids picked players for basketball games, I was the last one they chose. The one time I inadvertently hit a home run during a game at school—I didn't mean to do it—I ended up crying while running around the bases because I didn't know how else to react to the cheers, the excitement, directed at something I did. It just couldn't be me.

But Rano had enemies too. There were two Mexican kids who were jealous of him. They were his age, three years older than me. One was named Eddie Gambits, the other Rick Corral. One time they cornered me outside the school.

"You José's brother," Eddie said.

I didn't say anything.

"Wha's the matter? Can't talk?"

"Oh, he can talk all right," Ricky chimed in. "He acting the *pendejo* because his brother thinks he so bad. Well, he ain't shit. He can't even run."

"Yeah, José's just a *lambiche,* a kiss ass," Eddie responded. "They give him those ribbons and stuff because he cheats."

"That's not true," I finally answered. "My brother can beat anybody."

"Oh, you saying he can beat me," Eddie countered.

"Sure sounds like he said that," Ricky added.

"I'm only saying that when he wins those ribbons, *esta derecho,*" I said.

"It sounds to me like you saying he better than me," Eddie said.

"Is that what you saying, man?" Ricky demanded. "Com' on—is that what you saying?"

I turned around, and beneath my breath, mumbled something about how I didn't have time to argue with them. I shouldn't have done that.

"What'd you say?" Eddie said.

"I think he called you a punk," Ricky agitated.

"You call me a punk, man?" Eddie turned me around. I denied it.

"I heard him, dude. He say you are a punk-ass *puto*," Ricky continued to exhort.

The fist came at me so fast, I don't even recall how Eddie looked when he threw it. I found myself on the ground. Others in the school had gathered around by then. When a few saw it was me, they knew it was going to be a slaughter.

I rose to my feet—my cheek had turned swollen and blue. I tried to hit Eddie, but he backed up real smooth and hit me again. Ricky egged him on; I could hear the excitement in his voice.

I lay on the ground, defeated. Teachers came and chased the boys out. But before Eddie and Ricky left they yelled back: "José ain't nothing, man. You ain't nothing."

Anger flowed through me, but also humiliation. It hurt so deep I didn't even feel the fracture in my jaw, the displacement which would later give me a disjointed, lopsided, and protruding chin. It became my mark.

Later when I told Rano what happened, he looked at me and shook his head.

"You didn't have to defend me to those dudes," he said. "They're assholes. They ain't worth it."

I looked at him and told him something I never, ever told him again.

"I did it because I love you."

I began high school a *loco*, with a heavy Pendleton shirt, sagging khaki pants, ironed to perfection, and shoes shined and heated like at boot camp.

Mark Keppel High School was a Depression-era structure with a brick and art-deco facade and small, army-type bungalows in back. Friction filled its hallways. The Anglo and Asian upper-class students from Monterey Park and Alhambra attended the school.

They were tracked into the "A" classes; they were in the school clubs; they were the varsity team members and lettermen. They were the pep squads and cheerleaders.

But the school also took in the people from the Hills and surrounding community who somehow made it past junior high. They were mostly Mexican, in the "C" track (what were called the "stupid" classes), and who made up the rosters of the wood, print, and auto shops. Only a few of these students participated in school government, in sports, or in the various clubs.

The school had two principal languages. Two skin tones and two cultures. It revolved around class differences. The white and Asian kids (except for "barrio" whites and the handful of Hawaiians, Filipinos, and Samoans who ended up with the Mexicans) were from professional, two-car households with watered lawns and trimmed trees. The laboring class, the sons and daughters of service workers, janitors, and factory hands, lived in and around the Hills (or a section of Monterey Park called "Poor Side").

The school separated these two groups by levels of education: The professional-class kids were provided with college-preparatory classes; the blue-collar students were pushed into "industrial arts."

The Mexicans assembled beneath the big, gnarled tree on the front lawn next to the gym and shop area. The well-off students usually had cars and hung out in the parking lot or the cafeteria. Those who were in between or indifferent couldn't help but get caught in the crossfire.

By the time I went to Keppel, I had become introspective and quiet. I wanted to be untouchable: nobody could get to me. I walked the halls facing straight ahead, a saunter in my step, only slightly and consciously glancing to the sides.

Keppel had a rowdy reputation among San Gabriel Valley schools. Fights all the time. I believe it related to the ingrained system of tracking and subdivisions. The teachers and administrators were overwhelmingly Anglo and whether they were aware of it or not, favored the white students.

If you came from the Hills, you were labeled from the start. I'd walk into the counselor's office for whatever reasons and looks of disdain greeted me—ones meant for a criminal, alien, to be feared. Already a thug. It was harder to defy this expectation than just accept it and fall into the trappings. It was a jacket I could try to take off, but they kept putting it back on. The first hint of trouble and the preconceptions proved true. So why not be proud? Why not be an outlaw? Why not make it our own?

Mama gazed out of the back porch window to the garage room where I spent days holed up as if in a prison of my own making.

She worried about me, although didn't really know what I was up to; to protect herself from being hurt, she stayed uninvolved. Yet almost daily she offered quips and comments about me not attending school.

Mama called on the former principal of my elementary school in South San Gabriel to talk to me. This was the same school where Mrs. Snelling performed seeming miracles for my brother. While Joe amounted to something, to Mama I turned out to be a smudge on this earth, with no goals, no interests except what got puked up from the streets.

Bespectacled and bow-tied, Mr. Rothro wore unpressed suits which hung on his tall, lean frame. Mama knocked and I invited them in. Mr. Rothro ducked under the doorway and looked around, amazed at the magnificent disorder, the colors and scrawl on every wall, the fantastic use of the imagination for such a small room. Mama left and Mr. Rothro, unable to find a place to sit, stood around and provided an encouragement of words. Some very fine words.

"Luis, you've always struck me as an intelligent young man," Mr. Rothro said. "But your mother tells me you're wasting away your days. I'd like to see you back in school. If there's anything I can do—write a letter, make a phone call—perhaps you can return at a level worthy of your gifts."

I sat on a bed in front of an old Royal typewriter with keys that repeatedly got stuck and a carbon ribbon that kept jumping off its latch. My father gave me the typewriter after I found it among boxes, books, and personal items in the garage.

"What are you doing?" Mr. Rothro inquired.

"I'm writing a book," I said, matter-of-factly.

"You're what? May I see?"

I let him glimpse at the leaf of paper in the typewriter with barely visible type, full of x's where I crossed out errors as I worked. I didn't know how to type; I just punched the letters I needed with my index fingers. It took me forever to finish a page, but I kept at it in between my other activities. By then I actually had a quarter of a ream done.

"What's the book about, son?" Rothro asked.

"Just things . . . what I've seen, what I feel, about the people around me. You know—things."

"Interesting," Rothro said. "In fact, I believe you're probably doing better than most teenagers—even better, I'm afraid, than some who are going to school."

He smiled, said he had to go but if I needed his help, not to hesitate to call.

I acknowledged his goodby and watched him leave the room and walk up to the house, shaking his head. He wasn't the first to wonder about this enigma of a boy, who looked like he could choke the life out of you one minute and then recite a poem in another.

Prior to this, I tried to attend Continuation High School in Alhambra—later renamed Century High to remove the stigma of being the school for those who couldn't make it anywhere else. After a week, they "let" me go. A few of us in Lomas fought outside with some dudes from 18th Street who were recruiting a section of their huge gang in the Alhambra area. But Continuation High School was the last stop. When you failed at Continuation, the only place left was the road.

Then my father came up with a plan; when he proposed it, I knew it arose out of frustration.

It consisted of me getting up every day at 4:30 A.M. and going with him to his job at Pierce Junior College in the San Fernando

Valley—almost forty miles away on the other side of Los Angeles. He would enroll me in Taft High School near the college. The school pulled in well-off white kids, a good number of whom were Jewish. My father felt they had the best education.

I didn't really care so I said sure, why not?

Thus we began our daily trek to a familiar and hostile place— the college was located near Reseda where the family once lived for almost a year. The risk for my father involved me finding out what he really did for a living. Dad told us he worked as a labora- tory technician, how a special category had been created at Pierce College for him.

My father worked in the biology labs and maintained the sci- ence department's museum and weather station. But to me, he was an overblown janitor. Dad cleaned the cages of snakes, taran- tulas, lizards, and other animals used in the labs. He swept floors and wiped study tables; dusted and mopped the museum area. Dad managed some technical duties such as gathering the weather station reports, preparing work materials for students, and feeding and providing for the animals. Dad felt proud of his job—but he was only a janitor.

I don't know why this affected me. There's nothing wrong with being a janitor—and one as prestigious as my dad! But for years, I had this running fantasy of my scientist father in a laboratory car- rying out vital experiments—the imagination of a paltry kid who wanted so much to break away from the constraints of a society which expected my father to be a janitor or a laborer—when I wanted a father who transformed the world. I had watched too much TV.

One day I walked into the college's science department after school.

"Mr. Rodriguez, you have to be more careful with the place- ment of laboratory equipment," trembled a professor's stern voice.

"I unnerstan' . . . Sarry . . . I unnerstan'," Dad replied.

"I don't think you do, this is the second time in a month this equipment has not been placed properly."

I glanced over so as not to be seen. My dad looked like a lowly peasant, a man with a hat in his hand—apologetic. At home he was king, *el jefito*—the "word." But here my father turned into somebody else's push-around. Dad should have been equals with anyone, but with such bad English . . .

Oh my father, why don't you stand up to them? Why don't you be the man you are at home?

I turned away and kept on walking.

The opportunity for me to learn something new became an incentive for attending Taft High School. At Keppel and Continuation, I mainly had industrial arts classes. So I applied for classes which stirred a little curiosity: photography, advanced art, and literature. The first day of school, a Taft High School counselor called me into her office.

"I'm sorry, young man, but the classes you chose are filled up," she said.

"What do you mean? Isn't there any way I can get into any of them?"

"I don't believe so. Besides, your transcripts show you're not academically prepared for your choices. These classes are privileges, for those who have maintained the proper grades in the required courses. And I must add, you've obtained most of what credits you do have in industrial-related courses."

"I had to—that's all they'd give me," I said. "I just thought, maybe, I can do something else here. It seems like a good school and I want a chance to do something other than with my hands."

"It doesn't work that way," she replied. "I think you'll find our industrial arts subjects more suited to your needs."

I shifted in my seat and looked out the window.

"Whatever."

The classes she enrolled me in were print shop, auto shop, and weight training. I did manage a basic English literature class. I walked past the photography sessions and stopped to glimpse the students going in and out, some with nice cameras, and I thought about how I couldn't afford those cameras anyway: *Who needs that stupid class?*

In print shop I worked the lead foundry for the mechanical Linotype typesetter. I received scars on my arms due to splashes of molten lead. In auto shop, I did a lot of tune-ups, oil changes, and some transmission work. And I lifted weights and started to bulk up. The one value I had was being the only Mexican in school— people talked about it whenever I approached.

One day at lunchtime, I passed a number of hefty dudes in lettered jackets. One of them said something. Maybe it had nothing to do with me. But I pounced on him anyway. Several teachers had to pull me off.

They designated me as violent and uncontrollable; they didn't know "what to do with me."

After school, I walked to Pierce College and waited for Dad to finish his work so we could go home, which usually went past dark. I spent many evenings in the library. But I found most books boring and unstimulating.

I picked up research and history books and went directly to the index and looked up "Mexican." If there were a few items under this topic, I read them; I read them all.

Every day I browsed, ventured into various sections of shelves; most of this struck me with little interest. One evening, I came across a crop of new books on a special shelf near the front of the library. I picked one up, then two. The librarian looked at me through the side of her eye, as if she kept tabs on whoever perused those books.

They were primarily about the black experience, works coming out of the flames which engulfed many American cities in the 1960s. I discovered Claude Brown's *Manchild in the Promised Land,* Eldridge Cleaver's *Soul On Ice,* and the *Autobiography of Malcolm X.* I found poetry by Don L. Lee and Leroi Jones (now known as Haki R. Madhubuti and Amiri Baraka, respectively). And later a few books by Puerto Ricans and Chicanos: Victor Hernandez Cruz's *Snaps* and Ricardo Sanchez's *Canto Y Grito: Mi Liberacion* were two of them. Here were books with a connection to me.

And then there was Piri Thomas, a Puerto Rican brother, *un camarada de aquellas*—his book *Down These Mean Streets* became a living Bible for me. I dog-eared it, wrote in it, copied whole passages so I wouldn't forget their texture, the passion, this searing work of a street dude and hype in Spanish Harlem—a barrio boy like me, on the other side of America.

2. Bomb the Suburbs: Subway Scholar

WILLIAM UPSKI WIMSATT

It was supposed to say "SUBWAY SCHOLAR." Riding the Jackson Park–Englewood El train on the South Side of Chicago, it was the last landmark you'd see before plunging into the subway downtown. Two-and-a-half stories up, spanning the backs of four factory buildings, in blockbuster letters too close and too big to ignore, you'd read it: S-U-B-W-A . . .

One night last week I was up there working on the "O." The "O" was on a building all by itself, an entire landing of the fire escape. Earlier that day, I had stood with janitor clothes, an orange reflector vest, a yellow hard hat, and two gallons of white priming paint. I pretended I was painting over the graffiti. When the trains came by, I would wave to the motormen. A lot of them waved back.

So there I found myself that night, waiting for the bus, wearing white shorts and T-shirt, carrying two full bags across the city to a dark industrial alley with trains thundering overhead. The alley's full of everything you'd expect to find: falling-apart machines, stray ghosts, dogs, goblins, garbage, and me.

Some of my friends were supposed to come, especially my friend Chris, but he backed out at the last minute because there were supposed to be thunderstorms. I didn't mind a thunderstorm. I like painting in the rain. The better not to be seen with.

I climb the fire escape still wearing all white. Cloudy sky, no sign of rain. I take my all-black painting clothes out of the bags. I pull them on over the whites and strap a respiratory mask across my face. I feel warm and invisible in the night.

Which is a stupid way to feel. I've been caught painting up here before. The police check the alley with searchlights, especially this fire escape which is the main way writers climb up onto the tracks. So every time a train comes by with all its lights on, which is every couple minutes until about 2 A.M., sometimes around curves, sometimes up from the subway, the fire escape is lighted up and I have to run down and crouch out of view of the motorman.

So I'm up there painting the inside of the "O" for like half an hour. It's around midnight—I'm painting this scene of a girl playing in an overgrown lot—when I'm caught off guard by this worker train. The city's been doing track repairs in this area all summer and a couple times a night, worker trains just stop up here, sometimes for twenty minutes and do God-knows-what—I never stick around to find out.

I creep down the fire escape part way, curl up behind my paint bags and try to pass for a shadow should a cruiser decide to turn into the alley. I'm frozen there a few minutes tryna be patient when I get the impulse to check behind me. Next to the fire escape, ten feet below me and ten feet to the rear, is this freight train embankment that I sometimes use as an escape route. And right there, right on the edge of the embankment is a scraggly looking man crouching perfectly still, looking up at me and smoking a cigarette. So here we are in this abandoned alley in the middle of nowhere. I'm staring this guy down and he's staring me down, and ten seconds go by and neither of us moves. I can't see his face very well. There's a cigarette in front of it. Suddenly he stands up and with the flash of a pocket camera he tries to take a picture of me. I barely turn fast enough to hide my face.

So I'm like who the fuck is this? How long has he been here? What is he after? And what makes it weird, a similar thing happened the night before. I was lying in the same place and this bum walks into the alley maybe 150 yards beyond the freight embankment. He leans against a supporting beam, stands there for about fifteen minutes, smokes a cigarette looking right at me, and then he leaves. Without seeing me. I had thought.

And what makes it weirder, a week before, we were painting the "SCH." It was me, Chris, and this dumb-ass fifteen-year-old kid I brought along named Finesse. It would have been bad enough if Finesse was his graffiti name. It was the name his parents gave him. When the trains would come, me and Chris would be hiding in these crevices down the tracks. Finesse's ass wouldn't even hide. He would just keep playing on the fire escape, being all loud, borrowing cans to write his ugly, wack name everywhere, being all theatrical and shit. So I get really mad at this kid. I make him go climb up the fire escape and wait for us on the roof. Then everything's cool for a while. We're painting. Painting. Painting. All of a sudden, Finesse comes hurtling down off the roof in a panic.

Oh Lord. Here he comes again.

"There's a body on the roof. A body on the roof. A dead body."

"Finesse," I say. "Leave. Me. The Fuck. Alone."

"NO. NoNoNoNo. I'm serious. I'm serious. There's a body. I'm serious. I'm not joking. You gotta believe me. I ain't going up there."

We all climb up onto the roof. "There it is," Finesse says, pointing into a dark corner. Sure enough, there are the outlines of a body slouched in the darkness.

We tiptoe up to it. It doesn't move. We try talking to it. It doesn't move. We try kicking it. It still doesn't move. All of a sudden, here's Finesse. A beam of some kind is shooting out of Finesse and landing on the body. Finesse is pissing on the body!

"The fuck are you doing!" I yell.

Finesse is not pissing on the body. Finesse is spraying mace on the body. He got it out of my jacket which I let him wear.

Oh shit. The body moves. Oh shit. The body moves again. Oh shit. The body is coming back to life. Finesse has maced the body back to life. We push each other down the fire escape. We're on the tracks arguing, tryna figure out what to do. A police car spots us and tilts its search beam at us. We scatter into the night.

We never figured out who the body was. So here I am one week later. As I scramble the cans into my bag, I'm racking my brain about the scraggly guy. Is he a stealth cop? A vagabond trying to collect the reward for my arrest? Is he The Body? I'm throwing stuff in my bag and I'm watching him. He's very agile. He hops down from the freight embankment by this special way I thought only graffiti writers knew about. And then he does something which seizes my blood. He runs toward the base of the fire escape.

I didn't even get a chance to grab my old-school paint. I grab my mask, dash up the fire escape, and vault onto the tracks. My escape route from here has been planned but the worker train is right there on the tracks (part of the setup?). I've already been seen, so fuck it, they're gonna have to catch me. I start leaping across the tracks, across the gaps and third rails, till I get to the catwalk, which lies in between the center tracks, and leads eventually into the mouth of the subway two blocks away. All of this happens in seconds. I flee down the catwalk as fast as any man being chased. The catwalk is two feet wide, flanked on either side by a third rail. There is a rumbling behind me. Train. I jump over to the other track. I'm on the incline going toward the tunnel, and I know the train driver has seen me but he doesn't stop. So I keep running and follow the red taillights into the mouth of the tunnel, whipping off my gloves and tossing them, along with my mask, into crevices along the wall. The headquarters of the Chicago Police Department is exactly two blocks away.

Just inside the subway tunnel, they have constructed a new subway line, not yet in service, which branches off from the tunnel I'm in, and opens out into this even more abandoned district over by the river—a perfect getaway. I run the new tunnel, which is longer than I expect, and perfectly clean. There are no tags in it yet. I'm still looking over my shoulder for the scraggly guy, even though there's no way he could have followed me—probably too many Freddy the 13th movies where the monster keeps jumping out at you just when you thought you were safe. I hop the razor wire, then I stash my black clothes (bad guys wear black), and follow the freight tracks across the river at 16th Street. I still haven't heard any police sirens. It's a beautiful cloudy night and the whole Chicago skyline is lighted up like a dozen blocks away. I'm thinking now my whole mission is shot and I won't be able to finish it before I go on the road in a month or so. I'm thinking I gotta bring a posse up there the next night and like kill this dude.

So I finally reach a busy street, Halsted. There's bus fare in my shoe. I take the Halsted bus to 55th, then the 55th Street bus home. All I can think is Whew.

No whew. There is a cop car sitting on my corner. It sits there for five minutes. I retrieve my keys from a stash spot two blocks away and when I return, the cop car is still there. I don't have any paint on my hands, I'm dressed like I go to Oberlin. There's no way they know I did anything. I'll just play it off. I walk past the cop car and stare the cops down and they stare me down and I go into my apartment, shower, eat, congratulate myself on the escape, and curse myself for losing my cans and not finishing the piece. Worry some more about who this guy is and how I can take care of him. Then I try to fall asleep. My parents are out of town so all's cool.

At 3:15, I'm still awake. I keep thinking about that cop car on my corner, sitting there for no apparent reason and about my friend who had to flee to California, because the cops were doing intelligence on him trying to set him up. And I have this faint feeling that as I was running away from the alley guy, he was yelling my name. Biiilllyy. Biilllyyy. And then I realize something that makes me sit up in bed. One of the bags I left on the fire escape had pockets in it which I didn't check. And suppose one of those pockets had something in it with my name on it. We are the only Wimsatt in the telephone book. And what if those cops on the corner were waiting there to testify that yes I did come home at 2 A.M. And what if, at this very moment, they were preparing to bust in on me and search my house?

Spread out in my room are seventy spray cans. Many of them are rare brands—the same rare brands I left on the fire escape. I frantically run around, trying to hide the paint in shopping bags behind clothes in my mother's closet, under dusty boxes in my father's study, and I'm running around the apartment with half the lights on, spray cans everywhere, when I hear someone clomping up the stairs. Clomp Clomp Clomp, I hear—I have pretty quiet neighbors, and I think for sure It's The Police. Why did I turn the lights on! The clomps come up to my door, and then they continue up the stairs. Ahh, so they're surrounding me, are they? A key turns in one of my upstairs neighbor's locks and I sigh a temporary relief. Unless . . . the neighbors are in on it too. I knew I shouldn't have gotten that paint on the outside of the building.

Two minutes later, the phone rings. 3:34 A.M. After four rings, I pick it up. My plan is to sound like I'm half asleep. ("The police, at this hour? Whatever you want it can wait till the morning. Click.") I'm not sure how doing this will help, but I picture it playing an important role in some desperate future court case.

"Hello," I yawn falsely.

"Billy!" my friend Chris shouts into the phone. "It was me. It was me."

I croak in disbelief.

"It didn't rain, so I decided to come piece with you. I thought you recognized me. I started taking pictures of you but you ran away from me, I kept shouting 'Billy, it's Chris.' But you kept running; I thought you got killed by that train."

We never finished the piece.

3. ZAMI: A New Spelling of My Name

AUDRE LORDE

When I was five years old and still legally blind, I started school in a sight-conservation class in the local public school on 135th Street and Lenox Avenue. On the corner was a blue wooden booth where white women gave away free milk to black mothers with children. I used to long for some Hearst Free Milk Fund milk, in those cute little bottles with their red and white tops, but my mother never allowed me to have any, because she said it was charity, which was bad and demeaning, and besides the milk was warm and might make me sick.

The school was right across the avenue from the catholic school where my two older sisters went, and this public school had been used as a threat against them for as long as I could remember. If they didn't behave and get good marks in schoolwork and deportment, they could be "transferred." A "transfer" carried the same dire implications as "deportation" came to imply decades later.

Of course everybody knew that public school kids did nothing but "fight," and you could get "beaten up" every day after school, instead of being marched out of the schoolhouse door in two neat rows like little robots, silent but safe and unattacked, to the corner where the mothers waited.

But the catholic school had no kindergarten, and certainly not one for blind children.

Despite my nearsightedness, or maybe because of it, I learned to read at the same time I learned to talk, which was only about a year or so before I started school. Perhaps *learn* isn't the right word to use for my beginning to talk, because to this day I don't know if I didn't talk earlier because I didn't know how, or if I didn't talk because I had nothing to say that I would be allowed to say without punishment. Self-preservation starts very early in West Indian families.

I learned how to read from Mrs. Augusta Baker, the children's librarian at the old 135th Street branch library, which has just recently been torn down to make way for a new library building to house the Schomburg Collection on African-American History and Culture. If that was the only good deed that lady ever did in her life, may she rest in peace. Because that deed saved my life, if not sooner, then later, when sometimes the only thing I had to hold on to was knowing I could read, and that could get me through.

My mother was pinching my ear off one bright afternoon, while I lay spread-eagled on the floor of the Children's Room like a furious little brown toad, screaming bloody murder and embarrassing my mother to death. I know it must have been spring or early fall, because without the protection of a heavy coat, I can still feel the stinging soreness in the flesh of my upper arm. There, where my mother's sharp fingers had already tried to pinch me into silence. To escape those inexorable fingers I had hurled myself to the floor, roaring with pain as I could see them advancing toward my ears again. We were waiting to pick up my two older sisters from story hour, held upstairs on another floor of the dry-smelling quiet library. My shrieks pierced the reverential stillness.

Suddenly, I looked up, and there was a library lady standing over me. My mother's hands had dropped to her sides. From the floor where I was lying, Mrs. Baker seemed like yet another mile-high woman about to do me in. She had immense, light, hooded eyes and a very quiet voice that said, not damnation for my noise, but "Would you like to hear a story, little girl?"

Part of my fury was because I had not been allowed to go to that secret feast called story hour since I was too young, and now here was this strange lady offering me my own story.

I didn't dare to look at my mother, half afraid she might say no, I was too bad for stories. Still bewildered by this sudden change of events, I climbed up upon the stool which Mrs. Baker pulled over for me, and gave her my full attention. This was a new experience for me and I was insatiably curious.

Mrs. Baker read me *Madeline*, and *Horton Hatches the Egg*, both of which rhymed and had huge lovely pictures which I could see from behind my newly acquired eyeglasses, fastened around the back of my rambunctious head by a black elastic band running from earpiece to earpiece. She also read me another storybook about a bear named Herbert who ate up an entire family, one by one, starting with the parents. By the time she had finished that one, I was sold on reading for the rest of my life.

I took the books from Mrs. Baker's hands after she was finished reading, and traced the large black letters with my fingers, while I peered again at the beautiful bright colors of the pictures. Right then I decided I was going to find out how to do that myself. I pointed to the black marks which I could now distinguish as separate letters, different from my sisters' more grown-up books, whose smaller print made the pages only one gray blur for me. I said, quite loudly, for whoever was listening to hear, "I want to read."

My mother's surprised relief outweighed whatever annoyance she was still feeling at what she called my whelpish carryings-on. From the background where she had been hovering while Mrs. Baker read, my mother moved forward quickly, mollified and impressed. I had spoken. She scooped me up from the low stool, and to my surprise, kissed me, right in front of everybody in the library, including Mrs. Baker.

This was an unprecedented and unusual display of affection in public, the cause of which I did not comprehend. But it was a warm and happy feeling. For once, obviously, I had done something right.

My mother set me back upon the stool and turned to Mrs. Baker, smiling.

"Will wonders never cease to perform!" Her excitement startled me back into cautious silence.

Not only had I been sitting still for longer than my mother would have thought possible, and sitting quietly, I had also spoken rather than screamed, something that my mother, after four years and a lot of worry, had despaired that I would ever do. Even one intelligible word was a very rare event for me. And although the doctors at the clinic had clipped the little membrane under my tongue so I was no longer tongue-tied, and had assured my mother that I was not retarded, she still had her terrors and her doubts. She was genuinely happy for any possible alternative to what she was afraid might be a dumb child. The ear-pinching was forgotten. My mother accepted the alphabet and picture books Mrs. Baker gave her for me, and I was on my way.

I sat at the kitchen table with my mother, tracing letters and calling their names. Soon she taught me how to say the alphabet forwards and backwards as it was done in Grenada. Although she had never gone beyond the seventh grade, she had been put in charge of teaching the first grade children their letters during her last year at Mr. Taylor's School in Grenville. She told me stories about his strictness as she taught me how to print my name.

I did not like the tail of the Y hanging down below the line in Audrey, and would always forget to put it on, which used to disturb my mother greatly. I used to love the evenness of AUDRELORDE at four years of age, but I remembered to put on the Y because it pleased my mother, and because, as she always insisted to me, that was the way it had to be because that was the way it was. No deviation was allowed from her interpretations of correct.

So by the time I arrived at the sight-conservation kindergarten, braided, scrubbed, and bespectacled, I was able to read large-print books and write my name with a regular pencil. Then came my first rude awakening about school. Ability had nothing to do with expectation.

There were only seven or eight of us little Black children in a big classroom, all with various serious deficiencies of sight. Some of us were cross-eyed, some of us were nearsighted, and one little girl had a patch over one of her eyes.

We were given special short wide notebooks to write in, with very widely spaced lines on yellow paper. They looked like my sister's music notebooks. We were also given thick black crayons to write with. Now you don't grow up fat, Black, nearly blind, and ambidextrous in a West Indian household, particularly my parents' household, and survive without being or becoming fairly rigid fairly fast. And having been roundly spanked on several occasions for having made that mistake at home, I knew quite well that crayons were not what you wrote with, and music books were definitely not what you wrote in.

I raised my hand. When the teacher asked me what I wanted, I asked for some regular paper to write on and a pencil. That was my undoing. "We don't have any pencils here," I was told.

Our first task was to copy down the first letter of our names in those notebooks with our black crayons. Our teacher went around the room and wrote the required letter into each one of our notebooks. When she came around to me, she printed a large A in the upper left corner of the first page of my notebook, and handed me the crayon.

"I can't," I said, knowing full well that what you do with black crayons is scribble on the wall and get your backass beaten, or color around the edges of pictures, but not write. To write, you needed a pencil. "I can't!" I said, terrified, and started to cry.

"Imagine that, a big girl like you. Such a shame, I'll have to tell your mother that you won't even try. And such a big girl like you!"

And it was true. Although young, I was the biggest child by far in the whole class, a fact that had not escaped the attention of the little boy who sat behind me, and who was already whispering "fatty, fatty!" whenever the teacher's back was turned.

"Now just try, dear. I'm sure you can try to print your A. Mother will be so pleased to see that at least you tried." She patted my stiff braids and turned to the next desk.

Well, of course, she had said the magic words, because I would have walked over rice on my knees to please Mother. I took her nasty old soft smudgy crayon and pretended that it was a nice neat pencil with a fine point, elegantly sharpened that morning outside the bathroom door by my father, with the little penknife that he always carried around in his bathrobe pocket.

I bent my head down close to the desk that smelled like old spittle and rubber erasers, and on that ridiculous yellow paper with those laughably wide spaces I printed my best AUDRE. I had never been too good at keeping between straight lines no matter what their width, so it slanted down across the page something like this:

A
   U
      D
         R
            E

The notebooks were short and there was no more room for any-thing else on that page. So I turned the page over, and wrote again, earnestly and laboriously, biting my lip,

L
   O
      R
         D
            E

half showing off, half eager to please.

By this time, Miss Teacher had returned to the front of the room.

"Now when you're finished drawing your letter, children," she said, "just raise your hand high." And her voice smiled a big smile. It is surprising to me that I can still hear her voice but I can't see her face, and I don't know whether she was Black or white. I can remember the way she smelled, but not the color of her hand upon my desk.

Well, when I heard that, my hand flew up in the air, wagging frantically. There was one thing my sisters had warned me about school in great detail: you must never talk in school unless you raised your hand. So I raised my hand, anxious to be recognized. I could imagine what teacher would say to my mother when she came to fetch me home at noon. My mother would know that her warning to me to "be good" had in truth been heeded.

Miss Teacher came down the aisle and stood beside my desk, looking down at my book. All of a sudden the air around her hand beside my notebook grew very still and frightening.

"Well I never!" Her voice was sharp. "I thought I told you to draw this letter? You don't even want to try and do as you are told. Now I want you to turn that page over and draw your letter like everyone . . ." and turning to the next page, she saw my second name sprawled down across the page.

There was a moment of icy silence, and I knew I had done something terribly wrong. But this time, I had no idea what it could be that would get her so angry, certainly not being proud of writing my name.

She broke the silence with a wicked edge to her voice. "I see," she said. "I see we have a young lady who does not want to do as she is told. We will have to tell her mother about that." And the rest of the class snickered, as the teacher tore the page out of my notebook.

"Now I am going to give you one more chance," she said, as she printed another fierce A at the head of the new page. "Now you copy that letter exactly the way it is, and the rest of the class will have to wait for you." She placed the crayon squarely back into my fingers.

By this time I had no idea at all what this lady wanted from me, and so I cried and cried for the rest of the morning until my mother came to fetch me home at noon. I cried on the street while we stopped to pick up my sisters, and for most of the way home, until my mother threatened to box my ears for me if I didn't stop embarrassing her on the street.

That afternoon, after Phyllis and Helen were back in school, and I was helping her dust, I told my mother how they had given me crayons to write with and how the teacher didn't want me to write my name. When my father came home that evening, the two of them went into counsel. It was decided that my mother would speak to the teacher the next morning when she brought me to school, in order to find out what I had done wrong. This decision was passed on to me, ominously, because of course I must have done something wrong to have made Miss Teacher so angry with me.

The next morning at school, the teacher told my mother that she did not think that I was ready yet for kindergarten, because I couldn't follow directions, and I wouldn't do as I was told.

My mother knew very well I could follow directions, because she herself had spent a good deal of effort and arm-power making it very painful for me whenever I did not follow directions. And she also believed that a large part of the function of school was to make me learn how to do what I was told to do. In her private opinion, if this school could not do that, then it was not much of a school and she was going to find a school that could. In other words, my mother had made up her mind that school was where I belonged.

How meager the sustenance was I gained from the four years I spent in high school; yet, how important that sustenance was to my survival. Remembering that time is like watching old pictures of myself in a prison camp picking edible scraps out of the garbage heap, and knowing that without that garbage I might have starved to death. The overwhelming racism of so many of the faculty, including the ones upon whom I had my worst schoolgirl crushes. How little I settled for in the way of human contact, compared to what I was conscious of wanting.

It was in high school that I came to believe that I was different from my white classmates, not because I was Black, but because I was me.

For four years, Hunter High School was a lifeline. No matter what it was in reality, I got something there I needed. For the first time I met young women my own age, black and white, who spoke a language I could usually understand and reply within. I met girls with whom I could share feelings and dreams and ideas without fear. I found adults who tolerated my feelings and ideas without punishment for insolence, and even a few who respected and admired them.

Writing poetry became an ordinary effort, not a secret and rebellious vice. The other girls at Hunter who wrote poetry did not invite me to their homes, either, but they did elect me literary editor of the school arts magazine.

By my sophomore year in high school, I was in open battle on every other front in my life except school. Relationships with my family had come to resemble nothing so much as a West Indian version of the Second World War. Every conversation with my parents, particularly with my mother, was like a playback of the Battle of the Bulge in Black panorama with stereophonic sound. Blitz- krieg became my favorite symbol for home. I fantasized all my dealings with them against a backdrop of Joan of Arc at Rheims or the Revolutionary War.

I cleaned my flintlocks nightly, and poured my lead-mold bul- lets after midnight when everybody else in my family was asleep. I had discovered a new world called voluntary aloneness. After mid- night was the only time it was possible in my family's house. At any other time, a closed door was still considered an insult. My mother viewed any act of separation from her as an indictment of her authority. I was allowed to shut my door to my room only while I was doing my homework and not for a moment longer. My room opened into the living room, and an hour after dinner I could hear my mother calling me.

"What's that door still closed about? You not finished your homework still?"

I came to the door of my room. "I'm still studying, Mother, I have a geometry test tomorrow."

"You can't bring the book and study out here? Look your sister working on the couch."

A request for privacy was treated like an outright act of inso- lence for which the punishment was swift and painful. In my junior year, I was grateful for the advent of television into our house. It gave me an excuse to retreat into my room and close my door for an acceptable reason.

When I finally went to bed, scenes of violence and mayhem peopled my nightmares like black and white pepper. Frequently I woke to find my pillowcase red and stiffened by gushing nose- bleeds during the night, or damp and saturated with the acrid smell of tears and the sweat of terror.

I unzipped my pillow-covering and washed it by hand surrepti- tiously every weekend when I changed my bed linen. I hung it on the back of the radiator in my room to dry. That pillow-covering became a heavy, unbleached muslin record of all the nightly blitzes of my emotional war. Secretly, I rather enjoyed the rank and pungent smells of my pillowcase, even the yeasty yellow stains that were left after my blood was washed away. Unsightly as they were, the stains, like the smells, were evidence of something living, and I so often felt that I had died and wakened up in a hell called home.

I memorized Edna St. Vincent Millay's poem "Renascence," all eight pages. I said it to myself often. The words were so beautiful they made me happy to hear, but it was the sadness and the pain and the renewal that gave me hope.

> For east and west will pinch the heart
> that cannot keep them pushed apart
> and he whose soul is flat, the sky
> will cave in on him, by and by.

My mother responded to these changes in me as if I were a foreign hostile.

I tried confiding in a guidance counselor at school. She was also the head of the English department, who kept telling me that I could do much better work if I tried, and that I could really be a credit to my people.

"Are you having trouble at home, dear?"

How did she know? Maybe she could help, after all. I poured my heart out to her. I told her all my unhappiness. I told her about my mother's strictness and meanness and unfairness at home, and how she didn't love me because I was bad and I was fat, not neat and well-behaved like my two older sisters. I told Mrs. Flouton I wanted to leave home when I was eighteen, or go away to school, but my mother didn't want me to.

The sounds of traffic outside the window on Lexington Avenue grew louder. It was 3:30. Mrs. Flouton looked at her watch.

"We'll have to stop now, dear. Why don't you ask your mother to drop in to see me tomorrow? I'm sure we can fix this little problem."

I didn't know which problem she meant, but her condescending smile was sweet, and it felt good for once to have a grownup on my side.

Next day, my mother left the office early and came to Hunter. The night before I had told her Mrs. Flouton wanted to see her. She fixed me with a piercing look from out of the corner of her tired eyes.

"Don't tell me you making trouble again in this school, too?"

"No, Mother, it's just about going to college." Somebody on my side. I sat outside the guidance room door while my mother was inside talking to Mrs. Flouton.

The door opened. My mother sailed out of the office and headed for the school exit without so much as a look at me. Oh boy. Was I going to be allowed to go away to school if I could get a scholarship?

I caught up with my mother at the door leading to the street.

"What did Mrs. Flouton say, Mother? Can I go away to college?"

Just before the street, my mother finally turned to me and I saw with a shock that her eyes were red. She had been crying. There was no fury in her voice, only heavy, awful pain. All she said to me before she turned away was, "How could you say those things about your mother to that white woman?"

Mrs. Flouton had repeated all of my words to my mother, with a ghoulish satisfaction of detail. Whether it was because she saw my mother as an uppity Black woman refusing her help, or both of us as a sociological experiment not involving human feeling, confidentiality, or common sense, I will never know. This was the same guidance counselor who gave me an aptitude test a year later and told me I should consider becoming a dental technician because I had scored very high on science and manual dexterity.

At home, it all seemed very simple and very sad to me. If my parents loved me I wouldn't annoy them so much. Since they didn't love me they deserved to be annoyed as much as possible within the bounds of my own self-preservation. Sometimes when my mother was not screaming at me, I caught her observing me with frightened and painful eyes. But my heart ached and ached for something I could not name.

4. Black Fire

NELSON PEERY

We moved to a poorer part of town a few miles away from my gang and the corner. It was like starting a new life. I registered in the junior high school as the only black kid. A black student, Ann, had attended the school some three years ahead of me. She was loved by the teachers. Pretty and talented, a brilliant, straight-A student, she graduated from junior high at thirteen, high school at sixteen and the university at nineteen. I knew about her. Black and female, this lovely, brilliant young woman had no place. The best job she could get was at the post office. America forced her frustration inward until it turned to bitter, morose self-doubt and ended in a general nervous breakdown.

Within a week, the teachers were asking me why I didn't apply myself as Ann did. Since Ann was black and a straight-A student, they couldn't understand why I wasn't making straight A's.

There at Fowell Junior High, I came to the conclusion that whites are strange folk. If the first black they met was a scholar, then all blacks were scholars. If the first was a criminal, then all were criminals. Anyone different from the first was an exception. I began to understand why my parents kept reminding us of the importance of putting "our best foot forward" when dealing with whites. It wasn't, as I assumed, to get along with them, but a good impression made it easier for the next black who came along.

At an early age I learned the game that becomes a serious part of every black person's social personality. We learned roles. One person with our peers, we became a totally different person around whites. It was impossible for them to know us, and this was our defense. I didn't know how our race could stay out of the schizophrenic ward, considering the split personalities they forced upon us.

I hated to go back to school. Eighteen, older than most of the other students, I was no longer part of their half-adult, half-child world.

It was my senior year and I had to have that diploma. I had already missed more than a month and my grades last semester had been terrible. The principal did not want to let me come back. I had been in military training, and war was drawing near. That made his position—as he expressed it—"uncomfortable." The schools adopted a policy of immediately graduating any senior who enlisted. He suggested I might think about that.

The guys in our little gang and the young women around us were changing. Being away for even a short while made it so clear. They were already giving up. The school routed the women to the home economics classes and trained them for nothing but maid service. The guys were routed to the shop classes and trained for factory work. Only grades of consistently B or above and the most vigorous protests by parents would move a black student into college preparatory classes.

Making out my program, I asked for the class in creative writing as an elective. The principal slowly looked over my very poor English grades and shook his head.

Determined to take the course, I decided to see the teacher in charge of the class. When the school day ended, I went down to her office and peered through the glass-paneled door. Sitting at her desk, wearing glasses, reading through a pile of manuscripts, the teacher appeared stern—almost frightening. With her iron-gray hair knotted at the back of her head, her sharp, middle-aged features looked almost hawklike. I decided not to try it, but she glanced at the door, smiled, and beckoned me in.

At her desk, I forgot the speech I was going to make.

"Ah, I—"

"My name is Miss O'Leary, Abigail O'Leary. What's yours?"

"Nelson. Nelson Peery."

"Well, sit down, Nelson. I'm glad you came in. I've got all this stuff to read. My God, don't you kids do anything interesting anymore?"

She pushed the pile of manuscripts aside and swung her chair around to face me, nodding to a chair beside the desk. I took it. She went on talking, interrupting herself with laughs that crinkled her face, making her look kind and pleasant. Finally, she stopped chattering about her class and asked, "What is it you want, Nelson?"

Her talk put me at ease and now I wanted to talk about all the things I had to tell the people. How they are used against one another, how the Fascists planned to take over the country, tell them . . . "Well, Miss O'Leary, I want to write. I want to get in your class, but I got some bad marks in English, and the principal said no."

She smiled again. "You use some bad English, but that's not important."

I completed the form she handed me and gave it back to her.

"Peery . . . Peery. Have you always lived in Minneapolis?"

"I lived in Wabasha before here."

"I thought I knew that name. Did you know Abigail Quigley?"

"Sure," I laughed. "Once I beat up her kid brother and she grabbed a shoe and chased me into a briar patch. She spent an hour crying for me and picking the needles out of my foot. Then she gave me candy to boot."

Miss O'Leary laughed. "She's my niece. She told me about that."

We talked and laughed about Wabasha until the sun set and darkness gathered outside. Saying good night, we shook hands warmly. my hand between the two of hers. I knew I had found a friend.

The next day I met Heidi in the hall and told her I was going to learn to write. She grabbed my hands and leaned close to me.

"I'm so glad, hon."

Her eyes were deep and damp. The students walked by, some looked; no one said anything. I fought down an urge to kiss her.

"See you tonight, huh?"

"Sure. Write true, won't you? Not like you hate everything . . ."

"I do hate everything."

She pressed against me for a second and hurried to her class. Chuck walked up behind me.

"One of these days, you're gonna lose sight of the world."
Before Miss O'Leary's class, Chuck and I went out for a smoke and
I ran in just as the bell rang. The chairs were arranged in a semi-
circle, and there were a few extra ones in the back. I walked toward
them, not anxious to sit near anyone.

"Nelson, your seat is right there." Miss O'Leary pointed to an
empty seat between two white girls.

I hesitated. She smiled.

"Hurry now, we only have an hour."

I slid into the seat. I slightly knew the brown-haired, plump
young woman to my right. To my left sat an aristocratic, very
blond young woman. she smiled and said, "My name's Katherine."

I was startled. Her voice was thick with the South. I glanced at
Miss O'Leary, thinking, "What the hell kind of trick is this?"

"What's your name?" the Southerner was asking.

"Ah . . . Nels. Nels Peery."

I swung my legs away from her. I didn't want to give anyone
any excuse to say anything about me. I was uncomfortable
between the two women, but no one else seemed to notice.

Class started. Miss O'Leary had a terrible, explosive temper, and
the students were afraid of her. After being angry, she would smile
and act as if nothing had happened. I shrugged it off, thinking it
was just her Irish temper. It was just Miss O'Leary.

The class was the last period of the day. No one seemed anxious
to leave. Everyone continued the discussion, genuinely interested
in one another's work.

Miss O'Leary motioned to me.

"You have a lot of catching up to do. As soon as you can, I want
you to hand in a piece on what happened to you during the summer."

Katherine came over. A bit embarrassed, she tried to start a conversation. "I thought you took a dislike to me because I'm from the
South. I wouldn't blame you, but I do want to be friends."

Miss O'Leary smiled. I knew she had placed me next to Katherine on purpose. I stopped being angry with her.

"Sure . . . I'm sorry. I didn't mean for you to think I didn't want to be friends. I . . ."

"I know," she said. "But none of my family ever believed in segregation or discrimination. That's why we left Shreveport."

Jolted to the bottom of my race consciousness, I smiled at her. These refugees from Jim Crow were white. I went out of my way to he friends with Katherine.

I loved our writing class. Miss O'Leary pulled material out of every student. She would start the day threatening, cajoling, praising, and coaxing the work out of us. She would lead us toward thinking we might be budding geniuses, then knock us down for thinking it.

I wrote from fear of not writing and from an overpowering urge to express myself. If I handed in something trite or trivial, she raised pure hell.

"My God! Don't you know any real people? Don't hand this sort of trite writing to me again. Here, read this—if you can understand it. You're lazy and writing is the hardest work in the world. If you want to work, all right. If you want to play, get out of this class."

As did the rest, I would leave swearing never to come back. I always did.

I handed in a short sketch of Ace and West Coast. Overjoyed, she said, "It's about time, you simpleton. Everybody lives and has so much to say. You have to learn to write. Keep writing about real people."

As the school year wore on, Miss O'Leary guided me toward social and political maturity. I realized in later years that she personified the last of a great and noble part of American intellectual development. The Christian socialists of her caliber are gone. They tried so desperately to turn the tide of war and social oppression by living Christianity and struggling to plant the seeds of social morality in everyone they touched. She was my first real teacher.

As soon as I finished one book, she handed me another. From Hawthorne's *The Scarlet Letter* through Du Bois's *Souls of Black Folk* to Sandberg's *The People, Yes!* and scores of books in between was an unending, exciting awakening.

A teacher commented that one of her students was becoming too friendly with a black athlete. Flushing to an angry red, Miss O'Leary told her to kindly stay out of her classroom, and not to bother speaking to her again. She learned that Negroes were not welcome even to visit the Park Avenue apartments where she lived. She invited me to tea that very evening, making sure the manager was aware of my presence. After tea, she showed me her old-fashioned apartment. I couldn't see any value in old flatirons and tea pots but listened respectfully as she explained the period and history of each. Then she showed me her real hobby. Opening a trunk full of manuscripts, she said, "These are my children. I've written sketches on nearly every student I've had since 1912."

Under her forceful hand, the class published a quarterly literary magazine, *Quest*. The envy of every high school in the country, *Quest* had won at least one National Scholastic first prize every year for the past eighteen years. Few knew what went into making that magazine. She wrung it out of those students: fussing, belittling, humiliating them until the young women cried and the guys would almost quit. They came back for more. *Quest* won the prizes and she would throw an ice cream and cake party.

As time came to start organizing for publication, Miss O'Leary made recommendations for the various posts of the magazine. The class discussed the recommendations and approved them. Hank Franklin, a brilliant, shy, nominal member of our gang, was chosen editor. J.C. Wiggins, another member of the gang, was chosen business manager. I was chosen literary coeditor; Chuck was co-opted from the art class to work with the art editor. Four young white women filled the remaining posts. After school, on the corner, we realized that we had a staff of black guys and white women. The class did not notice it. They elected according to talent and ability. Aware of it from the very beginning, we set out to make this the best magazine published in the country.

5. C.Y.C.L.E. Stories

PATRICIA FORD

The following selections are works written by students of LaSalle Street C.Y.C.L.E., Community Youth Creative Learning Experience. C.Y.C.L.E. is a nonprofit organization housed in Cabrini-Green, a low income housing development on Chicago's north side. The mission of C.Y.C.L.E. is educational enrich-ment/empowerment. These essays, poems, autobiographical sketches, anecdotes, and short stories were written during creative writing courses taught by Dr. Robert Boone. They reflect the wealth and creativity of the young African-American mind, while embodying the ethos of urban youth. Fatalism/death, cultural identity, racial pride, ethics, alienation, and family strength are some dominant themes.

This collection captures the capacity of inner-city kids to express their life experiences through traditional and nontraditional forms. Inner-city is usually a code word for poor, disadvantaged, and minority. This stereotype negates the inherent talents and abilities of promising urban youth who are seen as "at risk." Too often these students are viewed as glasses that are half empty versus half full. This deficit-driven approach does not tap into the valuable knowledge and experience that these students bring to the classroom.

The students featured here represent the beginnings of greatness. It is your responsibility as future teachers to promote, foster, and cultivate their fullest potential.

THE LIES OF THE MEDIA

The media has said a lot about low-income housing projects. They have said that most people who live in "projects" are single parents. That people here are predominantly black and on welfare. They are saying that when we grow up we can only look forward to occupations such as: drug dealers, prostitutes, and gang bangers.

People are saying that we have *no* ambition and people who raise children here were probably raised here themselves.

They say that our homes take up too much valuable space. Space that can be used for condominiums. They say we live in a space where garbage is *never* collected, elevators *never* work, crime *never* ends, and someone is *always* being killed.

There is crime in low-income projects, but not just in "projects." There is also crime in condominiums, in buildings where security guards patrol the area. Our buildings are ones that have been vandalized, mutilated, and disrespected. We do need repairs in our buildings, but instead of complaining, someone should bring the issue out in the open so something can be done about it.

The media has expressed a lot of false statements. . . . They say we have no ambition and will never amount to anything. Many people have overcome the lies, the rumors that have been said, and accomplished their goals.

"They don't care, they feel that what they do is wrong" [the media says]. I will tell you what's wrong. It's wrong for them to twist facts and transform them into vile lies. It's wrong for them to trample the hopes of a child who lives in the projects.

I know that I will not let what they say affect my future. I have solid ambitions and plans to pursue my goals to the end. I am going to be a doctor, and I will not let lies of the media hold me back.

Christine Hamilton
12th Grade

THE QUESTION

How long must I wait
until that dreadful date
the day where all must cease
with death, that evil beast.

How long must I wait
when tomorrow is too late
I'll never see it coming
it's quiet with no dreary humming
not like it is in make believe
it simply comes for you and leaves.
You never know when your turn is up
your life might not be a full cup.
You may leave with just a sip
so make it count, let it rip.

Kitian Hamilton
11th Grade

SOMETIMES IT'S BETTER TO FORGET

Sometimes you hear about children getting killed. Where I live all children are in danger. One child that was killed changed Cabrini-Green for a while.

When he was killed all the gangs had a peace treaty. Everyone was shocked. The little boy was going to school and got shot in the head. I myself was scared because I stay right across the street from where he was shot. It was a big thing.

See, kids today need parents that can help them in this world. I'm scared. I am now on my way to high school. I hope that will never happen to me. I will not forget that because he was only a little boy, he had a life in front of him.

Yaminah Sesley
7th Grade

MAYBE

Often when I look in the mirror, I feel
as if I have been cheated. Maybe
God made a mistake
when he made me black
with an eager mind.
Maybe I was meant
to be part of a
different race.
I feel the same as a
rickety car with a
brand new engine
inside. People see
only the outside
of me and never
bother to find out
what's inside.
Or, maybe I was meant to
be black. Maybe God created me
to prove people wrong. Maybe I was
created for God's special purpose.
Maybe God created me to be a
trellis to help blacks.
Maybe he created me
to bring together
the sparse population
of the black race.

Maybe God is black.
Perhaps I was blessed
to be the color of God.
Maybe being black
is not bad at all.

Jermaine Savage
9th Grade

WHAT IS BLACK?

Black is the faces of everyone I know.
What is Black?
Black is the faces of the children that I watch grow.
What is Black?
Black is the charcoal that burns in my grill.
What is Black?
Black is the love and sex appeal.
What is Black?
Black is the blood that streams through my veins.
What is Black?
Black is the cup of my many pains.
What is Black?
Black is the heat that is in my heart.
What is Black?
Black is what was there right from the start.
What is Black?
Black is me and my sense of pride.
What is Black?
Black is the strength and the power.
What is Black?
Black is the time that has passed upon every hour.
What is Black?
Black is the ground which I walk upon.
What is Black?
Black is the sky cover when there isn't any sun.
What is Black?
Black are my hands and feet.

Victor Idowu
11th Grade

MAMA'S STORY

Get up, kids.
and clean up this house.
Get out of that bed
before I cuss you out.

I work hard for y'all kids
trying to make ends meet.
And this is the thanks I get,
coming in finding y'all asleep.

Look at these dishes
stacked a mile high.
Look at my plant
dying because it's dry.

Look at the floors
full of mud and dirt.
Look at my table
dirty with dust

When I look on the wall
you wanna know what I see?
A roach walking on the wall
staring at me.

So don't get mad or don't
say that I'm trippin'.
But for not cleaning this house
y'all kids are fixing to get a whipping!

    Fred McNeary
    10th Grade

CHOCOLATE

When I'm assigned to write about my life (in detail), I get this unexplainable feeling that signals me to start digging deep for the good stuff. But you and I both know that life contains those dark bits and pieces. It's not often that I tell someone of my accomplishments, my secrets, my sins, my treasures, and my life.

I had ponytails and black shiny shoes to complement my brown eyes of awe. My younger days were spent comparing weirdoes with the plain folk. But never was my analysis of the weirdo and plain folk given verbally. I was the type of girl that kept my smart remarks and comments inside. It was difficult for me to express my thoughts aloud because I was afraid of what others may feel.

I remember the holidays so well. The main thing I remember is the people. I remember the toys, cookies, ornaments, and Easter baskets. But I would rather focus my attention on the people because they are what makes the world go around. Our house was full of people that were disorderly, happy, drunk, full of it, or just plain skeptical. Not once would you find a sanctified person—only hypocritical. Luckily my parents were wise enough not to let this variety of people influence my daily habits, or life would have been an abstract design of an anonymous artist.

It was the Christmas of 1986. The first Christmas with my younger sister Dominique. I must say I was a spoiled child when it came to receiving toys. My eyes were wide open at the colorful sight of Christmas lights. Wider than a little girl watching her grandmother open the wrapper of chocolate candy. Christmas was a joyous time for my family. I just can't get the thought off my mind of my little sister crying over my Barbie doll and Mama saying, "Oh give it to her, you know how she is." As if this one-year-old gained such a strong personality with such spark without having a touch of experience in life. But I take pride in Dominique. Being the only child for nine years, I needed that someone to add an extra taste of chocolate to my life.

There are times when I could really get down and party. It was my fourteenth birthday with a bash. I awakened December 22 to a lively tune of "Happy Birthday." Dominique sang like she had an accent of a southern white girl. Dad sang like a drunken hillbilly. But luckily Mama was there to sing with soul. Mama's voice flowed like rich chocolate being poured smoothly over a sweet tart. She placed a melody to all the happy birthdays in 1990.

I didn't know I was having a birthday party. I thought people in my family could care less for my birthday. Hooray for surprises. I must have been in another world because I was dancing to Madonna and I was serious with my dance movements. The night was wild as my cousins and I danced freely around the West Side apartment. Thank God my parents aren't strict when it comes to furniture because we danced on, under, next to, and around every piece of furniture. Any other organized family would only allow dancing with feet flat on the floor. The Ervin family has no self-control or limits when it comes to partying. We let loose.

When it came to the cutting of the Jewel's cake, there was trouble. The Jewel box said Devil's Food Cake but inside it was Angel Food Cake. I had a fit and my mother respected that. My mother ordered my dad to take the kids to Jewel and get a Devil's Food Cake—chocolate cake. The whole birthday gang was in Jewel in less than ten minutes. My father took his finger and inspected every Jewel box. By the end of the day, I had my chocolate cake. And that's how I see life, like chocolate.

It's sweet with a dark color.

Antevia Ervin
12th Grade

BASKETBALL

It was hot. My adrenaline was pumping and I was ready to score more shots. My homey, Bruce, was feeding me the ball 'cause he knew I had been training jump shots one after another. I would go flick my wrist like a fag and the ball met the hoop like love at first sight. Onlooking spectators would applaud, chanting different sayings such as "Kill 'em, boy," "All day," and "Show no mercy."

And I would, with great appreciation, give them what they wanted. The game had quickly ended and as usual my team won. The fellas felt the same energy and some started forming a krip line for a dunk. I was like, "Hey, that's me. Let me at it," but I hadn't expected—not even in my wildest imagination—what was about to occur.

I had stepped back to get a pretty good pick-up start for the dunk. Ball was in hand. Mind was determined. Upper body poised, but as you noticed, I said nothing about my feet, because they must not have been ready for anything. I ran and recall myself going up, but somehow that didn't happen. I was laid out in the air and could feel myself in an abnormal position, but it was too late. I was coming down. Faster, faster, fas——splat! *&%#.

All I heard was people laughing, pointing, jeering, and other things I couldn't make out, for the pain was blocking my senses. I slowly picked myself up, dusted what was left of me off, and said, "Fellas, it's time for this circus clown to go home!"

They just said "You're right," and watched me leave.

Neville Horton
10th Grade

THE BLACK CINDERELLA OF THE 80S

Once upon a time in the red projects in 1160, there lived a girl named Cinderella. She lived in a house that was clean but made ugly by her stepmother and stepsisters, Antevia, Kathy, and Brenda. They always were spoiled by their mother and got everything, but Cinderella never got anything. She always had to clean. But not all the time. Sometimes she told them, "Shut up. I ain't doing nothing. Just get out of my face."

Cinderella sometimes couldn't go outside. But she begged her stepmother to let her, for she had a love she couldn't afford not seeing. His name was Runde. He was concerned about her freedom. He was also rich. On weekends he would come and pick her up and take her places.

One day a letter came in the mail. Cinderella's stepmother read it. "Oh," she said, "we're invited to the ball tonight. The prince is going to pick a girl to marry."

"Wow," said Cinderella. "I'm actually going to a ball."

"You ain't going nowhere."

"Yes I am," said Cinderella. "You never let me go anywhere."

"I know," said her stepmother. "I'm just afraid he'll pick you instead of your sisters." When her stepsisters came home, their mother cursed them out and told them to get their own clothes for the ball.

When they left Cinderella started talking about them. "Those baldheaded zombies," she thought, "I'm going to go to the ball." She took out her sharp peach Michael Jordan outfit and Michael Jordan gym shoes. She discovered she didn't have any transportation. So she prayed to her fairy homegirl. Her fairy homegirl came. "Fairy homegirl," she said, "would you grant me some transportation to the ball?"

"Yes," she said, "as you wish." Right before Cinderella's eyes came a blue Mercedes. Cinderella was going to the ball in style. She put on her starter's jacket and sat in the back seat of the car. In the front was a chauffeur that looked almost like the singer Bobby Brown.

The chauffeur took Cinderella to the ball. When Cinderella stepped in the hall, she saw a lot of people there. Most people had on dresses and suits and some had on pants. She looked around for her stepmother and sisters. She saw all four of them walking in their Nike suits. Suddenly Cinderella felt a light in her face. She looked in the mirror. She looked different. She would not be recognized by her family. She saw Runde. She ran up to him and kissed him. He said, "Don't do that. I'm a prince. Everybody might see you."

Cinderella said in a soft voice, "I'm sorry."

"You might be the one I pick," Runde said. "I love you more than anyone here. What time do you have to be home?"

"Two o'clock," Cinderella said.

Cinderella and Prince Runde danced the whole night. Cinderella bent down to tie her shoe when the bell rang on the clock, "Ding!" Cinderella started running, but because one of her Jordans was not tied, it came off.

She ran all the way home. She didn't even think about the Mercedes. When she got home she went to bed. A knock came at the door. It was her stepmother and stepsisters. As they walked in they all said, "What a night! We went there for nothing. He danced all night with the girl with the Jordan suit on."

There came another knock at the door. Kathy, her ugliest stepsister, opened the door. "Prince Runde," she said, "What brings you here?"

"I've come for my princess," he said.

Cinderella flung herself into his arms and gave him a big kiss. "I believe you dropped this," Runde said. He placed on her foot her lost gym shoe. And he promised her that she would get every pair of Jordans that came out if she married him. She said yes. And before she left she said, "I'm glad to get out of this dump."

And everybody lived happily ever after.

Yasheka Williams
7th Grade

SOUL SISTERS

I write Soul Sister with a capital "S"
Then someone dares and asks me.
"Are you proud to have an African heritage?"
The only answer I could give was, "why yes."
The Soul Sister is an extravagant black woman.
With big, blazing, brown eyes.
And wide thumping thighs.
The BLACK WOMAN
is ALL WOMAN.
From her head to her toes.
Why is she so powerful?
No one knows.
Her black, curly hair and wide smile
With that sassy, classy kind of style.

The Soul Sister walks down the Avenue
Her heels clanking against the pavement and head held high.
While our strong black men whistle and hiss
cryin', "my, my, my."
The ancient black beauties came from the Motherland,
Cleopatra, Nefertiti, and even our bestest of friend.
Yes, we were then forced to America with its wicked ways.
But we kept our pride while being thought of as slaves.
All the Soul Sister had left was her memories of Africa.
Vivid headdresses, ancient pharaohs, the mighty pyramids.
But the spirit of it all flowed from the Atlantic Ocean to
America.
Right into my Soul Sister's heartbeat.

So no one can stop the Soul Sister, for she is of dominance.

Carrying in her soul the mightiness and confidence
And in her mind the intelligence.
So I am proud to be a sophisticated Soul Sister
So sophisticated we are worth more than just a dime.

And the future of the Soul Sister will never end
For she stands the test of time.

    Antevia Ervin
    10th Grade

FRESHMAN YEAR

Freshman year, I believe, was my hardest and the most devastating as far as my academics. It took a while for me to learn that the expectations of my teachers weren't always going to be told to me, as was done in grammar school. The one-on-one attention that I had grown accustomed to was no longer existent, and the competition was much stronger. Worst of all, I received my first D and F in an Honors Early World Literature class that I was taking. In grammar school I was the teacher's pet and the class valedictorian. In high school I was back at the bottom, only one of many. I'm a very strong-willed and optimistic person, so I decided to take the beginning of a horrible year and put it to my advantage.

I give more than needed in my school work so that in most cases I can exceed the teacher's expectations. My study habits are now more efficient. I highlight, outline, and instead of ignoring the little details I pay attention to them the most. My mother told me after she discovered me crying over my D and F that everyone makes mistakes and that no one is perfect. It was this day that I decided that I would try my best to never get another grade lower than a C. So far I have succeeded. In fact, I have taken Honors English all four years and have gotten no lower than a B for each semester.

At the age of fifteen I acquired a register position at a Dairy Queen. What I thought of as being simply a part-time job turned out to be one of the most strengthening experiences of my life. It took me a while to adjust to going to school, working at Dairy Queen four days a week, and babysitting on the side, but I did adjust.

After my first night of work all of my enthusiasm about working seemed to disappear and I just wanted to give up and quit. The store became crowded with customers, so I was constantly on my feet. After being lectured by my boss about the numerous mistakes I had made that night, I was told to help sweep and mop before I started washing the dishes. When I was finally finished it was almost midnight. I had to walk home because my bus had stopped running, and I still had homework ahead of me. Afterward, I decided that I would work harder to learn everything so that in the future my working days would not seem as difficult.

My perseverance was noticed by the owner. A couple of months after my sixteenth birthday I was asked if I would like to become a manager. I was very hesitant at first because if I accepted I would be the youngest manager there. I knew it would mean hard work and more responsibilities, but I decided I would not turn down the offer without trying. Ironically, I became his most valued employee and I retained my position the longest. My major duties were supervising the workers, opening and closing the store, and handling any problems that arose while I was managing. I remained at Dairy Queen until the store closed due to financial problems. Working under pressure, making good decisions, and deciding the best way to correct mistakes and problems are some of the many valuable lessons I have learned. I am sure these lessons will last me a lifetime.

I spend my free time with College Opportunity Program 1995, which I joined in the sixth grade. Its purpose is to find a group of highly motivated students who are from low-income minority families, and to help prepare them for college. I am an African-American from a low-income family and definitely a highly motivated person, so I was accepted into this program. Tutoring, business classes, art classes, and support groups are some of the many things I am involved in with the College Opportunity Program.

My goal is to attend college and then graduate school, so that I can obtain a Master's in Business Administration. Afterwards, I plan to excel in "Corporate America." My dream is to become president of a prominent company because I feel it would be a great accomplishment.

I want to earn a great amount of money so that I can help the unfortunate of today's society. It upsets me when I see people who are blessed and fortunate disregard the homeless and abused as if they are worthless and nonexistent, expecially when they have the money to spare. There have been many days when I would give, even though I was tired and had little to spare. I know how it feels when sometimes it seems as if the ends are not justifying the means, but contrary to that fact, I would still give even if I couldn't relate, simply because I have a heart. I understand that I cannot help everyone, but I intend to help as many as I can.

I am a very talented strong-minded African-American young woman who can accomplish exceptional things when given the chance. I have very high hopes and dreams for my future. I will only be satisfied when I have achieved everything that I want to in life.

Kimberlyn Walker
12th Grade

PSYCHOLOGY

When I get older, I know for a fact that I am going to be success-ful. What I plan to do is, after my four years of high school, go to college either at UCLA or the University of Illinois. After my four years of college are over, I plan to study to be a psychologist. Then I will go out into the world and make a life of my own and settle down and maybe have children. I made a promise to myself that I will never be poor and out of money again, and I intend to keep my promise.

The main reason I have chosen psychology is because of the neighborhood I live in. Why do the people around me do the things they do? Why would they want to take another life? I want to know what makes these people tick, so that maybe I can help them. I also like this profession because it will help me to recog-nize my own problems and to learn how to handle them. Finally, I want to be a psychologist to help all people. Not only the poor, black, and disadvantaged need help, but also the rich. In fact, they seem to have more problems than the poor. I want to be there to listen and help.

Tara Landers
8th Grade

6. Testing . . . 1, 2, 3

DEBORAH STERN

THE UPTOWN GUIDE TO THE LIFE OF YOUTH (UGLY)

The Uptown Guide to the Life of Youth test is designed for one purpose. The purpose of this test is to prove that all standardized tests are culturally biased. The results from the UGLY will depend on the experiences a person has had. Are your experiences similar to that of young people in Uptown? Well, good luck!

Written, compiled, and introduced by students at Prologue Alternative High School, Chicago, Illinois: Danielle Benson, Thomas Brisco, William Bronough, Trina Campbell, Dave Foster, Eson Freeman, LaTrece Freeman, Pierre James, Arennia Johnson, Cynthia Johnson, Robert Johnson, Tammie Mason, Dinh Nguyen, Mouey Ouen, Tasha Payton, Sharond Redmond, Barnabas Riviera, Sherri Rohrbacher, Indira Rutues, Anthony Strong, and Berneice Young.

1. Yang is a) street talk b) rhythmic music c) a liquor d) a basketball shoe
2. A person who is "properdopolis" is a) Greek b) cool c) from the city d) a bank worker
3. To "put a ghost move on" means a) to wear black b) to wear white c) to disappear d) to frighten
4. What does "putting head to bash" mean? a) to beat up someone b) to have sex c) to comb your hair d) to get high
5. "Do the Right Thing" is a) a song b) a movie c) a way to use cocaine d) both a and b
6. "Lampin" means a) lighting a match b) relaxing c) drinking heavily d) committing suicide
7. A "brother" is a) a homosexual b) your parole officer c) a joint d) a black person
8. "BOS" means a) Bowl Of Soup b) Bucket Of Shit c) Brother Of the Struggle d) Bitch On the Side

9. "To jet out" is to a) eat b) have sex c) go to the airport d) leave
10. A "bucket" is a) an old car b) a bike c) an El station d) a quick meal
11. What does "coppin" mean? a) to talk about someone b) to give information to the police c) to shoot someone d) to wear a hat
12. "Bum rush" is a) a group of people doing something b) a nice butt c) mugging a street person d) a bad trip on drugs
13. What does "spray" mean'? a) to kill someone b) to get busy c) to fix your hair d) to ridicule
14. Something that is "wack" is a) dangerous b) good c) the best d) bad
15. "Figures" refers to a) money b) drugs c) women d) all of the above
16. A "bud" is a) a football player b) marijuana c) a friend d) a hairstyle
17. What is a "hype"'? a) someone who is easily excited b) a drug addict c) a dance d) a conic section
18. "Hi-top fade" is a) a dance b) a gym shoe c) a hair style d) a kind of grafitti
19. "Hip-hop" music is a) rap b) house c) disco d) salsa
20. "8 Ball" is a) a bad situation b) Old English c) an inside joke d) an automobile
21. To be "puffin" is to be a) smoking cocaine b) kissing c) smoking cigarettes d) lacking money to pay the rent
22. "Are you bangin?" refers to a) shooting drugs b) playing ball c) dancing d) living on your own
23. "Word" is the same as a) "Hi" b) "Good-looking" c) "Could you spell it?" d) "Straight up"
24. "Man, let's pull up" means a) let's go b) take it off c) let's lift weights d) let's have sex
25. "Riding the white horse" is a) riding a bicycle b) riding the CTA c) using dope d) fantasizing
26. A "hook" is a) a miniskirt b) a gang member c) a good song d) cheap liquor
27. "Skeletor" means a) performing oral sex b) a skinny girl c) Halloween d) a mean drug dealer
28. When something is "def" it is a) real good b) dead c) hard of hearing d) stolen
29. When a woman "drops a load" she a) does the laundry b) washes the car c) has a baby d) uses the bathroom
30. "Packin" is a) getting ready to go on a trip b) gathering in a large group c) getting a six-pack of beer d) carrying some kind of weapon
31. "Posse" refers to a) a large animal from Africa b) criminals in an old Western movie c) a drink d) a group of good friends together
32. "Dope" refers to a) drugs b) a stupid person c) one of the Seven Dwarfs d) something you like a lot

33. "To bone" means to a) have sex b) bite into a chicken bone c) put a bone in your hair d) all of the above
34. When someone gets "dissed," he gets a) put out of the room b) beat up c) disrespected d) spit on
35. A "skeezer" is a) a female with loose morals b) a car part c) a video game d) a new hairstyle
36. "Ride on out" is the same as a) taking money b) leaving a place c) fighting someone d) taking out the trash
37. To "spit some game" is to a) go for a ride b) talk c) take drugs d) eat dinner
38. A "freak" is a) a woman b) a weird person c) a drug addict d) a cocktail
39. "Where's the bo?" means a) Where's the action? b) I'm hungry c) Where are the drugs? d) I am the coolest
40. "The Wild Thing" refers to a) working out b) taking a vacation c) participating in a riot d) having sex
41. A "crib" is a) jail b) home c) a fake ID card d) a gang member
42. "Folks" are a) relatives b) gang members c) police d) good looking girls
43. "Beware of the corn chip" refers to a) calories b) narcotics agents c) foot odor d) Mexican restaurants
44. You say, "Give me a square" when you want to a) smoke b) eat c) sleep d) go shopping
45. What is "young blood"? a) someone who dies at an early age b) a person who has taken an AIDS test c) a young kid d) a gang fight
46. What is a "happy stick"? a) a baseball bat b) a steady boyfriend c) a job d) a marijuana cigarette dipped in embalming fluid
47. "Green" refers to a) the government b) marijuana c) money d) a family member
48. "He got popped" means a) he got drunk b) he got hit in a football game c) he got robbed d) he got shot
49. What are "dividends"? a) the price of oral sex b) money c) fast cars d) popular Rap artists
50. "Shot some rock" means a) did drugs b) played basketball c) shot a gun d) both a and b
51. What does it mean to "take a chill pill"? a) snatch someone's purse b) die c) stop doing something d) pop pills
52. What is a "homey"? a) a friend b) a lover c) a housewife d) a residential part of the city
53. You say, "Give me a dime," when you want to a) smoke marijuana b) find a prostitute c) make a phone call d) jump a police officer

54. What are "jumpers"? a) shoes b) cockroaches c) drug addicts
d) suicide victims

55. What does it mean to "get swabbed"? a) to get hit with a Q-tip b) to
get hit hard c) to collect unemployment d) to be ridiculed

56. To what does "birdy" refer? a) a far-hit baseball b) a bird dog c) a
loose woman d) the middle finger

57. What is a "G"? a) a gang b) a gun c) something good d) a pimp

58. What are "duckies"? a) people who spend time together b) money
c) inexpensive drugs d) stoolpigeons

59. What is a "jimmy hat"? a) a cowboy hat b) a condom c) a small gun
d) a gang member's hat, signifying his membership in the gang

60. "To gank" means to a) fight in a gang b) cheat or deceive c) have sex
with d) kill

61. What is "Buffalo Stance"? a) a sex position b) a cool stand c) a shelter
for homeless people d) brandy

62. "Chickabook" is a) a black person with nappy hair b) soul food c) a
hair style d) a guard dog

63. "Lamb game" is a) a stupid rap b) lying in order to get sex c) a person
who will say anything d) all of the above

64. "A player" is a) a gambler b) a ladies' man c) an actor d) a cop

65. To "kick it" means to a) go with someone b) to fight c) to play football
d) both a and c

66. A "glazed donut" is a) a way to refer to a fat person b) a way to insult
a gang member c) stealing from a convenience store d) a liar

67. "Old G" refers to a) a former gang member b) an older woman trying
to act like a young girl c) someone's mother d) a gun

68. "Pop toppin" is a) a heavy drinker b) a person performing oral sex
c) acting violent d) breaking out of jail

69. To "geek up" is to a) persuade b) to study for a test c) to shoot drugs
d) get married

70. To "be down with" means a) you have a cold b) you are intimate with
someone c) you are familiar with something d) you hate something

Answers

1. a 2. b 3. c 4. a 5. d 6. b 7. d 8. c 9. d 10. a 11. c 12. a
13. a 14. d 15. a 16. b 17. b 18. c 19. a 20. b 21. a 22. a 23. d
24. a 25. c 26. b 27. a 28. a 29. c 30. d 31. d 32. d 33. a
34. c 35. a 36. b 37. b 38. a 39. c 40. d 41. b 42. b 43. c
44. a 45. c 46. d 47. c 48. d 49. b 50. d 51. c 52. a 53. a
54. a 55. b 56. d 57. b 58. b 59. b 60. b 61. b 62. a 63. d
64. b 65. a 66. b 67. c 68. b 69. a 70. c

THE LOVE TEST

(Lifting Our Vibrations Higher for Equality)

Many tests are altogether biased—especially intelligence tests. Intelligence tests are often biased because they are based on certain information which is part of a certain specific culture. When people of other cultures take these tests, they might fail them, because they haven't been exposed to the same information. Then, these people are considered to be unintelligent.

We think this bias is unfair. To prove our point, we have created a test which you will pass only if you're from *our* culture.

Introduction by Nubia Manning. Test considered and created by Andre Adams, Erika Akins, Darrell Allen, Courtney Alston, Ronald Banks, Katrina Banner, Elliott Baskerville, Marie Battle, Aziel Bell, Cherita Broughton, Stephanie Brown, Mary Buckley, Rachel Byrd, Cozetta Castleberry, Lavanda Coats, James Coleman, Sagan Cowan, Jamie Davis, Adrian Densmore, Latossha Farrior, Joe Gaither, Ida Garner, Patricia Gibson, Darryl Glinsey, Ronnisa Griffin, Kenyatta Hardy, Raymond Jackson, Cecil James, Carl Jones, Phillip Jones, Lamont Kent, Twana Lewis, Zipporah Lewis, Shannon Lomax, Nubia Manning, Tyronza McCline, Donyale McCray, Eddie McGee, Laquita McGoogin, Lashandra McKenzie, Charles Mean, Larry Morris, Tykeith Nelson, Contrell Palmer, Claudia Ratliff, Rhonda Reed, Octavious Roberson, Arnika Scott, Rashawn Sigle, Lewis Strong, Latasha Thomas, Wallace Todd, Negal Trotter, Christopher Tucker, Monica Tucker, Brandi Wallace, Tiffany Warr, Hosea West, Mario Wigfall, Linda Wilkins, Craig Williams, Dorothy Williams, Monique Wilson, Calvin Young, and Izelda. Students from DuSable High School, Chicago, Illinois.

1. "Tripping" means a) falling down b) talking nonsense c) taking a trip d) getting high
2. "Ends" is a) pants legs b) money c) shoes d) an overdose
3. "Chillin' " means a) killing b) relaxing with friends c) getting frostbite d) being rude to

4. A "crib" is a) a baby's bed b) someone's house c) both a and b
   d) none of the above

5. "Fifty ones"/"Five-o's" means a) 51st Street b) old people c) police
   d) a gang

6. "Homie" means a) go home b) get out of town c) friend d) ugly

7. If you want someone to "show some love," you are asking for a) a hug
   or handshake b) a kiss c) sex d) a love letter

8. A "hype" is a) a drug addict b) someone who is happy c) a
   heterogeneous mixture d) a new dance

9. A "player" is a) a DJ b) a gambler c) a drug dealer d) a ladies' man

10. "To bone" is a) to make chicken b) to have sex c) to cheat d) to beat
    up

11. A "tootsie roll" is a type of a) gang initiation ceremony b) dance
    c) haircut d) marijuana cigarette

12. If you are "blown," you have been a) discovered committing a crime
    b) convicted of a crime c) drinking and/or smoking drugs d) none of
    the above

13. A "187" is a) a malt liquor b) a gun c) a good alibi d) a gang code

14. "Snoop" is a) a beer b) a nosy person c) an informant d) a new dance

15. "Fimp" is a) a junky car b) a fat wimp c) money d) food

16. A "boody call" is a) a marriage proposal b) a singles bar c) an
    invitation to have sex d) a phone call

17. "G" stands for a) great b) gangster c) gorgeous d) green (as in
    money)

18. "Dokin" is the same as a) getting busy b) using the bathroom
    c) fighting d) dancing

19. A "dove sac" is a) a bag used to catch pigeons b) $20 worth of
    marijuana c) people getting ready to fight d) Mexican beer

20. A "ride" is a) a gang b) a sex partner c) a car d) the person who
    supports you

21. A "forty" is a) a term meaning "rent money" b) a soft drink c) an old-
    timer d) a beer

22. What is a "Nelson"? a) an action figure b) a prison sentence c) a type
    of candy d) a gun

23. A "hood rat" is a) a mouse b) a juvenile delinquent c) a promiscuous
    slut d) an excuse

24. A "blunt" is a) a heavy object used to hurt someone b) a marijuana
    cigarette c) a person of mixed race d) a fight that ends in a tie

25. If someone is "fresh," they a) look good b) are rude c) are young
    d) are right out of jail

26. "Wake up" is a) a talk show b) money c) a type of rap d) a drug

27. "Kay low" means a) a house b) "All right" c) "I'm unhappy" d) a hat
28. "Dank" is a) lunch b) breakfast c) a child's game d) marijuana

Answers

1. b   2. b   3. b   4. c   5. c   6. c   7. a   8. a   9. d   10. b   11. b   12. c
13. b   14. a   15. c   16. c   17. b   18. a   19. b   20. c   21. d   22. d   23. c
24. b   25. a   26. b   27. a   28. d

THE BALLS TEST

Basic Assessment of Learning and Living Straight

This test is designed to show you the faults in most tests. If you really look at it, most of the test questions given to students are based on one certain area or culture—but these tests are given to all students, many of whom live outside that area, and many of whom are outside that culture.

That's why we designed this BALLS test. This test is based on the terminology we use every day. Our intention is to give this test to people from other cultures and other areas. Your results on this test will thus prove that tests do not test intelligence. They test background.

We want to thank you for taking the BALLS test. Hopefully you'll pass it with flying colors. But probably, unless you're from our world, you won't!

1. If someone wants you to "hold that shit down," they are saying you should a) chill b) put the gun away c) look out d) make someone look foolish
2. "Girl" refers to a) a female b) cocaine c) a gun d) a gangbanger
3. A "skeezer" is a a) whore b) person who betrays a friend c) churchgoer d) rapper
4. An "old G" is a a) gangster b) gangmember c) mother d) alcoholic beverage
5. To "break a night" means a) to stay out all night b) to kill a police officer c) to get incarcerated d) alcoholic
6. "Geek" is a) a pipehead b) a good mother c) a good student d) a cheap narcotic
7. "Ready Rock" refers to a) a famous Chicago DJ b) an erect penis c) a popular dance step d) drugs
8. "Flakes" refer to a) cereal b) certain gang members c) police officers d) a particular social disease
9. A "square" is a) an uncool person b) an attractive man c) a place where drugs are sold d) a cigarette
10. If a person is "thick," they a) have a nice body b) are stupid c) are overweight d) are drunk

11. "Bussing" means a) smoking cocaine b) taking public transportation c) well-dressed d) having sex

12. "To be tripping" is to be a) having fun b) clumsy c) taking hallucinogenic drugs d) going on a trip

13. To be "packin' " is to a) be leaving home b) carrying drugs c) carrying a weapon d) be sexually excited

14. A "homey" is a a) friend b) ugly person c) neighbor d) dog

15. "5-0's" refers to a) $5 h) police officers c) $500 d) certain crimes

16. "To be smokin' " means a) to be driving a fast car b) to be wanted for a crime c) to look good d) to be a drug addict

17. "Bogush" means a) fake b) foul c) powerful d) sexy

18. "8 Ball" refers to a) Old English b) cocaine c) group sex d) paying customers

19. "To dis" means a) "Do this" b) to disrespect c) "Over here" d) "That's cool"

20. "Excuse me" means a) "I disagree" b) "I love you" c) "Pardon me" d) "Get out of my way"

21. "Dub" is a) $20 b) a streetperson c) a good song d) a lie

22. An "A.B." is a) an all right bitch b) a college degree c) a martial artist d) an abortion

23. "A shorty" a) someone short b) a baby c) anyone younger than you d) all of the above

24. "Dog you out" means a) disgust you b) do you wrong c) lock you out of the house d) take you to McDonald's

25. A "rock star" is a) a drug user b) a transvestite c) a drug dealer d) Arsenio Hall

26. "P.W." means a) "The posse, world-wide" b) pussy whipped c) peaceful world d) powder woman (female drug dealer)

27. "Pumpkin head" means a) intelligent b) well-dressed c) got beat up d) knows all the lastest dance steps

28. "Peace out" is the same as a) "Chill" b) "I'm leaving" c) "Peace to the world" d) "I got laid"

29. "Knocking the boots" is a) having sex b) visiting someone c) escaping jail d) going shopping

30. To "get salty" is to a) get revenge b) get a great hairstyle c) score drugs d) get angry

31. "You be trippin' " means a) you're high b) you are crazy c) you are getting mad d) you are cheating

32. "Hold 'em up, Joe!" means a) "Wait a minute" b) "This is a hold up" c) "I like your clothes" d) "I'm not stupid"

33. "I ain't no Boho" is the same as a) "I'm not a slut" b) "I'm an American" c) "I'm not on Public Aid" d) "I'm not stupid"

34. To "dance" is to a) party b) have sex c) fight d) do drugs
35. "How you living?" means a) "Where do you stay?" b) "How do you support yourself?" c) "What's up?" d) "Where do you get your drugs?"
36. "How you sound?" means a) "What are you listening to?" b) "What's on your mind?" c) "What do you mean?" d) "Where are you going?"
37. "I snoozed!" means a) I played it cool b) I didn't see it c) I took a nap d) I lied
38. To "get your money" is a) to have sex b) to rob someone c) to become employed d) to buy drugs
39. A "hood" is a) a neighborhood b) a criminal c) a popular style of jacket d) an alibi
40. "Dag Joe" is a) a warning b) a soldier c) an exclamation d) a prostitute
41. If something is "straight," you will a) most likely accept it b) want to escape it c) want to fight it d) most likely be bored by it
42. You say, "Here comes agua!" when you see a) your mother b) a bar c) a police officer d) trouble
43. "Check you later" means a) "I'll see you soon" b) "I'll fight you" c) "I don't have time for this" d) "Let's get high"
44. "Slang" refers to a) selling crack and cocaine b) street talk c) a person who cheats d) respect
45. If someone is "pimped out," they a) are deceitful b) are abused c) are well-dressed d) are greedy
46. If a person is "bussin out," they a) look good b) are fat c) look angry and aggressive d) are hungry
47. "The dozens" are a) welfare paperwork b) insults c) recipes d) a women's group
48. To "dog somebody out" is to a) beat them at their own game b) mislead them c) use them d) criticize them
49. "Conk" is a) a hairstyle b) seafood c) knocking someone out d) drunk
50. If a hat is "broke," it a) is old b) is ugly c) signifies a gang affiliation d) has hair grease on it
51. "Ends" refers to a) murders b) cigarettes c) money d) difficult situations
52. "Mickey D" is a a) cartoon character b) restaurant c) preacher d) gangster
53. If you are "kickin' it," you a) are fighting b) having a relationship c) arguing d) posing or pretending
54. "The Man" does not mean a) the principal b) an important man c) a police officer d) Michael Jackson

55. If you are "percolating," you are a) upset b) scheming c) biding your time d) dancing
56. "Hoochie" refers to a) a promiscuous girl b) cheap liquor c) hide out d) the police are coming
57. "Cop a squat" means a) have a cigarette b) sit down c) hide out d) the police are coming.
58. "She can blow" means a) she is an addict b) it may rain on your parade c) she can sing d) she is working
59. If a girl is "around the way," she is a) pregnant b) from the neighborhood c) a nuisance d) adorable

Answers

1. a   2. b   3. a   4. c   5. a   6. a   7. c   8. b   9. d   10. a   11. c   12. a
13. c   14. a   15. b   16. c   17. a   18. a   19. b   20. a   21. a   22. d   23. c
24. a   25. a   26. b   27. a   28. b   29. a   30. d   31. b   32. a   33. d
34. c   35. c   36. c   37. b   38. a   39. a   40. c   41. a   42. c   43. a   44. a
45. c   46. a   47. b   48. d   49. a   50. c   51. c   52. b   53. b   54. d
55. d   56. a   57. b   58. c   59. b

City Issues

PART II

If there is no struggle, there is no progress. Those who profess to favor freedom, and yet deprecate agitation, are men who want crops without plowing up the ground. They want rain without thunder and lightning. They want the ocean without the awful roar of its many waters. This struggle may be a moral one; or it may be a physical one; or it may be both moral and physical; but it must be a struggle. Power concedes nothing without a demand.
—FREDERICK DOUGLASS

When you control a man's thinking you do not have to worry about his actions. You do not have to tell him not to stand here or go yonder. He will find his "proper place" and will stay in it. You do not need to send him to the back door. He will go without being told. In fact, if there is no back door, he will cut one for his special benefit.
—CARTER G. WOODSON

Let a new earth rise. Let another world be born. Let a bloody peace be written in the sky. Let a second generation full of courage issue forth; let a people loving freedom come to growth.
—MARGARET WALKER

It is a very grave matter to be forced to imitate a people for whom you know—which is the price of your performance and survival—you do not exist. It is hard to imitate a people whose existence appears, mainly, to be made tolerable by their bottomless gratitude that they are not, thank heaven, you.
—JAMES BALDWIN

Chaos and Opportunity

Toni Morrison's dazzling portrayal of urban extremes in her novel, *Jazz*, brings the city to life as complex, dynamic, trembling and real:

> Daylight slants like a razor cutting the buildings in half. In the top half I see looking faces and it's not easy to tell which are people, which the work of stone masons. Below is shadow where any blasé thing takes place: clarinets and lovemaking, fists and voices of sorrowful women. A city like this one makes me dream tall and feel in on things . . . I'm strong. Alone, yes, but top-notch and indestructible.

> Nobody says it's pretty here; nobody says it's easy either. What it is, is decisive, and if you pay attention to the street plans, all laid out, the City can't hurt you . . . you have to be clever to figure out how to be welcoming and defensive at the same time. When to love something and when to quit.

In Morrison one feels vitality and degradation, alienation and cherishing, and something of what John Dewey had in mind when he wrote to his wife from Chicago in 1894: "Chicago is the place to make you appreciate at every turn the opportunity which chaos affords."

Carl Sandburg marked Chicago indelibly as:

> Hog Butcher for the World,
> Tool Maker, Stacker of Wheat,
> Player with Railroads and the Nation's Freight Handler,
> Stormy, Husky, Brawling,
> City of the Big Shoulders

Sandburg's Chicago—aching with nostalgia now—is full of youthful spit: laughing, fierce, vibrant, bareheaded, sweating, overdoing it, "lapping for action." Its brashness somehow appeals, its confidence, as he portrays it, inspires. And still Sandburg's romance was not blind. He also wrote:

> . . . they tell me you are brutal and my reply is: On the faces of women and children I have seen the marks of wanton hunger.

And in "Halsted Street Car" he invites artists to ride the trolley with him, to

> Find for your pencils
> A way to mark your memory
> Of tired empty faces.
> After their night's sleep,
> In the moist dawn
> And cool daybreak,
> Faces
> Tired of wishes,
> Empty of dreams.

Sandburg's was a city of contradictions, but a city in its youth, before confidence had turned completely to arrogance, brashness to bullying. It was in many respects a great city.

Ours is a different city altogether, perhaps a city in decline, certainly no longer tool maker, hog butcher, stacker of wheat—no longer the youthful city of the big shoulders. It is still a city of courage, energy, and imaginative space, but its shoulders have slumped precipitously. What are we to make of today's proposals to revitalize the city firmly rooted in the tradition of bread and circuses? Legalized gambling, riverboats, casinos with twenty-four-hour child-care provided—these are increasingly rolled out as economic development schemes. How are we to understand policies that destroy neighborhoods for the putative goal of saving them—the historic Maxwell Street Market crushed to expand the athletic fields of the University of Illinois, for example, memories of aggression in foreign lands? And what can we say about the twisted, tangled pathway toward funding city schools, and the ragged band of characters trembling and lurching down that road together—a spectacle rehearsed in broad outline in every city from New York to Los Angeles?

Don DeLillo offers arresting images of modern cities, atomized and yet dense with a hostile, if occasionally hopeful, edginess. He writes:

"Where I live, okay, there's a rooftop chaos, a jumble, four, five, six, seven stories, and its water tanks, laundry lines, antennas, belfries, pigeon lofts, chimney pots, everything human . . . little crouched gardens, statuary, painted signs. And I wake up to this and love it and depend on it. But it's all being flattened and hauled away so they can build their towers."

"Eventually the towers will seem human and local and quirky. Give them time."

"I'll go and hit my head against the wall. You tell me when to stop."

"You'll wonder what made you mad."

"I already have the World Trade Center."

"And it's already harmless and agelesss. Forgotten-looking. And think how much worse . . . [if] there was only one tower instead of two . . . Wouldn't a single tower be much worse?"

"No, because my big complaint is only partly size. The size is deadly. But having two of them is like a comment, it's like a dialogue, only I don't know what they're saying."

"They're saying, 'Have a nice day.' "

Still, we love big cities.

We love their energy and buzz.

We love the way they pulse and hurry and drive at all hours.

We love Lower Wacker. We love rushing up State Street, bicycling home on Martin Luther King Drive, cruising along 43rd Street.

We love Chicago's straight alleyways and marvel at her crooked politicians.

We love the lake and the river.

Ah, yes, the river. That brings to mind the recent Chicago flood—an urban disaster, a crisis of subbasements, deeply felt but largely unseen.

A danger of city living, of course, is that it can mediate against any sense of a palpable, living world—a world of air and water and earth. It can give a distorted sense of power in which people treat nature—as Martin Heidegger once said—as if it were nothing more than a gigantic gas station; we lose, then, an important sense of relatedness and connectedness to place, to time and history, to a sense of integration in community. Standing in a New York concrete playground during the Mount St. Helen's volcanic eruption, a friend remarked, "I can't believe this is happening in America." The city creates an illusion of living outside of nature, apart from the world. The city as mirage.

Nelson Algren wrote of politics in his famous love poem to his home, *Chicago: City on the Make:*

> Not that there's been any lack of honest men and women sweating out Jane Addam's hopes here—but they get only two outs to the inning while the hustlers are taking four. When Big Bill Thompson put in the fix for Capone he tied the town to the rackets for keeps.
>
> So that when the reform mayor who followed him attempted to enforce the Prohibition laws, he wakened such warfare on the streets that the Do-Gooders themselves put Thompson back at the wheel, realizing that henceforward nobody but an outlaw could maintain a semblance of law and order on the common highway. Big Bill greeted his fellow citizens correctly then with a cheery, "Fellow hoodlums!"
>
> The best any mayor can do with the city since is just to keep it in repair.
>
> Yet the Do-Gooders still go doggedly forward, making the hustlers struggle for their gold week in and week out, year after year, once or twice a decade tossing an unholy fright into the boys. And since it's a ninth-inning town, the ball game never being over till the last man is out, it remains Jane Addams' town as well as Big Bill's. The ball game isn't over yet.

Jane Addams' town. What a great sound. Addams was one of our greatest dissenters—a socialist, early feminist, pacifist, and activist. She has been sanitized and defanged with the rosy glow of history, but it is important to remember that she was a fighter and a builder, that she did not follow a path already laid out. When she established Hull House in Chicago a century ago, she argued that building communities of care and compassion required more than "doing good," more than volunteerism, more than the controlling stance of the benefactor. It required human solidarity, a oneness with others in distress. She had this in mind when she opened her settlement house and lived there with families of crisis and need, saw the world through their eyes, and in fighting for their humanity, recovered much of her own.

There are countless men and women today sweating out Jane Addams' hopes, naming situations and circumstances as unacceptable, acting on their own consciousness and concern to repair deficiencies, to right wrongs. A photographer named Leise Ricketts, for example, initiated a project she calls "Drive-By Peace." She distributes cameras to young people in public housing, teaches them after school and on weekends the art of her craft, the tools of her trade. Her first assignment is always for the kids to photograph a safe place—recently, one youngster took a picture of his room, another of her mother's lap, a third of the cover of a favorite book. She is positing peace and safety as possible, something to expand and strive for.

Jamie Kalven, a writer and activist, created a program called Turn-A-Lot-Around—a citizen action project in which vacant lots are turned into gardens one lot at a time, through the collective physical labor of neighbors. Jamie is expanding the notion of environmental racism even as he names space and labor as two wasted resources in the city.

And Hal Adams, another friend, has built a stunning adult literacy project in which mothers are writing autobiographical sketches and portraits, and in the process making problems that had been experienced as personal and private, public, shared, and social. This literacy project has developed other dimensions—*The Journal of Ordinary Thought* is an irregular publication of their writings, used as a reader in some classrooms, distributed throughout the community. The participants, having found common cause, have also created social and political dimensions to their work. They have struggled together to close a crack house, for example, and to rid their community of guns. Literacy became a vehicle for deeper participation as citizens, and learning to read became linked to claiming and changing the world.

These wildly diverse projects have certain common edges. Each is built on a sense of dialogue and not monologue; participants expect to *be* changed, not merely to *bring* change. Each assumes an intelligence in people; each sees and builds upon possibility and not merely deficit. Each is premised on solidarity and not service, on a sense of community as shared and constructed and proven, not merely proclaimed. Each is dug-in, long-term, and local. And each is the work of a city teacher.

Adrienne Rich, the dazzling New York essayist, teacher, and poet describes three prototypes of modern middle-class city-dwellers. One she calls the "paranoiac"—to arm yourself with mace and triple-lock doors, to never look another citizen in the eye, to live out a vision of the city-as-mugger, dangerous, depraved, and unpredictable with, she notes, "the active collaboration of reality."

The second choice she calls the "solipsistic," to create, if you are able, a small fantasy island "where the streets are kept clean and the pushers and nodders invisible," to travel by taxi to dinner or the theater, and to "deplore the state of the rest of the city,"—filled with pollution and violence and foreigners—"but remain essentially aloof from its causes and effects."

These two prototypes are painfully familiar—each of us has experiences with a paranoid neighbor or colleague, someone filled with suspicion and alarm; many of us have even felt the perverse, attractive pull of that particular stance. Each of us has experienced, as well, those self-absorbed urbanites, the ones with the breezy air and the uncomplicated view of city life—"I love Chicago," they say, without a hint of irony or paradox as they rush from cab to health club to carry-out. Theirs is a comfortable and convenient assumption: my small, personal, privileged experience is the equivalent of the entire human experience.

Adrienne Rich posits a third possibility, an alternative to these ultimately destructive and delusional choices, something she herself struggles to name—"a relationship with the city which I can only begin by calling love." This is neither a romantic nor a blind love, but rather a love mixed "with horror and anger . . . more edged, more costly, more charged with knowledge . . . Love as one knows it sometimes with a person with whom one is locked in a struggle, energy draining but also energy replenishing, as when one is fighting for life, in oneself or someone else. Here was this damaged, self-destructive organism preying and preyed upon. The streets were rich with human possibility and vicious with human denial."

In order to live fully in the city, Rich concluded, she must above all ally herself with human possibilities, she must not run from, but seek out the webs of connection, weave them thicker and stronger and tighter. She would embrace the unmapped, the complex, the imaginable. This may be helpful for those of us who believe in a future for the city and for city schools. Can we develop relationships that we might begin by calling love? Can we develop that love—energy draining and energy replenishing—in a struggle for human possibility, for life itself? Can we imagine a world that could be otherwise?

Can city schools be saved?

If we continue the current course—the profoundly inequitable distribution of educational resources leaving most city schools starved and desperate (Chicago's DuSable High School in the shadow of Robert Taylor Homes spends six thousand dollars per year per child; the Gold Coast's New Trier High School spends twelve thousand); the existence of a range of tangled and self-interested bureaucracies sitting atop city schools, each capable of working its narrow will against any notion of the common good, and thereby rendering many schools lifeless places, hopeless and gutless; the presence of a culture of contempt for city kids, distant from communities and families, deadening for students and enervating for teachers—then the answer is certainly not. If, on the other hand, we create the collective capacity to imagine a dramatically different world, and summon the collective courage to sustain that vision as we work toward making that imagined world real, then the answer is absolutely yes. It's a tall order, to be sure, a complex matter of political will and social commitment to begin, but it is possible.

Deborah Meier, the pioneering principal of Central Park East Secondary School in Spanish Harlem, argues that what is required is "tough but doable: generous resources, thoughtful and steady work, respect for the diverse perspectives of the people who work in and attend our schools and, finally, sustained public interest in and tolerance for the process of reinvention." This is a good framework with which to begin.

The crisis in the schools today is selective. There simply is no teacher shortage in Winnetka, but in Chicago we are desperate for qualified, outstanding teachers. There is no huge command-style bureaucracy in Glencoe, while in Chicago its presence is unmistakable. And on and on: the crisis of school resources is particular; the crisis of school culture is specific; the crisis of school management is distinct.

Similarly, the school crisis is not a natural phenomenon. In this time of unexpected earthquakes, devastating hurricanes, and Biblical floods, it is well to remember that the schools we have are neither acts of God nor freaks of nature, neither accidental crack-ups nor natural disasters. We have got the schools we built, and we are reaping the crisis we ourselves have sown.

Not surprisingly, this unnatural, selective school crisis is a crisis of the poor, of the cities, of Latino and African-American communities. All the structures of privilege and oppression apparent in the larger society are mirrored in our schools: Chicago public school students, for example, are overwhelmingly children of color—sixty-five percent are African-American, twenty-five percent are Latino—and children of the poor—sixty-eight percent qualify for federal lunch programs. More than half of the poorest children in Illinois (and over two-thirds of the bilingual children) attend Chicago schools. And yet Chicago schools must struggle to educate children with considerably less human and material resources than neighboring districts.

Illinois in effect has created two parallel systems—one privileged, adequate, successful, and largely white, the other disadvantaged in countless ways, disabled, starving, failing, and predominantly African-American. When former Governor James

Thompson called Chicago schools a "black hole" as he rejected appeals for more equitable support, he excited all the racial justifications and tensions inherent in that situation. And when a host of politicians continually call Chicago schools "a rat hole," "a sink hole," and "a dark hole," they are just following suit.

The artist and social critic Jules Feiffer captures much of this tragedy perfectly in a recent cartoon. Voice bubbles emerge from the television news:

"How do you feel about being back in school?"

"We get no books. The books they give us are out of date. Classes are overcrowded. They closed the library. We got more weapons than we got teachers. The teachers are threatening to go on strike. And they cut the school budget."

"And you feel this is unfair?"

"Damn right it's unfair. I'm WHITE."

The purpose of education in a democracy is to break down barriers, to overcome obstacles, to open doors and minds and possibilities. Education is empowering and enabling; it points to strength, to critical capacity, to thoughtfulness and expanding capabilities. It aims at something deeper and richer than simply imbibing and accepting the codes and conventions, acceding to whatever common sense society posits. Education asks "Why?"—which is beyond "What?" or "How?" The larger goal of education is to assist people in seeing the world through their own eyes, interpreting and analyzing through their own experiences and reflective thinking, feeling themselves capable of representing, manifesting, or even, if they choose, transforming all that is before them. Education, then, is linked to freedom, to the ability to see and also to alter, to understand and also to reinvent, to know and also to change the world as we find it. Can we imagine this at the core of city schools?

If city school systems are to be retooled, streamlined, and made workable, and city schools are to become palaces of learning for all children (Why not? Why does "palaces" sound so provocatively extravagant?), then we must fight for a comprehensive program of change: Educational resources must be distributed fairly. Justice—the notion that all children deserve a decent life, and that the greatest need deserves the greatest support—must be our guide.

School people must find common cause with students and parents. We must remake schools by drawing on strengths and capacities in communities rather than exclusively on deficiencies and difficulties. We must focus on problems as shared and social, and solutions as collective and manageable. "Saving," then, is not the right word at all. We must talk of solidarity rather than "services," people as self-activated problem-solvers rather than passive and pacified "clients." We must note that the people with the problems are also the people essential to creating solutions.

We must, all of us, get angry at the injustices and the obstacles, and become proactive in opening new possibilities. Anyone who is waiting for someone else to get it right (the union, the school board, the legislature, the mayor) before taking action, will wait forever. The challenge is to act now, to build whatever alliances we can, to change this corner of this school right now.

7. Saving Our Cities from the Experts

SAM SMITH

If you take the long-term view of things, it may be of some comfort to realize that the neighborhoods of medieval Damascus were controlled by gangs who wore distinctive colors and specialized in robbery, looting, and assassination.

On the other hand, most of us live in the short term, so it may be more relevant to recount a few things that have occurred since I started working on this article:

- A gang of youths in my city, Washington, D.C., fired more than thirty shots into a crowded indoor market, killing a fifteen-year-old presumed to be their target and wounding eight others.
- A dozen New York City police officers were arrested for running a drug shakedown and protection racket. Many other officers knew about it and said nothing.
- The President of the United States proposed that public housing tenants in Chicago and elsewhere give up their Fourth Amendment rights and sign leases permitting warrantless searches of their homes.
- It was revealed that the only way you could get into D.C. public housing over the past few years has been by bribing a public housing official.

Because of stories like these, I hear more people asking whether there is a future for the American city.

If we feel ambivalent about cities, it is perhaps because they are big enough to contain all the contradictions of life itself—and life, Ralph Waldo Emerson noted, is "evermore beauty and disgust, magnificence and rats."

If we are fearful, we have companions in the poet Shelley, who called hell a city "much like London," and Thomas Jefferson, who saw American cities as "a pestilence to the morals, health, and liberties of man."

And if we decide to pack up and leave, we are certainly not alone. Since 1970 one-third of the people in Cleveland and Detroit have moved out without being replaced. Atlanta, Baltimore, and Philadelphia each has lost about twenty percent of its population, Chicago seventeen percent. St. Louis has lost half of its citizens since 1950.

And if we do leave, where will we go? To another city, or something barely distinguishable from it. Even when we speak of the suburbs, we are increasingly only describing a change of address, not a new life. Crime, congestion, racial conflict, worries about schools and pollution are all problems that no longer stop at city limits. We now choose between kinds of urban life, not between cities and something else.

FLEEING TO THE SUBURBS

That cities have problems is nothing new. One of the functions of cities has always been the efficient exploitation of labor, producing a continual struggle between exploiters and exploited. And there has always been crime. Architectural critic Charles Lockwood quotes a New York City mayor who declared in 1839: "This city is infested by gangs of hardened wretches" who "patrol the streets making night hideous and insulting all who are not strong enough to defend themselves."

The question of urban life has consistently been one of competing virtues and faults, but what is happening now suggests a new stage in American urban history: the growing perception that our country's major cities are not worth the trouble.

The commercial advantage of cities has been eroded by the suburbanization of business to malls and office parks, the communications advantage eroded by technology like fax machines and computer networks, and the cultural advantage appropriated by television and VCRs. Perhaps most important, we have increasingly come to see some who still need cities—immigrants and the unassimilated native poor—as threats to the common good, endangering our lives and wasting our tax dollars.

These changes in the city have been a long time coming. The streetcar and then the automobile destroyed the compact city in which people walked to work. In its place came suburbanization, the husband leaving the neighborhood for employment and the wife staying home, leading eventually to what one writer described as the modern centaur: half woman, half station wagon. These changes, which also reflected cheap energy and what we now see as a dismal misunderstanding of environmental impact, accelerated dramatically after World War II, placing enormous strains on the city. While the suburbs were enjoying an intended boom, the cities were being involuntarily decimated—socially, physically, and economically.

As freeways stabbed city neighborhoods, federal housing programs provided easy suburban money—while at the same time systematically shunning urban neighborhoods with a self-fulfilling prophecy of decline and deterioration. Businesses, manufacturing jobs, and residents drifted or were forced outward, and in their place a vast internal migration of poor southern blacks, fleeing oppression and seeking opportunity, arrived in northern cities to share tense space with the blue-collar whites the suburban boom had left behind. The national response to these developments turned sharply pessimistic following the riots of the sixties. In place of the hopeful rhetoric of the war on poverty, a language of urban despair arose. Rather than repair the damage to our cities it seemed simpler, and certainly less dangerous and more profitable, to rebuild the American city somewhere else. As early as 1972, *Fortune* declared that "Downtown Has Fled to the Suburbs."

THE MISGUIDED EFFORTS OF URBAN RENEWAL

Meanwhile, inside the old cities, the political response was not to deal with the social implications of what was happening or to respond imaginatively to the economic challenge of the new suburbs, but rather to change the look of the place—to focus on physical solutions to what were deep social and economic problems.

Behind this attempt was what author Richard Sennett has called a search for "the purified community." Describing the psychology of urban planners in *The Uses of Disorder,* Sennett says, "Their impulse has been to give way to that tendency, developed in adolescence, of men to control unknown threats by eliminating the possibility for experiencing surprise."

Even the best American minds felt the impulse. William O. Douglas wrote a Supreme Court decision in 1954 upholding the country's first massive urban renewal project, which included the brutal clearing of 551 acres of a Washington, D.C., community. Said Douglas: "The experts concluded that if the community were to be healthy, if it were not to revert again to a blighted or slum area, as though possessed by a congenital disease, the area must be planned as a whole."

Assumptions like this brought waves of urban renewal, freeways, convention centers, stadiums, subways, pedestrian malls, waterfront developments, and, most recently, proposals for casino and riverboat gambling—all in the name of urban progress and a healthier tax base.

Few of these schemes would ever come close to realizing the claims made on their behalf. Even the rise of black urban politicians did little to change the course of the American city; many became exuberant boosters of edifice economics. The black mayor may have been king, but the white business community still ran the parliament.

In the past forty years, powered by visions of sparkling new cities, we remade the urban landscape. In the name of clearing slums and blights, we have gutted many vital urban communities, replacing them with gargantuan concrete complexes for parking cars, playing sports, or doing business. Most of this has been done in the name of attracting new employment, but even when the jobs came, it didn't necessarily help the city much. For more than a decade Washingtonians heard Mayor Marion Barry brag of bringing employment to the city, yet when the final score was in, all the new private jobs—sixty thousand of them—went to mostly white suburbanites, while employment of D.C. residents, who are mostly black, actually declined fifteen thousand.

Even midsized towns have become enamored of this big-project approach. *The Casco Bay Weekly,* an alternative newspaper in Portland, Maine, commented: "There's been a piranha-like feeding frenzy to build aquariums ever since Baltimore revitalized its waterfront with a big and fancy fish house in 1981. Every town and city in search of touro-dollars since has erected new aquariums. . . . The bandwagon is picking up speed and Portland is desperately trying to hop aboard. But how many big fish can the American public be expected to look at? Our guess is that when you reach a certain concentration, the allure of fish watching drops off dramatically. If every midsized city in the nation builds a glitzy aquarium, why should anyone come to Portland to watch fish?"

WHAT REALLY NEEDS FIXING

This emphasis on physical solutions to urban woes exemplifies what British critic G. K. Chesterton once described as "the huge modern heresy of altering the human soul to fit its conditions, instead of altering human conditions to fit the human soul."

The alternative to misguided urban politics, in the nice distinction made by urban sociologist Clause Fisher, is policies for urban people. What we call urban policy usually involves the manipulation of data that, in the end, explains far less than it pretends to, judging the urban experience on economic, physical, or statistical factors that may move in directions quite separate from urban dwellers' cultural and emotional wishes.

For each of us there is a public and a private city. Some live primarily in the former and typically describe the city with concrete numbers—so many of some problem per hundred thousand people, for example. Many of us, however, know the city as a collection of specific places, people, and stories—our favorite corner of the park, Gus the grocer, memories of the big snowstorm.

Urban policy seeks to improve a city's numbers rather than the real stuff of individual lives. The result is that many plans still implicitly assume that part of the solution is a "better" class of people moving to the place being planned. We do not yet require human impact statements that might reveal a plan's true cost in higher rents, ethnic and economic change, effect on existing social patterns and neighborhood institutions, or access to places that matter.

Each of us can map our own private city by placing a pin in a map for each location we have visited over the past several months. This personal city might include only a small portion of the metropolis, a fact that suggests one of the prime assets of city life: choice. In a city we can create our own village, and we can select our own family.

It is this flexibility—this sense of many possibilities—that per-haps best distinguishes the traditional city not only from rural and small town America but even from the life of the newer suburbs. The traditional city offers new opportunities, which in turn are accompanied by risks. Arnold Weinstein, who teaches a course on the city and the arts at Brown University, points out that a number of qualities of the city—anonymity, chance encounters, and numerous exchanges—can have both happy and sad endings. We can be free of prying neighbors but we can also be lonely; we can get a good job and we can be mugged. This very level of risk may self-select for the city a more aggressive, unconventional, and ambitious resident.

It is also important to bear in mind that the characteristics we ascribe to the city may actually be characteristics primarily of American cities, reflecting cultural traits such as competitiveness and violence. In many European cities, the upper middle class congregates in the center of town and the poor live in the suburbs. Americans traditionally have been more antiurban than Euro-peans, which may, it has been suggested, make it more difficult for us to commit ourselves to the improvement of our cities.

THE CITY AS A GOOD PLACE TO LIVE

Cities' enduring service to our conflicting urges for both security and excitement makes even the grimmest among them magnets for new residents. Even as people approaching middle age—who have used cities successfully for their own careers and other purposes—flee to the quiet, comfort, and safety of another place, the artist, the ambitious new immigrant, the drug dealer who will someday cash in his chips for a legal business, and the young college grad move in and begin the urban story again.

Yet it is now difficult, in the midst of the litany of urban tragedies played up on the local evening news, to recognize—let alone celebrate—this traditional urban tale. Even in progressive political circles, urban politics has become largely a grim matter of legislative panhandling, subsidizing survival, and mitigating damage. Fatalism creeps into most of our talk of urban affairs.

Consider, for example, the Los Angeles riots. In the millions of words pouring out after the uprising you could easily search in vain for one sentence implying that anyone—victim, participant, or would-be reconstructionist—had any real hope for our inner cities other than partial salvation through moral conversion or partial recovery through endless subsidy.

But what if, just for a moment, we had put aside our fatalism and asked ourselves a different sort of question: How could we turn South Central L.A. into a good place to live?

It is a revolutionary question because, by asking it, we bring the people of South Central L.A. out of the shadows of stereotypes, statistics, and sob stories. We begin to view their problems as we might that of a neighbor rather than that of an abstract crisis to which we must dutifully but futilely tithe in the name of doing something.

The people living in a poor community like South Central L.A. are mostly normal people in abnormal circumstances. To be sure, such communities have an excess of social deviants, but they deviate from their own community's norms as well as those of America in general. It is one of the libels of our times to assert that the failure of the poor urban communities is a failure of morality or of courage. Walk down any inner-city street in America and you'll find more people with more courage, resilience, and integrity than you'll find in your average TV newsroom, corporate headquarters, or government offices. These are people who every day have to face the most extraordinary strains on their dignity and self-respect.

The first, easiest, and cheapest positive step we can take is to eradicate phrases like "ghetto pathology," "at risk," "culture of poverty," and "permanent underclass" from our vocabulary. This is powerfully self-fulfilling rhetoric and an alibi for our indifference. Until we see city communities as real places with real people entitled to the pursuit of life, liberty, and happiness, we will continue to regard them as targets of triage rather than as an integral part of our society. We will see them as inevitable victims rather than as probable survivors.

To free ourselves from the urban crisis we must first free ourselves from the idea that an unhappy ending is inevitable.

BACK TO THE NEIGHBORHOOD

If change is to occur, there must first be a political mechanism for it. One of the primary characteristics of our political system is the isolation of the citizen from the politician. This wasn't intended by the country's founders. The first Congress represented only forty thousand people; there are six hundred thousand people in the average congressional district today. Citizens today lack access to politicians, and politicians, responsible for oversized political units, rely heavily on bureaucrats who are unresponsive to the citizen.

Neighborhood government offers an antidote to the gap between government and governed. There is, after all, little reason to cling to the notion that the solution to our problems is to spend more money on a centralized form of urban government that has increasingly shown its incompetence.

Neighborhood government is also pragmatic politically. Much political dissatisfaction comes from residents' inability to make their concerns felt at city hall. Problems are specific; big city government by its nature is general. If you don't fit the mold, you get left behind.

One way to quickly and dramatically shift the power in a city away from city hall and to the neighborhoods is to create elected neighborhood councils with real power, including the power to sue the city government, to run community programs and businesses, to contract to provide services now offered by city hall, and to have some measure of budgetary authority over city expenditures within its boundaries. Not the least among their powers should be a role in the justice system, since it is impossible to recreate order in our communities while denying communities any say in maintaining it.

Budgetary authority (not the actual money) could be granted over, say, one percent of a community's pro rata share of a city budget. In D.C., this would mean an extraordinary $1 million for a neighborhood of twenty thousand people. Federal revenue sharing of a similar magnitude could produce another million dollars for every community of twenty thousand in the country. Consider what could be done in your own community for $2 million a year and then try to figure out what happens to the money now.

While one community might choose to spend its money on education, another might choose more police patrols or recreation facilities. There would be mistakes, but they would be our mistakes, easier to understand and to rectify. By permitting error we would also be permitting genius, which other neighborhoods could follow.

CITIES TAKING CARE OF THEMSELVES

The city is changing, whether we do anything about it or not. Some say new communications technologies, especially telecommuting, spells the end of cities as we know them. Telecommuting, however, is far more adaptable for some businesses than others (the greatest private contributors to the gross national product are real estate and retail trade, neither an easy candidate for telecommuting). And *Wired* magazine recently added the concept to its Hype List on the eminently practical grounds that "most employees still believe that physical visibility is necessary for promotions and this will keep telecommuting from catching on."

But such changes tend to obscure the fact that we are not experiencing the replacement of the city so much as its transformation.

What is really occurring is a diaspora of urban culture so pervasive that towns like Burlington, Vermont, and Lancaster, Pennsylvania, are cropping up in business magazines as centers of urban economic opportunity.

If other cities are losing out in this transformation, it may be as much a result of the entropy of imagination as anything. The eminent urban observer Jane Jacobs in her *Cities and the Wealth of Nations* argues that "economic life develops by grace of innovating; it expands by grace of import-replacing." By this, Jacobs means the process of becoming more and more self-sufficient. Jacobs talks about urban development officials who "work so hard to attract industries into moribund economies which for seemingly mysterious reason are too passive to generate industries of their own." It is this passive approach—easily identified by the obsession with attracting rather than creating new business—that characterizes the economy of many of America's older cities.

Consider, for example, zip code 20032, one of the poorest in Washington, D.C., with a per-capita income of $9,039. By American standards that's not much, but it's greater than the per-capita gross domestic product of Israel and almost as much as that of Italy and the United Kingdom. The total household income of this one poor neighborhood is $370 million a year. What happens to that $370 million after it gets to the neighborhood is vital to what happens to the people who earn it. At present much of it simply flows into the community and out again.

The key to urban economic revival is the development of self-generating economies. Small business is at the heart of self-generating economies, as local people are hired and then can keep the money in the community by spending it at other small businesses. Yet most cities have encouraged, through rezoning and other techniques, the removal of small businesses that employ city residents to make space for larger corporations whose workforce is heavily suburban. The importance of such economies tends to be disregarded because they don't have the visible form of a single corporation or factory. Yet the impact can be dramatic.

If all of Washington's taxi drivers worked for a single company, they would form the largest firm in the city. You'd never guess it from public policy, which is far more concerned with regulating the drivers than with encouraging them.

Overregulating businesses in municipalities has also caused a drop in jobs. Over the past few years Washington, D.C., has lost thousands of jobs through overregulating (or too-rigid enforcement of the laws regarding) street vendors, cabs, art studios, street performers, interior decorators, and home occupations. Every time someone thinks of a way to make money outside of working for a major corporation, a city council member comes up with a law to make it as difficult as possible. The result is a reduction in employment, more "illegal" activity, and a growing tendency toward industry concentration, since only the most powerful firms are equipped to deal with the regulatory morass. Thus the economic space between being homeless and being a junior partner is slowly emptied.

JUSTICE AND THE 'HOOD

The problems of the city are intimately related to the problem of crime: the failures of our cities contribute to crime, and crime contributes to the failure of cities. The question is how to interrupt this destructive cycle. The conventional answers—more police and more jails—not only haven't worked, they are beginning to bankrupt a number of cities.

At the core of the problem is a miserable, ineffective, unconstitutional, and hypocritical "war on drugs." In truth, the drug problem is really an outward and visible sign of a multitude of other crises, many of which we show little inclination to confront. Where there are drugs there are bored, underpaid, or unfulfilled workers; teenagers without hope; parents alone and adrift; graduates without moral vision. Drugs are a symptom of the city without community; education without meaning; a culture without purpose. And increasingly, drugs and mental illness go together.

The war itself has been a failure. We are no longer fighting the war on drugs to save the lives of addicts or to protect citizens accidentally in its line of fire. If we were, we would certainly notice the hypocrisy of demanding a tougher approach to violent crime while jamming our court system with minor drug cases. Just as in Vietnam, we really are fighting the war in order to justify the decision to have begun it in the first place. We are fighting to protect the jobs and the budgets of those who still insist, in the face of massive evidence to the contrary, that the drug war will work.

One of the worst products of this war has been its contribution to urban violence. Drive-by shootings, assaults in schools, and random attacks on innocent persons have resulted in growing demands for harsh retribution. Most middle-class citizens, however, are unaware of the degree to which poorer urban America is already under paramilitary occupation. They don't know about the de facto driving violation known as DWB—driving while black. White middle-class citizens do not match the profile of a drug courier; they don't go to schools where the police—in a bizarre perversion of Officer Friendly—offer black students advice on how to behave when they're stopped by the police (as most of them will be); they don't wake up in the middle of the night with the National Guard shining spotlights on their homes or live close enough to a crack house to have their door mistakenly broken down by a SWAT team. Thus, there remains the stunningly inaccurate myth that we have not been tough enough on urban crime.

The truth is that we long ago reached the outer limits of law enforcement's ability to deal with urban crime. As one police official put it, what the police do is arrest people and "we already have more arrests than we know what to do with." What we have failed to do is to deal with the culture of crime and its alternatives.

Here is one small example: Washington, D.C., recently became exercised over the increase in guns and violence in its schools. With great fanfare, the mayor announced a program that would add more police officers to schools that had experienced the most problems. Few noticed that there were other schools, also in high-crime areas, that had not experienced unusual violence and had not been placed under intense police patrol. Why were these schools different? I asked the chief of security for the schools.

Without hesitation, he replied, "Good management." In other words, the school system was using the police to compensate not just for violent kids, but for poor principals as well—including one who returned a weapon to a gun-toting student at the end of the day.

There are other cultural causes to be found in this story. One of the reasons given for the inability to control guns in the schools is that some of the buildings have as many as fifty exit doors. How does one introduce a feeling of community in a building so huge that it has fifty exit doors?

Instead of dealing with such issues, we once again call upon the police to replace the former functions of family, community, school, and church. The irony is that the drive for family and community is so strong among the young that they manufacture a surrogate for what has disappeared. They call it a gang.

On the other hand, the imaginative introduction of positive alternatives can have encouraging results. One of the most significant may be the teaching of mediation and conflict resolution. A teacher in this field, Kathy Owen, notes that many of the young simply lack the skills or language to respond other than physically to being "dissed." Her work has been so successful that one of her high school students, upon hearing a bus driver and a passenger in the midst of a heated dispute, walked to the front of the bus and announced, "I am a trained mediator. I think I can help you." And she did.

We also need to find ways to restore the role of the community in social order. Most law and order stems from personal and community values or peer pressure of one sort or another—not law enforcement. Community courts and neighborhood constables or sheriffs are one way of re-creating community law and order. Community courts could deal with misdemeanors using correctives such as community work and various forms of restitution.

Neighborhood constables or sheriffs could have the power of arrest and become symbols not of the city's law and order, but of the community's. Strange as this idea might seem, downtown business districts and shopping malls regularly practice it; their constables are called security guards. New York City's 42nd Street project employs some forty public safety officers all linked by radio to the city police. In the first two years, thanks also to a community court that could handle minor offenses quickly, pickpocketing and purse snatching in the area dropped by forty-two percent. Other urban neighborhoods are entitled to similar protection.

THE CURSE OF ZONING

One of the largest unacknowledged urban problems is zoning. Current zoning laws generally are blithely indifferent to decades of accumulated ecological knowledge, to the changing status of women, to the need for new economic opportunity. The bias is against mixed-use neighborhoods, home employment, and technological experimentation and innovation—and in favor of a socially, environmentally, and economically unsound emphasis on isolated single-family residential living.

Edmund Fowler, a Canadian urban scholar and author of *Building Cities That Work*, notes that in most large North American cities, vast areas remain largely unused during weekdays and come to life only at night and on weekends. As Fowler points out, our thinly settled segregated city has encouraged us to want mobility—the ability to get what we need—rather than access, which is having what we need where we need it. I once asked a transportation expert to name the single most efficient mode of mass transit. His reply: "Stop people from moving around so much." Nothing we can do with mass transit can match the effect of lessening the need for people to travel.

To live the way we do takes enormous amounts of space. Marcia Lowe of the Worldwatch Institute reports that while the New York metropolitan region's population has grown only five percent in twenty-five years, developed areas have increased by sixty-one percent, "consuming nearly a quarter of the region's open space, forests, and farmlands."

Paradoxical as it sounds, agriculture and wilderness are an essential part of a city. Not only do they contribute to ecological balance, they offer solid social, economic, and psychological advantages as well. One place that understands this is Oregon, which passed a land use act in 1973 that required each of the state's 242 cities to "adopt plans that use urban land efficiently, while protecting prime farm and forest lands," reports the magazine *City Watch*. "The anchor of this program is a tool known as an urban growth boundary. The UGB is a line that sharply defines the border between urban and rural. . . . New development is severely limited or prohibited outside the line."

Of course, you can also grow things in the city. Hong Kong, one of the world's densest cities, raises forty-five percent of its own vegetables. One survey of Harlem found a thousand lots that might be used for urban gardens were they not filled with trash, toxic material, and drug dealers. Harlem's agriculturists have generated so much enthusiasm with their current projects that there's talk of establishing vineyards to produce the grapes for a Chardonnay de Harlem.

The more we advance into new and creative thinking about the ecology of cities, the more we find ourselves drifting closer to other things—our work, our food, our environment, and our neighbors. As we change our focus, we find ourselves rejoining the crowd—rediscovering the virtues of density. One study found that per-capita energy use in a low-density city is twice that in a high-density city.

After college, I lived in a rooming house in Washington's Capitol Hill neighborhood that housed five single tax-paying young people. Today the house is occupied by one family. My neighborhood restaurant, gas station, dry cleaner, and mom-and-pop grocery store are gone, all carefully excised from the urban landscape in the name of a better Capitol Hill. But however much more upscale the ambience is now, there has been a hidden economic cost: fewer businesses per block and fewer taxpayers per square foot. One futurist business newsletter has already identified the revival of boardinghouses as one of the trends of the nineties.

Granny flats (accessory apartments in homes) as well as reviving the practice of taking in boarders could increase density and community in our cities. The boarder tradition played a major role in the growth of the American city, providing newcomers with an inexpensive place to stay while adding a source of income for those who had lived in the city long enough to own a house.

There are, of course, many other housing solutions—among them cohousing—but accessory apartments and rooming houses are particularly noteworthy because they are examples of the many urban solutions that do not require high technology, massive bureaucracies, or huge expenditures.

CLEANING UP THE PLACE

In the 1960s, in the wake of riots four blocks away, a block club was formed in our neighborhood. The name—the Northeast Progressive People's Association—reflected the grandiose politics of the times but the first project, suggested by a neighbor whose own backyard was paved with cracked cement across which rats would scurry in the yellow glow of the crime-fighting lights, was that we get some grass seed and plant it in all the bare spots of our community.

Ever since, when I read of a politician, journalist, or urban policy wonk condemning "cosmetic approaches" to city problems, I wince. The hubris of many experts includes the assumption that others can wait as patiently as they can for things to improve.

Later, when I was president of our elementary school's parent association, the regional superintendent bragged to our board that her staff had painted their office. I immediately asked, "Where did you get the paint? We'd like to paint our school, too." She came through, and we—parents, students, and teachers—painted the inside of the school for a whole weekend.

It is easy to lose sight of such little things in the complexity of urban America, but they are important. Buried in the news following the L.A. riots were details of a $3.6 billion recovery plan offered by two of the city's most notorious gangs, the Bloods and the Crips. Here, included among larger proposals, are a few of their ideas:

- All pavements/sidewalks in Los Angeles are in dire need of resurfacing
- We want a well-lit neighborhood. All alleys shall be painted white or yellow.
- All trees will be properly trimmed and maintained. We want all weeded/shrubbed areas to be cleaned up and properly nurtured. New trees will be planted to increase the beauty of our neighborhoods.
- All schools shall have new landscaping and more plants and trees around the schools; completely upgrade the bathrooms, making them more modern, provide a bathroom monitor to each bathroom [who] will provide freshen-up toiletries at a minimum cost to the students.

At a time when white America—and even much of black America—was wallowing in a postapocalyptic vision of the city fostered by movies and the evening news, at least some at ground zero were envisioning a place of beauty.

BROADENING THE TOP

At the other extreme, there are matters that need to be tended to that are much larger than any individual city. The whole structure of the federal government is antiurban and, by corollary, antipoor and antiminority. The Senate is so segregated that if it were a school system it would be facing court-ordered busing.

How do we start to change this? One solution would be to create additional states carved out of metropolitan areas. The efforts of Washington, D.C., and Puerto Rico for statehood could set a precedent. There is nothing particularly radical in this—ask the folks in West Virginia, Maine, or other states that were formed out of existing states.

There is also the vexing problem of distributing tax dollars fairly. One of the soundest approaches is federal revenue sharing, under which federal monies are redistributed to states and localities with relatively few strings attached. The concept, gutted during the Reagan years, could be revived with the addition of grants to neighborhoods that have elected governing bodies.

There has also been some talk of and experimentation with regional tax pooling (under which revenues are redistributed to a region's neediest jurisdictions). And the existence of enormous differences in property tax revenues between cities and suburbs is at the heart of many regional fiscal inequities. The resolution of this problem may well have to await a Supreme Court that recognizes that communities as well as individuals can be discriminated against and that neighborhoods may be entitled to affirmative remedies just as much as an individual or a class based on race or sex.

NEW PLACES AND OLD STORIES

One instructive alternative to the conventional urban or suburban community is a neotraditional village such as Kentlands, designed by Andres Duany and Elizabeth Plater-Zyberk on a 352-acre plot in Gaithersburg, Maryland. Their plan is based on the traditional grid system with narrow streets. Schools, shopping, parks, and recreational facilities are within walking distance of the homes.

Wandering around Kentlands recently, I accidentally drove into an adjacent development of conventional suburban townhouses. What immediately signaled my error was not just the comparative blandness of the architecture but the rows of cars in front of each abode. At Kentlands, with its garages on the alley, the automobile is far less intrusive.

At the same time, there was a similarity between the two developments not usually mentioned in the generally well-deserved praise of Kentlands and similar efforts. In neither place, it seemed, was there a story. Nor was there any sign of serendipity. Nowhere was there cause to ask, "Now how did that come to be there?" Or "What's that for?"

For the moment, Kentlands reminds one of Arthur Schlesinger Jr.'s remark that a community without history is like a person without memory. Clearly, in ten or twenty years there will probably be more interesting tales from Kentlands than from its neighboring suburban development, but what will they be? Will the varied, historically inspired architecture define the outer limits of the community's eccentricity, or will it inspire human variation as well? Will it be a community or only a subdivision with a twist?

And why do we tend to be more impressed by new developments like Kentlands than we are by the communities they deliberately copy? The very perfection of the place reminds us of the greatest quality of older cities and towns—an incalculable gift of surprise, quirkiness, and chronological character—along with the fathomless wealth of stories and mysteries to be found there.

It is, after all, the cities we now disparage that inspired the neo-traditionalist architects, just as much of what we need to do to save our cities involves little more than adapting urban practices and habits of earlier eras.

We have in recent decades been so intent on making our cities neat and orderly that we have forgotten that the city's major contribution is its random potential for opportunity. Our goal has been physical order and fiscal benefits; the results have been social disorder and huge deficits.

This was a big mistake, but, in the end, it was not the fault of the physical form of the city or its economy or even its size. Rather, it came about because too few were allowed to decide too much. Without functioning citizens you cannot have functioning cities. As Shakespeare said, "The people are the city." And, as Jane Jacobs added, "Cities have the capability of providing something for everybody, only because, and only when, they are created by everybody."

8. City Lights

LEWIS H. LAPHAM

Each person, withdrawn into himself, behaves as though he is a stranger to the destiny of all the others. His children and his good friends constitute for him the whole of the human species. As for his transactions with his fellow citizens, he may mix among them, but he sees them not; he touches them, but does not feel them; he exists only in himself and for himself alone. And if on these terms there remains in his mind a sense of family, there no longer remains a sense of society.
—ALEXIS DE TOCQUEVILLE

During the first two weeks of May, I listened to a great many politicians worry about the scenes of urban apocalypse in South-Central Los Angeles, but the more often they mentioned "the crisis of the cities" or "the need for meaningful reform," the less convincing I found their expressions of concern. Most American politicians neither like nor trust the temperament of large cities, and their habitual animosity showed through the veneer of the speeches. They said what they were supposed to say—"healing the wounds of racial injustice," "a tragedy for us all," "human suffering," "rebuilding America's destiny"—and although many of them even went to the point of promising money—"enterprise zones," "relief funds," "bank loans"—it was clear that they would rather have been talking about something else. President George Bush appeared briefly in Los Angeles on May 7 and 8, a week after rioting and fire had laid waste to roughly fifty square miles of the landscape, and his palpable uneasiness defined the tenor of the response from the leading manufacturers of the country's conscience and opinion. What he said wasn't much different from what everybody else said (cf. the anguish in *Time* and *Newsweek*, Governor Bill Clinton's campaign statements, the anguish on

Nightline and *Meet the Press,* Governor Pete Wilson's press conferences, the anguish of Dan Rather), but Mr. Bush has a talent for
embodying a falsity of feeling that lends itself to almost any
solemn occasion, and his performance in Los Angeles admirably
represented the attitudes of a social and political class that regards
the city as its enemy. He arrived among the ruins of Vermont and
Western avenues at dawn on Thursday, riding in a heavily armed
limousine under the protective escort of the Secret Service, the
LAPD, and the National Guard. His advisers allowed him to
remain in the neighborhood for no longer than three hours in the
early morning, before too many people were abroad in the streets,
and his entourage had gone before most of the local residents
knew that it had come. Walking through streets still sour with the
smell of smoke, the President was obviously disturbed by what he
saw of the wreckage, and his unscheduled remarks veered off in
the direction of unfamiliar emotion. Speaking to a small congrega-
tion in a Baptist church, he said, "We are embarrassed by interracial violence and prejudice. We are ashamed. We should take
nothing but sorrow out of all of that and do our level best to see
that it's eliminated from the American dream."

Clearly the President was chastened by the sorrow and resentment of the people to whom he spoke, but his words were somehow tentative and contingent, as if they could be withdrawn on a
month's notice. C-Span's television cameras followed him on his
pilgrim's progress through the ashes of an urban slum, and as I
watched him keep to his schedule of condolence I understood that
it was a small, drawing-room story about George Bush (his education, conduct, and deportment), not a large and tragic story about a
society that could inflict upon itself the despairing ruin of South-
Central Los Angeles.

By Friday morning the President had recovered his optimism
and his sense of political proportion. He announced a gift of $19
million (for clinics and schools and the harrying of drug dealers)
and he went to a hospital to visit a fireman severely wounded by
gunfire on the first night of the rioting. Partially paralyzed and
unable to speak, the fireman lay on his bed watching Mr. Bush

sign autographs and hand out tie pins. The President was cheerful but nervous, and in a moment of awkward silence he said to the fireman's wife, "This is fantastic. We're glad to be here. Absolutely."

To the wife of another fireman injured in the riots, the President, still trying to make polite conversation and meaning to show that he, too, was acquainted with grief, spoke of the heavy seas that had come last October to Kennebunkport: "I'm sorry Barbara's not here. She's out repairing what's left of our house. Damn storm knocked down four or five walls. She says it's coming along."

The American ruling and explaining classes tend to live in the suburbs, or in cities as indistinguishable from suburbs as West Los Angeles and the government preserves of Washington, D.C., and their fear and suspicion of the urban landscape (as well as the urban turn of mind) would have been well understood by the gentlemen who founded the republic in Philadelphia in 1787. The idea of a great city never has occupied a comfortable place in the American imagination. Much of the country's political and literary history suggests that the city stands as a metaphor for depravity—the port of entry for things foreign and obnoxious, likely to pollute the pure streams of American innocence. Virtue proverbially resides in villages and small towns, and for at least two hundred years the rhetoric of urban reform has borrowed its images from the Bible and the visionary poets. Under the open sky (or a reasonable facsimile thereof) the faithful gather by the firelight to denounce the metropolitan sewers of crime and vice, and every now and then a knight errant—Jimmy Carter, Ralph Nader, Gary Hart, Ross Perot, et al.—rides off toward the dark horizon under the banners of redemption.

A similar bias informs the romantic spirit of American literature and provides the plots for popular melodrama. With remarkably few exceptions, the writers of genius decry the foul and pestilent air of the city, and instead of staying in town to paint the portraits of society they wander off into the wilderness in search of spiritual salvation. Thoreau beside his pond, Melville in the vastness of the southern ocean, Hemingway off the coast of Cuba—all of them glad of their escape from the stench of commerce in Boston and New York.

The conventional hero of the western or detective story (sometimes known as John Wayne or Humphrey Bogart, at other times taking the alias of Gary Cooper, Clint Eastwood, or Harrison Ford) rides into the dusty, wooden town and discovers evil in even the most rudimentary attempts at civilization. The hero appears as if he were a god come to punish the sin of pride and scourge the wicked with a terrible vengeance. After the requisite number of killings, the hero departs, leaving to mortal men and women (i.e., wretched citizens) the tedious business of burial, marriage, and settlement.

The movies and television series delight in showing the city as a killing ground. Predators of every known species (pimps, real estate speculators, drug addicts, prostitutes, dissolute prosecuting attorneys, and venal police captains) roam the streets as if they were beasts drifting across the Serengeti Plain. The successful protagonists learn to rely on their animal instincts. If they make the mistake of remaining human (trusting to the civilized virtues of tolerance and compassion) they die a fool's death in the first reel.

Given the preferred image of the city as godforsaken heath, it's not surprising that so many American cities come to look the way the audience wants and expects them to look. The proofs of worldly ruin give credence to the theorems of transcendental grace. If American cities have the feeling of makeshift camps, littered with debris and inhabited, temporarily, by people on the way to someplace else, it is because we conceive of them as sulfurous pits in which to earn the fortune to pay for the country rose garden and the house with the view of the sea. The pilgrims come to perform heroic feats of acquisition and then to depart with the spoils to the comforts of Florida or the safety of Simi Valley.

To the extent that we measure the distance between the city and the suburbs as the distance between virtue and vice, we confuse metaphysics with geography, and so imagine that blessedness is a property of the right address. During the Cuban Missile Crisis of 1962, in the early afternoon of the day on which the thermonuclear judgment was believed to be well on its way north from

Havana, the city editor of the *New York Herald Tribune* sent me into Times Square to ask random citizens for opinions on their impending doom. Most of the respondents expressed a degree of anxiety appropriate to the circumstances, but I remember a woman from Lake Forest, Illinois, who told me that I had addressed my question to the wrong person, and who smiled as agreeably as President Bush handing out tie pins in the Los Angeles hospital room. "I wish I could help you," she said, "but I don't live here, you see. I'm just visiting from out of town."

The spirit of the age is feudal, and the fear of the cities allies itself not only with the fear of crime and disease and black people but also with the fear of freedom. The energy of the city derives from its hope for the future and the infinite forms of its possibility. The city offers its citizens a blank canvas on which to draw whatever portraits of themselves they have the wit and courage to imagine. Nobody asks them to constantly explain their purpose, and they remain free to join the minorities of their own choosing. Among people whom they regard as their equals, who share the same passions for seventeenth-century religious painting or Edwardian licentiousness, they can come and go in whatever direction their spirit beckons. The freedom of the city is the freedom of expression and the freedom of the mind.

So precious are these freedoms that the citizens judge the city's squalor as a fair price for its promise. What suburban opinion deplores as unmitigated abomination—bad air, poverty, noise, crowds, crime, traffic, heavy taxes, exorbitant rents, cynical government—the citizen accepts as the cost of liberty. It is in the nature of great cities to be dangerous, just as it is the nature of the future to be dangerous. The complexity of life in the city engenders in the inhabitants an equivalent complexity of thought and a tone of mind that can make a joke a paradox and contradiction.

The ideal of the city as an expression of man's humanity to man never has enjoyed much of a constituency in the United States. The stones of Paris and London and Rome speak to the citizenry's high regard for the proofs of civilization. If it is possible to walk calmly through the streets of those cities late at night, it is not only because the government gladly spends money on public fountains but also because the other people in the streets take pride in their civility. Americans take pride in the building of roads and weapons systems as well as in their gifts for violence. We know how to mount expeditions—to the Persian Gulf or the California frontier or the moon—but we lack a talent for making cities.

The broad retreat to the suburbs over the last twenty or thirty years correlates to the fear of the future and the wish to make time stand still. The politics of the Nixon, Reagan, and Bush administrations made manifest a San Diego realtor's dream of Heaven and defined the great, good American place as an exclusive country club. Expressions of the same sentiment take forms as various as the judgments of the Rehnquist courts, Senator Jesse Helms's suspicions of the National Endowment for the Arts, the ascendance of conservative and neoconservative socioeconomic theory, the sermons of George Will, and the division of the county of Los Angeles into a series of residential enclaves (Bel Air, Beverly Hills, Pasadena, etc.) as fiercely defended (by gates and electronic surveillance and regiments of liveried police) as the feudal manors of medieval Europe. As the larger business corporations come to employ as many people as lived in Renaissance Florence, they acquire the character of fiefs and dukedoms, and by shifting their headquarters into landscapes luxurious with English lawns and avenues of trees, they signify the splendor of their superiority—both moral and financial—to the urban mob.

Whenever I read in the papers that yet another corporation has quit New York City for a country estate in Virginia or Connecticut, I think of the United States receding that much farther into the past. The company of the elect becomes too quickly and too easily estranged from the democratic argument. Already protected from chance and uncertainty by the walls of bureaucratic protocol, the ladies and gentlemen of executive rank become ever more fearful of strangers—of Al Sharpton and Puerto Rican Day parades as well as of rats, pestilence, and crime—and their distrust of the city soon resembles the contempt so often and so smugly expressed by Vice President Quayle.

The fear is contagious, and as larger numbers of people come to perceive the city as a barren waste, the more profitable their disillusion becomes to dealers in guns and to the political factions that would destroy not only New York and Chicago but also the idea of the city. During the decade of the 1980s the federal government reduced by sixty percent the sum of money assigned to the nation's cities. Official Washington embraces the ethos of an expensive suburb, and the reductions embodied a cultural prejudice as well as a political doctrine. The same bias shows up in seminars conducted by professors of urban science who blandly announce—invariably with many smiling references to the wonders of modern telecommunications—that the United States no longer has need for large cities. From the point of view of civil servants and Baptist ministers, the revelation might be construed as good news, but not from the point of view of anybody still interested in freedom.

The hatred of cities is the fear of freedom. Freedom implies change, which implies friction, which implies unhappiness, which disturbs the nervous complacency of the admissions committee at the country club. Because the city promises so many changes and transformations (a good many of them probably dangerous or unhealthy), the act of decision presents itself as a burden instead of an opportunity. Confronted with the dilemma of making moral and existential choices, the friends of Vice President Quayle and Chief Justice Rehnquist seek to escape their confusion by declaring freedom the enemy of the state. They prefer the orderliness of the feudal countryside, where few strangers ever come to trouble the villagers with news of Trebizond and Cathay.

In the whole of the editorial autopsy conducted by the news media in the days following the Los Angeles riots, I never heard anybody say anything about the popular hatred of the freedoms of a great city. I know that the topic is not one that the political and intellectual authorities like to discuss, but without at least mentioning it in passing, the familiar indices of poverty and crime make little sense. Until we learn to value the idea of the city, we can expect to see the streets paved with anger instead of gold.

The more well-intentioned the reforms announced by the politicians and the more theatrical the anguish of *Newsweek* or Barbara Walters, the more clearly I could hear the voice of suburban triumph. The guests assembled on a lawn in Arlington or Kennebunkport nod and frown and piously confuse New York or Los Angeles with the Inferno imagined by Dante or Mel Gibson. A drift of smoke on the horizon confirms them in their best-loved suspicions and excuses their loathing for the multiplicity of both the human imagination and the human face.

9. The Pedagogy of Poverty Versus Good Teaching

MARTIN HABERMAN

Why is a "minor" issue like improving the quality of urban teaching generally overlooked by the popular reform and restructuring strategies? There are several possibilities. First, we assume that we know what teaching is, that others know what it is, that we are discussing the same "thing" when we use the word, and that we would all know good teaching if we saw it. Second, we believe that, since most teachers cannot be changed anyway, there must be other, more potent, teacher-proof strategies for change. Third, why bother with teaching if research shows that achievement test scores of poor and minority youngsters are affected primarily by their socioeconomic class; affected somewhat by Head Start, school integration, and having a "strong" principal; and affected almost not all by the quality of their teachers?

THE PEDAGOGY OF POVERTY

An observer of urban classrooms can find examples of almost every form of pedagogy: direct instruction, cooperative learning, peer tutoring, individualized instruction, computer-assisted learning, behavior modification, the use of student contracts, media-assisted instruction, scientific inquiry, lecture/discussion, tutoring by specialists or volunteers, and even the use of problem-solving units common in progressive education. In spite of this broad range of options, however, there is a typical form of teaching that has become accepted as basic. Indeed, this basic urban style, which encompasses a body of specific teacher acts, seems to have grown stronger each year since I first noted it in 1958. A teacher in an urban school of the 1990s who did not engage in these basic acts as the primary means of instruction would be regarded as deviant. In most urban schools, not performing these acts for most of each day would be considered prima facie evidence of not teaching.

The teaching acts that constitute the core functions of urban teaching are:

- Giving information
- Asking questions
- Giving directions
- Making assignments
- Monitoring seatwork
- Reviewing assignments
- Giving tests
- Reviewing tests
- Settling disputes
- Punishing noncompliance
- Marking papers
- Giving grades

This basic menu of urban teacher functions characterizes all levels and subjects. A primary teacher might "give information" by reading a story to children, while a high school teacher might read to the class from a biology text. (Interestingly, both offer similar reasons: "The students can't read for themselves," and "They enjoy being read to.") Taken separately, there may be nothing wrong with these activities. There are occasions when any one of the fourteen acts might have a beneficial effect. Taken together and performed to the systematic exclusion of other acts, they have become the pedagogical coin of the realm in urban schools. They constitute the pedagogy of poverty—not merely what teachers do and what youngsters expect but, for different reasons, what parents, the community, and the general public assume teaching to be.

Ancillary to this system is a set of out-of-class teacher acts that include keeping records, conducting parent conferences, attending staff meetings, and carrying out assorted school duties. While these out-of-class functions are not directly instructional, they are performed in ways that support the pedagogy of poverty. Since this analysis deals with the direct interactions characteristic of urban teachers and their students, I will limit myself to a brief comment about how each of these out-of-class functions is typically conceptualized and performed in urban settings.

- *Record-keeping* is the systematic maintenance of a paper trail to protect the school against any future legal action by its clients. Special classes, referrals, test scores, disciplinary actions, and analyses by specialists must be carefully recorded. This slant is the reason that teachers are commonly prejudiced rather than informed by reading student records; yet the system regards their upkeep as vital. (In teacher preparation, neophytes are actually taught that student records will reveal such valuable information as students' interests!)
- *Parent conferences* give parents who are perceived as poorly educated or otherwise inadequate a chance to have things explained to them.
- *Staff meetings* give administrators opportunities to explain things to teachers.
- *Assorted school duties* are essentially police or monitoring activities that would be better performed by hired guards.

The pedagogy of poverty appeals to several constituencies:

1. It appeals to those who themselves did not do well in schools. People who have been brutalized are usually not rich sources of compassion. And those who have failed or done poorly in school do not typically take personal responsibility for that failure. They generally find it easier to believe that they would have succeeded if only somebody had *forced* them to learn.
2. It appeals to those who rely on common sense rather than on thoughtful analysis. It is easy to criticize humane and developmental teaching aimed at educating a free people as mere "permissiveness," and it is well known that "permissiveness" is the root cause of our nation's educational problems.
3. It appeals to those who fear minorities and the poor. Bigots typically become obsessed with the need for control.
4. It appeals to those who have low expectations for minorities and the poor. People with limited vision frequently see value in limited and limiting forms of pedagogy. They believe that at-risk students are served best by a directive, controlling pedagogy.
5. It appeals to those who do not know the full range of pedagogical options available. This group includes most school administrators, most business and political reformers, and many teachers.

There are essentially four syllogisms that undergird the pedagogy of poverty. Their "logic" runs something like this:

1. Teaching is what teachers do. Learning is what students do. Therefore, students and teachers are engaged in different activities.
2. Teachers are in charge and responsible. Students are those who still need to develop appropriate behavior. Therefore, when students follow teachers' directions, appropriate behavior is being taught and learned.
3. Students represent a wide range of individual differences. Many students have handicapping conditions and lead debilitating home lives. Therefore, ranking of some sort is inevitable; some students will end up at the bottom of the class while others will finish at the top.
4. Basic skills are a prerequisite for learning and living. Students are not necessarily interested in basic skills. Therefore, directive pedagogy must be used to ensure that youngsters are compelled to learn their basic skills.

REFORM AND THE PEDAGOGY OF POVERTY

Unfortunately, the pedagogy of poverty does not work. Youngsters achieve neither minimum levels of life skills nor what they are capable of learning. The classroom atmosphere created by constant teacher direction and student compliance seethes with passive resentment that sometimes bubbles up into overt resistance. Teachers burn out because of the emotional and physical energy that they must expend to maintain their authority every hour of every day. The pedagogy of poverty requires that teachers who begin their careers intending to be helpers, models, guides, stimulators, and caring sources of encouragement transform themselves into directive authoritarians in order to function in urban schools. But people who choose to become teachers do not do so because at some point they decided, "I want to be able to tell people what to do all day and then make them do it!" This gap between expectations and reality means that there is a pervasive, fundamental, irreconcilable difference between the motivation of those who select themselves to become teachers and the demands of urban teaching.

For the reformers who seek higher scores on achievement tests, the pedagogy of poverty is a source of continual frustration. The clear-cut need to "make" students learn is so obviously vital to the common good and to the students themselves that surely (it is believed) there must be a way to force students to work hard enough to vindicate the methodology. Simply stated, we act as if it is not the pedagogy that must be fitted to the students but the students who must accept an untouchable method.

In reality, the pedagogy of poverty is not a professional methodology at all. It is not supported by research, by theory, or by the best practice of superior urban teachers. It is actually certain ritualistic acts that, much like the ceremonies performed by religious functionaries, have come to be conducted for their intrinsic value rather than to foster learning.

There are those who contend that the pedagogy of poverty would work if only the youngsters accepted it and worked at it. *Ay, there's the rub!* Students in urban schools overwhelmingly do accept the pedagogy of poverty, and they do work at it! Indeed, any teacher who believes that he or she can take on an urban teaching assignment and ignore the pedagogy of poverty will be quickly crushed by the students themselves. Examples abound of inexperienced teachers who seek to involve students in genuine learning activities and are met with apathy or bedlam, while older hands who announce, "Take out your dictionaries and start to copy the words that begin with *h*," are rewarded with compliance or silence.

Reformers of urban schools are now raising their expectations beyond an emphasis on basic skills to the teaching of critical thinking, problem solving, and even creativity. But if the pedagogy of poverty will not force the learning of low-level skills, how can it be used to compel genuine thinking? Heretofore, reformers have promulgated change strategies that deal with the level of funding, the role of the principal, parent involvement, decentralization, site-based management, choice, and other organizational and policy reforms. At some point, they must reconsider the issue of pedagogy. If the actual mode of instruction expected by school administrators and teachers and demanded by students and their parents continues to be the present one, then reform will continue to deal with all but the central issue: how and what are students taught?

The pedagogy of poverty is sufficiently powerful to undermine the implementation of any reform effort because it determines the way pupils spend their time, the nature of the behaviors they practice, and the bases of their self-concepts as learners. Essentially, it is a pedagogy in which learners can "succeed" without becoming either involved or thoughtful.

THE NATURE OF URBAN CHILDREN AND YOUTH

When he accepted the 1990 New York City Teacher of the Year Award, John Taylor Gatto stated that no school reform will work that does not provide children time to grow up or that simply forces them to deal with abstractions. Without blaming the victims, he described his students as lacking curiosity (having "evanescent attention"), being indifferent to the adult world, and having a poor sense of the future. He further characterized them as ahistorical, cruel and lacking in compassion, uneasy with intimacy and candor, materialistic, dependent, and passive—although they frequently mask the last two traits with a surface bravado.

Anyone who would propose specific forms of teaching as alternatives to the pedagogy of poverty must recognize that Gatto's description of his students is only the starting point. These are the attributes that have been enhanced and elicited by an authoritarian pedagogy and do not represent students' true or ultimate natures. Young people can become more and different, but they must be taught how. This means to me that two conditions must pertain before there can be a serious alternative to the pedagogy of poverty: the whole school faculty and school community—not the individual teacher—must be the unit of change; and there must be patience and persistence of application, since students can be expected to resist changes to a system they can predict and know how to control. Having learned to navigate in urban schools based on the pedagogy of poverty, students will not readily abandon all their know-how to take on willy-nilly some new and uncertain system that they may not be able to control.

For any analysis of pedagogical reform to have meaning in urban schools, it is necessary to understand something of the dynamics of the teacher/student interactions in those schools. The authoritarian and directive nature of the pedagogy of poverty is somewhat deceptive about who is really in charge. Teachers *seem* to be in charge, in that they direct students to work on particular tasks, allot time, dispense materials, and choose the means of evaluation to be used. It is assumed by many that having control over such factors makes teachers "decision makers" who somehow shape the behavior of their students.

But below this facade of control is another, more powerful level on which students actually control, manage, and shape the behavior of their teachers. Students reward teachers by complying. They punish by resisting. In this way students mislead teachers into believing that some things "work" while other things do not. By this dynamic, urban children and youth effectively negate the values promoted in their teachers' teacher education and undermine the nonauthoritarian predispositions that led their teachers to enter the field. And yet, most teachers are not particularly sensitive to being manipulated by students. They believe they are in control and are responding to "student needs," when, in fact, they are more like hostages responding to students' overt or tacit threats of noncompliance and, ultimately, disruption.

It cannot be emphasized enough that, in the real world, urban teachers are never defined as incompetent because their "deprived," "disadvantaged," "abused," "low-income" students are not learning. Instead, urban teachers are castigated because they cannot elicit compliance. Once schools made teacher competence synonymous with student control, it was inevitable that students would sense who was really in charge.

The students' stake in maintaining the pedagogy of poverty is of the strongest possible kind: it absolves them of responsibility for learning and puts the burden on the teachers, who must be accountable for *making* them learn. In their own knowing but crafty way, students do not want to trade a system in which they can make their teachers ineffective for one in which they would themselves become accountable and responsible for what they learn. It would be risky for students to swap a "try and make me" system for one that says, "Let's see how well and how much you really can do."

Recognizing the formidable difficulty of institutionalizing other forms of pedagogy, it is still worthwhile to define and describe such alternative forms. The few urban schools that serve as models of student learning have teachers who maintain control by establishing trust and involving their students in meaningful activities rather than by imposing some neat system of classroom discipline. For genuinely effective urban teachers, discipline and control are primarily a *consequence* of their teaching and not a *prerequisite* condition of learning. Control, internal or imposed, is a continuous fact of life in urban classrooms—but, for these teachers, it is completely interrelated with the learning activity at hand.

GOOD TEACHING

Is it possible to describe a teaching approach that can serve as an alternative to the pedagogy of poverty? I believe that there is a core of teacher acts that defines the pedagogy one finds in urban schools that have been recognized as exemplary. Unlike the directive teacher acts that constitute the pedagogy of poverty, however, these tend to be indirect activities that frequently involve the creation of a learning environment. These teaching behaviors tend to be evident more in what the students are doing than in the observable actions of the teacher. Indeed, teachers may appear to be doing little and at times may, to the unsophisticated visitor, seem to be merely observers. Good teaching transcends the particular grade or subject and even the need for lessons with specific purposes.[1]

[1] James D. Raths, "Teaching Without Specific Objectives," *Educational Leadership*, April 1971, pp. 714–20.

Whenever students are involved with issues they regard as vital concerns, good teaching is going on. In effective schools, the endless "problems"—the censoring of a school newspaper, an issue of school safety, a racial flare-up, the dress code—are opportunities for important learning. In good schools, problems are not viewed as occasions to impose more rules and tighter management from above. Far from being viewed as obstacles to the "normal" school routine, difficult events and issues are transformed into the very stuff of the curriculum. Schooling is living, not preparation for living. And living is a constant messing with problems that seem to resist solution.

Whenever students are involved with explanations of human differences, good teaching is going on. As students proceed through school, they should be developing ever greater understanding of human differences. Why are there rich people and poor people, able and disabled, urban and rural, multilingual and monolingual, highly educated and poorly educated? Differences in race, culture, religion, ethnicity, and gender are issues that children and youths reconsider constantly in an effort to make sense of the world, its relationships, and their place in it. This is not "social studies." All aspects of the curriculum should deepen students' basic understandings of these persistent facts of life.

Whenever students are being helped to see major concepts, big ideas, and general principles and are not merely engaged in the pursuit of isolated facts, good teaching is going on. At all levels and in all subjects, key concepts can be made meaningful and relevant. Students cannot be successful graduates without having at some point been exposed to the various forms of knowledge. Historians deal with the nature of sources; artists, with texture, color, and design. A fundamental goal of education is to instill in students the ability to use various and competing ways of understanding the universe. Knowing how to spell is not enough.

Whenever students are involved in planning what they will be doing, it is likely that good teaching is going on. This planning involves real choices and not such simple preferences as what crayon to use or the order in which a set of topics will be discussed. Students may be asked to select a topic for study, to decide what resources they will need, or to plan how they will present their findings to others. People learn to make informed choices. Following directions—even perfectly—does not prepare people to make choices and to deal with the consequences of those choices.

Whenever students are involved with applying ideals such as fairness, equity, or justice to their world, it is likely that good teaching is going on. Students of any age can, at some level, try to apply great ideals to their everyday lives. The environment, war, human relationships, and health care are merely a few examples of issues that students can be thinking about. Determining what should be done about particular matters and defending their ideas publicly gives students experience in developing principles to live by. Character is built by students who have had practice at comparing ideals with reality in their own lives and in the lives of those around them.

Whenever students are actively involved, it is likely that good teaching is going on. Doing an experiment is infinitely better than watching one or reading about one. Participating as a reporter, a role player, or an actor can be education. Constructing things can be a vital activity. We need graduates who have learned to take action in their own behalf and in behalf of others.

Whenever students are directly involved in a real-life experience, it is likely that good teaching is going on. Field trips, interactions with resource people, and work and life experiences are all potentially vital material for analysis. Firsthand experience is potentially more educational than vicarious activity, *provided* it is combined with reflection.

Whenever students are actively involved in heterogeneous groups, it is likely that good teaching is going on. Students benefit from exposure to cultural as well as intellectual heterogeneity, and they learn from one another. Divergent questioning strategies, multiple assignments in the same class, activities that allow for alternative responses and solutions all contribute to learning. Grouping in schools is frequently based on artificial criteria that are not used in life. Grouping can either limit or enhance students' self-concept and self-esteem and thus has a powerful effect on future learning.

Whenever students are asked to think about an idea in a way that questions common sense or a widely accepted assumption, that relates new ideas to ones learned previously, or that applies an idea to the problems of living, then there is a chance that good teaching is going on. Students are taught to compare, analyze, synthesize, evaluate, generalize, and specify in the process of developing thinking skills. The effort to educate thoughtful people should be guided by school activities that involve thought. The acquisition of information—even of skills—without the ability to think is an insufficient foundation for later life.

Whenever students are involved in redoing, polishing, or perfecting their work, it is likely that good teaching is going on. It is in the act of review, particularly review of one's own work, that important learning occurs. This technique may involve an art project or a science experiment as well as a piece of writing. The successful completion of anything worthwhile rarely occurs in a single trial. Students can learn that doing things over is not punishment but an opportunity to excel.

Whenever teachers involve students with the technology of information access, good teaching is going on. Teachers, texts, and libraries as they now exist will not be sufficient in the future. Computer literacy—beyond word processing—is a vital need. As James Mecklenburger points out, "Electronic learning must play a more important part in the mix, even at the expense of customary practices. Today, students and educators alike can create, receive, collect, and share data, text, images, and sounds on myriad topics in ways more stimulating, richer, and more timely than ever before."[2]

Whenever students are involved in reflecting on their own lives and how they have come to believe and feel as they do, good teaching is going on. Autobiography can be the basis of an exceedingly powerful pedagogy—one that is largely discarded after early childhood education. When critics dismiss my characterization of the pedagogy

[2] James A. Mecklenburger, "Educational Technology Is Not Enough," *Phi Delta Kappan,* October 1990, p. 108.

of poverty as an exaggeration, I am reminded of an immense sign hanging in an urban high school that has devoted itself totally to raising test scores: "We dispense knowledge. Bring your own container." This approach is the opposite of good teaching, which is the process of building environments, providing experiences, and then eliciting responses that can be reflected on. Autobiographical activities are readily extended into studies of family, neighborhood, and community. What could be more fundamental to subsequent learning than self-definition? Urban schools, in the way they narrowly structure the role of the teacher and restrict the content to be taught, too frequently repudiate the students and their home lives. The vision of good teaching as a process of "drawing out" rather than "stuffing in" is supported by diverse philosophies, including, most recently, feminist theories of the teaching/learning process.[3]

THE REWARDS OF NOT CHANGING

Taken individually, any of these indicators of good teaching is not a sufficient basis for proposing reform. We all know teachers who have done some of these things—as well as other, better things—for years. Taken together and practiced schoolwide and persistently, however, these suggestions can begin to create an alternative to the pedagogy of poverty.

Unfortunately, we must recognize that it may no longer be possible to give up the present authoritarianism. The incentives for the various constituencies involved may well have conditioned them to derive strong benefits from the pedagogy of poverty and to see only unknown risk in the options.

In the present system, teachers are accountable only for engaging in the limited set of behaviors commonly regarded as acts of teaching in urban schools—that is, the pedagogy of poverty. Students can be held accountable only for complying with precisely what they have specifically and carefully been directed to do.

[3] Madeleine Grumet, *Women and Teaching* (Amherst: University of Massachusetts Press, 1988), p. 99.

Administrators can be held accountable only for maintaining safe buildings; parents, only for knowing where their children are. Each constituency defines its own responsibilities as narrowly as possible to guarantee itself "success" and leave to others the broad and difficult responsibility for integrating students' total educations.

Who is responsible for seeing that students derive meaning and apply what they have learned from this fragmented, highly specialized, overly directive schooling? It is not an accident that the present system encourages each constituency to blame another for the system's failure. My argument here is that reforms will "take" only if they are supported by a system of pedagogy that has never been tried in any widespread, systematic, long-term way. What prevents its implementation is the resistance of the constituencies involved—constituencies that have a stake in maintaining their present roles, since they are, in effect, unaccountable for educating skilled, thoughtful citizens.

Continuing to define nonthinking, underdeveloped, unemployable youngsters as "adults" or "citizens" simply because they are high school graduates or passers of the General Education Development (GED) examination is irresponsible. Education will be seriously reformed only after we move it from a matter of "importance" to a matter of "life and death," both for society and for the individuals themselves. Graduates who lack basic skills may be unemployable and represent a personal and societal tragedy. However, graduates who possess basic skills but are partially informed, unable to think, and incapable of making moral choices are downright dangerous. Before we can *make* workers, we must first *make* people. But people are not *made*—they are conserved and grown.

10. Transforming Schools into Powerful Communities

DEBORAH MEIER

Our schools represent a lesson in creating a powerful community. In both the elementary schools and the high school, we have made possible strong relationships between and among people. There is no point in labeling these relationships cognitive or affective. They are relationships around issues, around life, around things that matter to young people.

A community embodies the hopes of human beings. You cannot learn to play tennis if you have never seen it played. You cannot teach children the power of wonderful ideas if they have not been immersed in a community that cares about wonderful ideas, that believes in them, that explores them, and that puts them into practice.

Intellectually and morally, we are a serious and respectful community. Despite the fact that I speak as an expert on middle schools, I started out as a prekindergarten and kindergarten teacher. I have come to believe that there is nothing children need in the middle grades that they do not also need for the rest of their lives. Children may need some things more than others at different ages. Every age I have worked with, however, seems to me to be critical. I have come to the conclusion that children, and human beings in general, need and deserve a decent environment at every single age. Whether they are six or sixty, people are more amazingly alike than they are different.

We finally did an in-depth study of the first seven graduating classes of Central Park East (CPE) Elementary School graduates—students who had completed sixth grade between 1978 and 1985. It took a lot of work to track down all those youngsters, but we did it. Of the first 135 we reached 119. We managed to have phone conversations with most of them, and long face-to-face interviews with about forty, plus conversations with many of their families. It turns out that even though they left our school following sixth grade, before the onslaught of adolescence, and most went on to pretty terrible schools (schools that do not graduate most of their incoming ninth graders), the CPE students survived. In fact, ninety percent managed to earn high school diplomas, and another six percent received general education diplomas. We did not have any direct relationship with them after they were twelve years old—nevertheless, contrary to the usual proportions in high schools, two-thirds went on to college.

Reading the interviews is a reminder of what counts. It is a reminder that a powerful community can have a transformative impact on other human beings at any age. People who care, who have access to young people for an extended period of time and who create a community around them, for them and their families, have an enormous effect. The impact of a good school is evident not only among children, nor only in the acquisition of academic skills; it has an effect on the entire constellation of family and student beliefs in their powers and their ability to handle the world around them.

I saw a television program some years ago that remains a metaphor for what I am talking about. The interviewer asked some high school dropouts, seventeen or eighteen years old, whether they knew anyone who had ever graduated from college. These three dropouts said no. I thought, what an odd thing to say. They had been in school for almost twelve years, and had had somewhere between twelve and fifty teachers, all of whom had graduated from college. On the other hand, this was not a strange statement at all. The youth did not include any of those teachers among the people they knew because they did not know their teachers. The fundamental fact in our school, and in schools like ours, is that at times the children may be angry with us, they may hate us, they may love us, they may be disgusted with us, they may want us "out of their faces"—but they include us among the world of people they know. We are part of their universe. We are part of the web of influences in their lives.

Curiosity is one of the things that keeps us alive. We wonder why. We wonder what tomorrow will bring. Our intellectual curiosity about the world around us, our interest in it, our noticing that this or that is an amazing fact, an amazing idea—this is what makes each day memorable. Pursuing our interests develops habits of mind that give us hope, that sustain us through pain. It is fundamental to our health. Immersing children in a culture in which such habits are valued is health-promoting, more health-promoting than any health-ed course or program ever invented.

Children go to institutions called high schools, created for a variety of reasons a century ago, which fail to sustain their curiosity. Instead they drive young people mad. Students develop ways of adjusting, techniques for handling madness, which we then attribute to their hormones. None of us, at any stage in our life cycle, would survive well in such institutions. No other institution we know of, even the army or prison, is organized so mindlessly. In no other institution do we change supervisors and peer groups every forty-five minutes, or engage in a totally different activity every time the bell rings, without any particular sequential order.

This kind of high school could not conceivably be an institution intentionally created to give our minds good exercise and to help us develop intellectually serious habits, not to mention intellectually serious connections with people. Young people go to schools in which adults are allowed no time to act as serious mentors. Teachers are not models of people who engage in serious discussion, because students never see teachers engage in serious discussions, debates, or arguments about things that we teachers would like to see students argue about.

The typical high school is a setting in which the adults and the students are not members of the same community. Instead, they exist in two unconnected communities inhabiting the same building. We have abandoned them in adolescence to a community in which there are no adults to have an influence on them. Then we decry the fact that they create a peer culture that does not have the values we as adults want them to have. This is insanity. We commit a crime in spending our resources to create institutions that foster habits so adverse to the physical and emotional health of young people.

In our school we decided to reverse all of that. We have created a high school that is essentially like a good kindergarten. All we really did was to adopt the practices that I knew worked in prekindergarten and kindergarten and keep them going through elementary school, through middle school, and all the way up through twelfth grade. We should not be surprised to find that this works. If we look at universities like Oxford and Cambridge or other elite universities we find that they are informed by the same ideas.

Students at Oxford, for example, have a central tutor, someone who knows them well and who helps to orchestrate a powerful learning community around them. The assumption is that novices learn from experts. Students are surrounded by and immersed in a community of people who are more expert than they are. That is what we did in our high school and our middle school. Youngsters stay with the same small cluster of teachers for at least two years. Each child has a principal adviser who knows him or her and the child's family well. I am an adviser myself.

The culture of the schools includes an understanding that young people need to learn from their families. We believe all families have things to teach their young. A school that implies to young people that the adults in their life outside of school are not worth respecting has lost an important ally. We find many ways to tell the children's families that they are important.

If the parents' first contact with school, their first conference with a teacher or administrator, makes them feel more powerful, more useful, more knowledgeable, and better able to help their youngster, they are likely to come back for more. If, however, coming to school is only a political act, to show the school you care, then parents with busy lives, who feel tired and defeated, find it difficult to visit the school—and each time it gets harder. All this just to show teachers you care? Parents need some strength and hope that they can do well for their children.

School size is a major drawback to creating sane and healthy learning environments. The size of the school should be based on the number of teachers who can gather around a table together. That means no more than 250 or 300 students, or 15 to 20 adults. I do not mean that this is the right size for a "program" or a "house." It is the ideal size for an ongoing, life-giving, healthy school.

No matter how many good programs there are, or how brilliantly conceived, because of their context they often turn into a charade. It is the *culture* of the school, not its programs, that counts. To create a culture is not easy; it takes a lot of face-to-face encounters. We built big buildings because we had some other idea in mind—factory-style efficiency—and because of the cost of space in large urban areas. But the buildings exist. What we want to do is use them to house small communities, each with sufficient autonomy to create for young people a living model of what it is like to be in control of one's environment, to have strong, stable, and continuous relationships.

Big buildings need not be our enemy. They can contain small schools. The building of which I am the official principal has over a thousand pupils. It houses, however, three separate schools, each with its own parent association, its own school head, its own operating life.

We need not put only children between the ages of eleven and fifteen together. There are different strengths and weaknesses at different ages; mix them up. It is a wonderful fact of life in our building that our adolescents see four-year-olds and seven-year-olds and that the young children see older adolescents, and look up to them as models. This reminds us of the basic idea that learning takes place when we have contact with people who are more expert than we are, when our community is composed of various stages of expertise.

Finally, we need to see our buildings as places that can house services other than education. Instead of assuming that the school, the board of education, and the principal must run all the services that children need, why not share these buildings with others? Let the building house health services, and family services, and after-school services. For school people to pretend to take on all the tasks only exhausts us, drowns us, makes us ineffective. Let us create a school culture that acknowledges its limits, and collaborate with other experts whose services children need. The power of the school is not a matter of bricks and mortar, but of the human relationships we create that give young people the courage and ability to create other healthy relationships on their own. We should help them to establish such relationships beyond the boundary of our school but we should not pretend to be more than we are.

11. Children of Value: We Can Educate All Our Children

CONSTANCE CLAYTON

The black family and the urban public schools share more than their children. The "plight" of each has been assayed in apocalyptic terms and chronicled in the reports of myriad researchers, panels, commissions, and task forces. A new generation of academics has cut its teeth on elaborate analyses written for publication, tenure, and self-promotion.

After the critics have retreated into their academic and bureaucratic havens, black families and the metropolitan public schools are left to confront the same situation as before—and more often than not, each other. However, all is not quite the same. In ways sometimes subtle and sometimes not, the researchers have suggested that the plight of the black family and that of the urban public schools are not only related but are causally so. Thus, a seeming conundrum: Is the black family to blame for the plight of the public schools? Or have public schools caused the plight of the black family? Neither happens to be the case, but merely posing the issue in that manner is a phenomenon worth exploring.

The paramount public policy issue today is whether this country accepts as inevitable the existence of a permanent underclass. Encoded in much of the rhetoric of concern about the "plight" of the nation's public schools, and about the family life and home environment of the children who attend these schools, is a considerable degree of ambivalence over a more fundamental question: whether this society seriously intends or even desires to educate the mostly black and Latino children who now occupy the majority of seats in its large urban school systems.

There are those who still question in their hearts the proposition that "all children can learn" and who adhere to the belief that the cultural deficits of some children are too deeply embedded to be overcome. However, that ambivalence also may reflect an intuitive recognition that the absence of a commitment to educate the underclass allows for results that mask significant questions that would otherwise arise about the political economy. As Michelle Fine of the University of Pennsylvania noted, the much-discussed subject of "dropouts" presents an excellent example of this masking:

> What would happen, in our present-day economy, to these young men and women if they all graduated? Would their employment and/or poverty prospects improve individually as well as collectively? Would the class, race, and gender differentials be eliminated or even reduced? Or does the absence of a high school diploma only obscure what would otherwise be the obvious conditions of structural unemployment, underemployment, and marginal employment disproportionately endured by minorities, women, and low-income individuals?

Whatever its bases, the ambivalence about the worthiness of the clientele of the urban schools has structured both the diagnosis and the prescription. First, only failure is perceived as significant. It is highly unlikely that much will be said about the tens of thousands of high-school students who graduated this past June and who will go on to succeed in higher education, the armed forces, and the public and private sectors. Their achievements (along with those of the parents and teachers who supported them) will go unheralded, unable to fit into the language of failure.

Second, although couched in terms of parental choice, many of the proposed responses to the "problem" sound very much like a prescription for the abandonment of urban public schools. Whether intended or not, proposals for tuition tax credits, vouchers, and metropolitan busing plans would facilitate middle-class flight from the urban "inner-city" public classrooms for seemingly greener pastures in suburban, private, and parochial schools.

Proposing abandonment of the public schools would be unthinkable if the children served by those schools were white and middle class, or if the public schools involved were on neatly manicured campuses in well-to-do suburbs. Regardless of their relative performance on conventional measures of achievement, persistence, and success, deserting these schools would be deemed an unacceptable response. Rather than being seen as populated by "children at risk," they would continue to be seen as serving and caring for children *of value*.

Perhaps the question answers itself, but it still deserves to be asked: Are there not children of value in the urban public schools? If so, why would we countenance abandonment?

The children-of-value formulation differs from the notion of children at risk. The at-risk designation no doubt began as a well-intentioned attempt to focus attention and resources on those children most in need. This original purpose loses much of its efficacy as the number of those "at risk" approximates, surpasses, and then exceeds by far the children judged not to be. In those instances, "at risk" becomes as much a misnomer as the term "minority" in a school that is *majority* black and Latino. The continuing vitality of both appellations can be explained either by linguistic inertia or by a political judgment that the term implies a status so fundamental and lasting as to be impervious to change.

It is important to note, however, that the children-at-risk rhetoric is more than a mere misnomer. The children-at-risk rubric locates the problem at the level of the individual child, with the implicit suggestion that this is where the solution must begin. This notion is often accompanied by dreary statistics on the number of children who live in poor, single-parent (generally female-headed) households characterized by high unemployment, low educational attainment, and other indicators of marginal or lower socioeconomic status. This litany produces a not-too-subtle and virtually irresistible temptation for schools to join the *"if only"* chain, a rationale used to explain and excuse less than satisfactory outcomes.

Much of the impetus for school desegregation came from those who believed, conscientiously, that the academic performance of black children could be improved significantly *if only* black children and white children attended the same schools. We know now that even in the absence of second-generation problems, desegregation is no panacea.

The generally negative rendition of black family life sent out yet another siren call. *If only* the children were different (or had different parents from a different social class, race, or neighborhood), schools would succeed!

There is at least one major problem with that position: the empirical evidence shows that it is demonstrably wrong. The "effective schools" literature is replete with examples showing that, on the terms by which success is currently measured, there are schools with students of these families that have succeeded in the past and are succeeding now. As the late Ronald Edmonds (belatedly acknowledged as the founder of the effective-schools movement) asked nearly a decade ago:

> How many effective schools would you have to see to be persuaded of the educability of poor children? If your answer is more than one, then I submit that you have reasons of your own for preferring to believe that basic pupil performance derives from family background instead of school response to family background. . . . Whether or not we will ever effectively teach the children of the poor is probably far more a matter of politics than of social science and that is as it should be.

That analysis still holds true. Educating the children in urban schools is no "mission impossible." Nor is it a mystery. Given the tools, skills, and resources, teachers can insure that students become actively involved and, thereby, more effectively involved in learning. Margaret Wang, director of the Temple University Center for Research in Human Development and Education, and others have demonstrated that "adaptive instruction," drawing on new insights from cognitive science and research on teaching, can work when given the chance.

Individual schools can be made to work in terms that are important and measurable. Effective schools share common traits that are identifiable and replicable: a school climate conducive to learning, high expectations, emphasis on basic skills and time-on-task, clear instructional objectives, and strong instructional leadership. The mini-industry that has grown up around the effective schools' applied research can now deliver virtually a turnkey operation. Moreover, James Comer and his colleagues at the Yale Child Study Center have demonstrated by example how explicit recognition of the child-development role of the school, coupled with what is known about social and behavioral science and education, can be employed to overcome poor motivation, low self-esteem, discipline problems, and even perceived learning disabilities.

School districts, too, can perform better when the will exists. Across the country, new leadership is recapturing urban school districts from disrepair, decay, and red ink, rebuilding both infrastructure and instructional programs. Formerly controversial decisions establishing critical minimums for the curriculum, devising new measures and instruments for assessment and evaluation, and ending social promotions have contributed demonstratively to building the framework for educational improvement.

Because we know that classrooms, schools, and school districts can work, and we know how to make them work, it is not unreasonable to conclude, as Edmonds did, that the continued "plight" of the urban public schools must reflect an unwillingness to make the fundamental political decision about whether a permanent underclass is acceptable and necessary.

Those whose interests are served by masking the unwillingness of society to pursue the redistributive policies necessary to deal with the underclass phenomenon often find aid and comfort among educators who have become frustrated by disappointing results from even the most carefully drafted and expertly implemented school improvement programs. Presented with the choice of either accepting responsibility for repeated failure or blaming the parents and children they serve, these educators choose the latter.

Many of us now recognize that behavior as the false choice that it is and refuse to become or to blame the victim. In short, by unmasking and acknowledging the question of perpetuating an underclass, we go about the business of school improvement and education reform fully cognizant of the Sisyphean nature of our task. Simply put, we commit ourselves to educate children who are real, if not ideal; the children we have, rather than the ones we do not.

The school improvement and education reform agenda is both long and concrete. It includes:

- Early childhood programs to provide interventions at the point at which they will do the most good and have the most lasting value
- Continuity of instruction efforts to increase time-on-task, increase both student and teacher attendance, reduce "pullout" programs and other school-day interruptions
- Attention to the middle years and the special needs, concerns, and developmental processes of those young adolescents who are often overlooked when educators focus upon the elementary and high schools
- Regulatory reform initiatives designed to create an environment freed of the vague drafting, inconsistent interpretation, overlapping jurisdiction, and inflexible audit procedures that often combine to prohibit preventive intervention, require premature termination of services, and encourage programs designed to be audit-proof even if not pedagogically sound

Even that partial agenda is ambitious. Its completion would be an accomplishment of considerable magnitude. Nonetheless, such an accomplishment would have a pyrrhic quality unless educators are willing to engage the broad spectrum of issues involving the underclass. Educators could commit themselves to the politically risky course of open advocacy for children, particularly those children whose horizons are being constrained by their conscription into the underclass.

If it is to be authentic, that advocacy would have to be seen as consistent with and falling within the institutional mission of the public school. Thus, an explicit component of that undertaking would have to be to promote social improvement. Once part of the mission, advocacy for social change would be included in both the hidden and the official curriculum. Those who are willing to eschew the teaching of core values or to pretend that no values are being taught now are likely to find this a development of calamitous portents. Teaching would have become truly a subversive activity.

Authentic advocacy would mean breaking with established orthodoxy even when that would entail some version of secular heresy. For example, the current debate around bilingual education assumes a consensus about the rightful place of English as the exclusive national language. Schools could enter the national language debate on the side of those who oppose the explicit or de facto imposition of a national language.

Educators are in a unique position to challenge that consensus by arguing that to treat the language spoken in a child's home as "un-American" or otherwise illegitimate is cultural chauvinism and has nothing to do with education. They must encourage a reexamination of how schools respond to children from non-English-speaking homes. By so doing they will take an important step toward affirming the worth and dignity of the children they must reach to teach.

Most important, advocacy for children will require that educators cease their tacit collaboration with those who suggest that the causes for educational shortcomings reside with individual children or with their parents. Educators can do this by reiterating loudly and clearly the simple yet profound admission offered by Ronald Edmonds:

> We can, whenever and wherever we choose, successfully teach all children whose schooling is of interest to us. We already know more than we need, in order to do this. Whether we do it must finally depend on how we feel about the fact that we haven't [done so] so far.

Whether the children of the underclass, who are becoming the predominant clientele of urban public schools, are allowed to be educationally successful is a matter for society to decide. The future of urban public schools depends less on the development of a new pedagogy than on the emergence of a new politics. Without this, the chances in life of those children will be determined less by their mastery of the three R's than by their ability to prevail over the myriad obstacles created by a fourth—race; less by former Education Secretary William Bennett's trinity of C's (content, character, and choice) than by the pervasive and confining realities of class.

These realities compel a new relationship between black families and public schools. That relationship would be one dedicated to responding to the urgent problems of race and class and the common ground on which they meet: poverty.

12. Social Justice Unionism

NATIONAL COALITION OF EDUCATION ACTIVISTS

Public education is at a crossroads and so, too, are our unions. Our society's children face deepening poverty and social dislocation. Our schools face a growing crisis of confidence as they confront greater challenges and higher expectations with declining resources. Our unions face powerful political opponents, the punishing consequences of economic hard times, and a crisis of identity caused, in part, by uncertainty about our capacity to rise to the demands of the day.

As the organized core of the teaching profession, education unions remain central to resolving these crises. While there is some promising movement in new directions, the prospects for the future are far from certain.

Much is at stake. The rights of education workers and the interests of public education are under attack and must be defended and strengthened. But relying on strategies which in the past secured better lives for our members is no longer enough.

Economic hard times pose a sustained threat to hopes for improvement in the social welfare. Savage inequalities in the public education available to children of different racial and class backgrounds reflect growing social and economic polarization—and squander the potential of our youth. Gaps between schools and the communities they serve are widening. The price of continued decay in public education and social well-being will be paid in reduced prospects for a democratic future.

With the stakes so high for ourselves and for our country, we have good reason to respond urgently to calls for reform. Yet too often that response has been reactive and timid. While some bold innovations have shown that union initiatives can make a crucial difference, those initiatives have been the exception rather than the rule. Too often, unions have resisted reform efforts or have uncritically followed the lead of others, rather than raising the voices of educators and school communities. Too rarely does reform constructively affect our classrooms or our schools, with teachers and educators leading the way. Too many have been quick to blame children and their communities for school failure, and slow to identify educational policies and classroom practices that, in the long run, serve those who want to see public schools die out or be sold off to the highest bidder.

Prevailing definitions of educational success and failure remain overly preoccupied with standardized test scores or focused on narrow conceptions of economic competitiveness. Instead, reform should be driven by standards of equity and social justice, including high expectations and educational excellence for all. The ideals that led us to organize our unions and fight for economic justice—indeed, that led many of us to enter teaching in the first place—are no less compelling than in the past: a desire to help children; hope for the future; service to community; and a conviction that public education is a cornerstone of society's commitment to opportunity, equity, and democratic participation. But these ideals can not be served by business-as-usual in our schools or in our unions. Both demand new vision.

Without a broader conception of the interests of teachers and of teaching, our unions will find themselves on ever more shaky ground, defending fewer jobs and shrinking privileges against repeated attacks. Without a better partnership with the parents and communities that need public education most, we will find ourselves isolated from essential allies. Without a new vision of schooling that raises the expectations of our students and the standards of our own profession, we will continue to founder. Without a new model of unionism that revives debate and democracy internally and projects an inspiring social vision and agenda externally, we will fall short of the challenges before us.

KEY COMPONENTS OF SOCIAL JUSTICE UNIONISM

Social justice unionism retains the best of traditional unionism, borrows from what has been called "professional unionism," and is informed by a broader concept of our members' self-interests and by a deeper social vision. Social justice unionism should:

1. *Defend the rights of its members while fighting for the rights and needs of the broader community and students.*

The interests of education workers are best served by defending public education while simultaneously working to transform it. Unions of education workers need to accept some responsibility for the problems in public schools. We need to use our resources, membership, and power at the bargaining table and in the legislative arena to help resolve these problems.

For example, education unions should fight to extend collective bargaining laws to the sixteen states that currently lack them, so that unions can better protect teachers and teaching. Yet they also need to be willing to reconsider contract language that proves to be an obstacle to school reform.

2. *Recognize that the parents and neighbors of our students are key allies, and build strategic alliances with parents, labor unions, and community groups.*

Instead of promoting policies that may alienate the communities where our students live, we should forge alliances and resolve differences whenever possible.

Because parents play a central role in the education of their children and are our strongest political allies, education unions should work to insure that parents are full partners in our schools. Unions should advocate for significant parent and community involvement on local school governing bodies, and should urge staff to promote parental involvement in school activities. Where racial and cultural differences exist between our members and the communities they serve, the union should work proactively to close the gap. For example, unions should urge schools to communicate with the parents in their native language, to secure child care and transportation for meetings and conferences, and to schedule meetings at times and places accessible to parents. Unions should lobby for legislation which would allow parents paid time off from their jobs for conferences and school activities.

Education unions should also work to unite all staff members at a school. They should build ongoing alliances with a wide range of groups, from other public service unions to the broader labor movement, churches, community and social organizations, advocacy groups, and business and political groups that support public schools. Such alliances are necessary to defeat budget cutbacks, fight for adequate and equitable funding of public education paid for by progressive tax reforms, and advocate for comprehensive school reform. Our unions must also participate in alliances taking up other issues affecting our students, such as job programs, housing, health care, recreation, safety, and antiviolence and antiracism initiatives.

3. *Fully involve rank-and-file members in running the union and initiate widespread discussion on how education unions should respond to the crises in education and society.*

Only by changing the culture of our unions will they become a force for changing the culture of our schools. Many local education unions need to move from a "service" model—where inactive members are passive recipients of services provided by the paid staff—to a model where a mobilized membership takes active responsibility for union affairs. Members often feel that their union is as distant from them as the school administration. Communication is too often one way, with union newspapers and newsletters rarely seeking opinions or input. Some local and state apparatuses are dominated by cliques of individuals, making entry into union activities difficult for new members or rank-and-file activists. While democratic structures formally exist in virtually all education employee unions, such structures on their own do not ensure democratic practices or membership involvement. Bureaucratic styles and parliamentary obstacles can too easily thwart a concerned member. Unions need to constantly encourage membership involvement and mobilization.

4. *Put teachers and others who work in classrooms at the center of school reform agendas, ensuring that they take ownership of reform initiatives.*

Those who work in schools and classrooms on a daily basis are in the best position to implement and evaluate school reform initiatives. Unfortunately, unions have not ensured that the voices of these educators are adequately heard. Unions need to allocate sufficient resources to promote reform initiatives and build grassroots support for them.

Just as we demand that school administrators empower staff to make educational policy decisions, union leaders must equip their members to make decisions at local school levels. This means being open to changes in contract language that inhibits reform, and committing resources to train members for active, decisionmaking roles at the school level. While the union has a responsibility to protect the rights of all its members, only by moving more decision-making power to the school site will there be enough initiative and expertise to make school reform successful. Such a transfer of the locus of power, if done properly with adequate training, could also bring historically disenfranchised union members back into our organizations.

5. *Encourage those who work with children to use methods of instruction and curricula that will promote racial and gender equity, combat racism and prejudice, encourage critical thinking about our society's problems, and nurture an active, reflective citizenry that is committed to real democracy and social and economic justice.*

Too often, schools fail to challenge students intellectually, dull their creativity, and bore them to a point of alienation from learning. Moreover, the difference in achievement levels between children of color and their white counterparts is totally unacceptable. Education unions should work with communities of color to address this grave problem.

Unions need to give higher priority to classroom and schoolbased practices that promote better education and equity for all students. These include: changes in curricula that affirm a child's home language and culture while teaching English and respect for all cultures; practices that promote gender equity; teacher training in the reduction of prejudice, including homophobia; alternatives to tracking and ability grouping; and school restructuring. In addition to the inherent merits of such practices, parents and communities who see unions promoting reforms that better serve their children's needs are more likely to support schools and teachers.

6. *Forcefully advocate for a radical restructuring of American education.*

Daily life for teachers must be changed from one of isolation and overextension with few standards and little accountability, to one of collaboration, reflection, high standards, and mutual accountability. For this to happen, schools must be radically restructured. Some of the components of this restructuring include: lower class sizes so students can establish more productive relationships with teachers; smaller schools; a substantial increase in collaborative planning and staff development time; peer mentoring and evaluation; new, more equitable forms of standards and performance assessment; faculty selection processes in which the staff and principal of a school have more power; sharply reduced bureaucracy at all levels; and the reintegration of administrators into classroom teaching on a regular basis. Unions should use their power at the bargaining table and in the legislative arena to fight for these measures.

7. *Aggressively educate and mobilize its membership to fight for social justice in all areas of society.*

Growing racial and class divisions are threatening not just our schools, but the very foundations of our society. Education unions, from the local to the national level, must address these divisions. Ultimately, such problems will only be adequately addressed by a massive social movement similar to the civil rights movement and the movement against the war in Vietnam. In the short term, however, much can be done—from creating classrooms that encourage students to critically reflect and act on social problems, to building coalitions that address specific social problems.

Education unions need to move beyond a crisis orientation and become part of ongoing, long-term coalitions. We must stress constant grassroots education and organizing and not just sporadic media blitzes. We must lobby behind the scenes but not forego militant public actions when necessary. We need to build bridges to political leaders and parties, but not rely too heavily on them. We need to work with others to build a political movement that is independent of the Democratic and Republican parties and that focuses on the fight for social and economic justice.

13. The Struggle for Decent Schools

BOB PETERSON

ORGANIZING FOR POPULAR POWER

In order to get anything done in society, particularly anything just and equitable, one must organize and organize and organize—and I might add, organize collectively. Of course it is essential to know what we are organizing for. Slogans such as "power to the people," or "community control," or "teacher empowerment" all sound nice on one level, but what is the purpose or politics that lie behind such calls for power? For many years in the South and much of the North, phrases such as state rights, local control, and even power to the people meant power to white people. "Community control" may mean control by those people who have the time and money to exercise that power, or perhaps control by a majority community that thinks English should be the only language used. As a teacher I use the term "teacher empowerment," but what does that mean in a community like Milwaukee where eighty percent of the teachers are of European origin while seventy percent of the students are of color?

We must organize for popular power—radical democratic institutions that put power in the hands of the most marginalized sectors of our society. This organizing should take place in our classrooms, school systems and society at large. As we organize we must simultaneously educate ourselves so that as we collectively win more power, we use different approaches to solving problems and running institutions than those currently used.

This is no easy task. The hierarchical nature of our society is very strong. A very small percentage of the population controls vast quantities of wealth and power in our society, and most of the rest of us are so well socialized as to not put up a fuss. Prejudices based on race, gender, class, religion, outright egomania, and individualism makes organizing for equity and justice very difficult.

One way to orient our organizing—to ensure that what energy we do use is used successfully—is to be clear about our goals and to relate our goals to what we see as the purpose of schooling. Historically, people have argued that in the United States schools have three purposes:

1. To educate our young people physically, mentally, and socially.
2. To equalize society and to provide opportunity for all.
3. To reproduce society's values, structures, and institutions.

There is a major problem with these three purposes: goal number three—to reproduce society—is in direct contradiction to number two—to equalize society—and sometimes to number one—to educate our young. Number two could be categorized as a democratic goal while number three is an elitist goal. Needless to say, those policies which have historically shaped our school system most reflect the third goal of reproducing our society. The domination of this third goal in educational policy matters has led to the current crisis in education. Ann Bastian and others have suggested in the book *Choosing Equality* that the crisis in education can be reduced in its simplest form as being twofold:

1. *A catastrophic failure to produce adequate schools for low-income students.* Fifty to eighty percent of our urban students drop out. This is a failure to ensure equality, the second goal mentioned above.
2. *A chronic failure to provide reasoning and citizenship skills to all students.* John Goodlad found that not even one percent of the instructional time in high school was devoted to discussion that requires some kind of response involving reasoning or perhaps an opinion from students. This is a failure to meet the first goal—truly educating our young.

This twofold crisis is deeply rooted in the very fabric of our hierarchical society. Moreover, even when progressives gain some degree of power, whether in the classroom, school, or in an entire school system such power is immediately compromised.

(153)

For example, Bill Ayers of Chicago writes in his excellent book, *The Good Pre-School Teacher,* about having power in an early childhood center in a working-class neighborhood in New York City with a staff that had a commitment to change gender biased language. He explains that in his center the word firefighter replaced fireman; that their dramatic play area had a poster of a black firefighter in action, and the block area had a unique collection of little figures including a white male nurse and a black female firefighter. But the power that he and his colleagues held was little match for reality. Across the street was a firehouse staffed exclusively with white, male firefighters. Bill's toddlers visited the firefighters, tried on their helmets, rang their bell, and got to know a few of them. Those of us who know young children know they are diligent classifiers and concrete observers. Reality is their most powerful teacher. The center's nonsexist language and nonracist materials were in conflict with some hard facts: for the children, the word "fireman" became a perfectly reasonable word for many situations. Sexist and racist social relations in our society are very powerful in our schools.

Or take our experience at Fratney School—La Escuela Fratney. A soon-to-be vacated school was the center of a community struggle—a successful struggle, and the implementation of a very bold innovative program. The first year we trained our staff in "democratic discipline" techniques, but despite long hours of planning and lofty goals, many of our classrooms were disrupted—some severely—by kids so damaged by society that they were threats to themselves and their classmates. Larry, for example, an abusive second-grader who brought razor blades to school, is himself abused and lives in a shelter. Violent social power relations in our society are being reproduced daily in our schools.

Or take the case of the few school districts or municipalities in our country where progressive pro-equality forces have taken power. Leaving aside for a moment the obvious problems such districts face with massive bureaucracies and uncooperative educators, let's speak to the more fundamental problem of resources that such schools lack. For example, for a period of time Milwaukee had a progressive mayor, county executive, and school super-intendent. But there was little money to do what needed to be done. A consultant group said it would take $500 million to rebuild the run-down schools in our city and to increase the number of classrooms so class size could be reduced, full-day kindergarten could be provided, and every school would have an art room, music room, and library. Five hundred million seems like a lot—but in fact it's less than the cost of one B-2 bomber, those low-flying offensive jets that military people say are going to be ineffective. And the Congress, which itself is bulging with millionaires, has ordered the construction of 132 such mechanical death birds. If instead Congress had established a National School Reconstruction Fund, the 132 largest cities in the country would get $500 million each to rebuild their schools. Think of the jobs it would create, the better learning conditions it would foster, the community centers for our alienated youth it could provide. But no, class interests and the obsession with militarism directly impacts on what progressives can do in education.

I must be clear about what I am *not* saying. I am not saying that progressive change in schools is impossible because of current power arrangements in our society. Nor am I saying that fundamental societal change must precede positive educational change. I *am* saying something that is obvious, although it's rarely mentioned in the reports of the many commissions on education. The problems of schools are directly connected to problems in society. Organizing for change in the schools, and in my opinion, teaching progressively, must therefore be tied to broad social movements in our nation.

THE CASE OF MILWAUKEE

To illustrate these points, I now turn to the case of Milwaukee. A few years ago things looked dismal in the Milwaukee Public Schools. All sectors of our city—businesses, community groups, and the media—regularly criticized the schools, particularly for gaps in achievement between white students and students of color. The administration had just spent nearly $1 million on development of a curricular initiative called Outcomes Based Education (OBE) and had conducted a fiasco of an in-service on this competency-based curriculum which had thousands of learner objectives. Many of us opposed the OBE initiative arguing that the large number and specificity of the objectives would weigh down classroom teachers, pushing us to cover many topics in a shallow manner and forcing a stress on literal recollection. A few years prior to OBE the reading textbook adoption process was underway. We were told a new basal would be adopted and that whole language options were nothing more than unworkable idealistic dreams. And also a few years ago, unbeknownst to most, the administration had written a plan to put a Madeline Hunter teaching training school into the soon-to-be vacated Fratney School site.

Most teachers looked at these developments in much the same way most other changes have been looked at in MPS: either with cynicism—"Oh, great, another pack of paper from central office for my circular file," or with hopelessness—"I know things are bad, but by God those people at central office are so out of touch with classroom life that they have managed to make things worse."

There were some of us, though, who viewed things a bit differently. Insulted by the disrespect the OBE curriculum project exemplified, we transcended our cynicism and became angry. We did not feel hopeless, but determined—determined that things had to and could get better if teachers and parents organized.

Propelled both by our anger and a vision of education that we sometimes caught a glimpse of in our own classrooms and those of our colleagues, we decided not to stick to the official script and docilely follow certain central office administrators into a regimented, lockstep curriculum. We met with school board members, passed out leaflets at the teachers' convention mobilizing teachers against OBE, testified at school board hearings, and wrote articles in *Rethinking Schools*. I am proud to say that because of these efforts and others, the reactionary curriculum project was dumped; teachers were given three options in reading instead of just the basal; ten whole language pilot projects were established;

and Fratney Street School was set up as demanded by the community.

When I use the word "we," I don't just mean the people involved with *Rethinking Schools,* or the community group that won Fratney, but a broader network of teachers and educators and parents who have been active not only with *Rethinking Schools* and Fratney, but in the efforts to promote whole language, a five-year black history project (the Martin Luther King Writing Contest), and continuing attempts to make the Milwaukee Teachers' Education Association more democratic and concerned with pedagogical issues.

Progressive movements in education in Milwaukee are not new. The honor roll of progressive efforts include: the massive antisegregation school boycotts of 1963 and 1964, the walkouts by Mexican and Puerto Rican students in the early 1970s to demand bilingual education, the movements to build new high schools in the black and Hispanic communities, the efforts to secure the rights of exceptional children by the Exceptional Education Task Force, the movement to institute equitable desegregation after the court order in 1976, and the struggle to save North Division High School. Two more mentioned above, *Rethinking Schools* and Fratney Street School, illustrate what can be done in the struggle for decent schools.

RETHINKING SCHOOLS

In 1986 a small group of teachers and community activists started to discuss the need for a progressive, education-focused journal. We wanted to stop being on the defensive all the time. We were tired of constantly trooping down to the school board meetings to stave off yet another attack on teachers and decent education programs. We also saw the need for people working for change in the schools to have a forum in which we could exchange ideas and analyses. Local publications that dealt with education—such as the daily press, the Milwaukee Teachers' Education Association *Sharpener* newsletter, and the University of Wisconsin-Milwaukee's *Met-*

ropolitan Education journal—didn't deal adequately with the important issues facing us. We decided to publish a mass distribution paper that dealt with both theory and practice and specifically with the politics of education in the Milwaukee school system.

We wanted to let the voice of those people most excluded from policy debates—teachers, parents, and students—be heard. We know that for educational reform to take place it has to be centered in the classroom. Teachers have to embrace it. Teachers who aren't open to new ideas need to be challenged both through critique and through examples of things that work. Thus, despite the financial hardship, we decided to distribute our paper for free because we wanted regular classroom teachers and administrators—not only those already committed to progressive change—to read it.

We published six thousand copies of the first issue, which focused on reading, in November of 1986. The eyes of classroom teachers were immediately caught by the bold front-page headline: "Surviving Scott-Foresman: Confessions of a Kindergarten Teacher." The article's author, Rita Tenorio, a bilingual kindergarten teacher, wrote that "administrators in MPS . . . and across the country are responding to pressure to improve our schools by pushing these flawed mechanistic [basal] methods even more! Thus they are extending the questionable basal reading program downward to kindergarten." As an alternative she laid out explicit ideas of what has come to be known as the "emergent reading" or "whole language" approach.

In an editorial in the same issue we outlined a critique that we continued to develop and deepen over the next two years. We criticized the "ritualistic and mechanical activities" of the basal, charging that "students experience reading as a drab prelude to equally drab paper and pencil activities. They come to view books as a source of boredom, rather than as a source of discovery and stimulation." Moreover, we charged that this "systems management" approach was "de-skilling teachers," depriving them of their proper role as teachers and the chance to "grapple with the difficult tasks of figuring out what and how to teach." Finally we quoted the famous labor organizer, Joe Hill, telling teachers,

"Don't Mourn, Organize"—saying that "the only realistic way for MPS elementary teachers to regain the independence they need to teach well is to organize around classroom issues. A serious effort would be to question the current MPS basal program. It is time for the basal system to be arraigned before the court of sound educational practices, with parents, students, and teachers occupying prominent places in the jurors' box."

The school system did not jump at the idea of putting teachers and parents in the "jurors' box." But by some fluke or coincidence, a few whole language proponents, myself included, were placed on the 1987/88 Reading Textbook Evaluation Committee. A loose network of teachers initially organized around *Rethinking Schools*—but eventually including individuals working in the Milwaukee Kindergarten Association, a newly formed chapter of Teachers Applying Whole Language, the Milwaukee chapter of the NAEYC (National Association for the Education of Young Children), the Ad Hoc Committee for Whole Language, and the reading committee of the Milwaukee Teachers' Education Association—began to speak out in favor of alternatives to the basal system. *Rethinking Schools* became a vehicle by which many teachers were educated about whole language and kept abreast of the political developments in the struggle against basal adoption. We ran articles like, "Should Children Read During Reading Instruction?" and "Recipe for Teaching Reading—Hold the Basal." We organized meetings with school board members and spent significant time talking privately with them. Teacher proponents of whole language testified at school board meetings.

Our editorials, at first, called for whole language to be considered in the adoption and then openly called for a postponement of the basal adoption. In one we critiqued the relationship between social promotion and the basal system. Finally, the month the adoption committee was to make its decision, our centerfold had a lengthy review of the *Report Card on Basal Readers* from the Commission on Reading of the National Council of Teachers of English.

Three of us on the adoption committee disagreed with the

majority so strongly that we issued a minority report, perhaps the first one in the history of textbook adoption in Milwaukee. We called for a whole language option and for pilots to be established. We continued to apply pressure, forming the Alliance for Whole Language. In June, 1988, the school board and the new superintendent finally decided to postpone the adoption of the basal and establish ten whole-language project schools. We felt vindicated.

After another year of adoption proceedings, teachers were given the option of choosing from one of three reading approaches—a basal approach, a literature-based approach, and a whole language approach. While the majority still choose the basal, we feel we have won a significant reform in securing the right of choice for teachers. Even more important, we made the issues of whole language and the nature of reading instruction a center of discussion in Milwaukee.[1]

Needless to say, *Rethinking Schools* has taken a great deal of effort, usually done after long days of teaching. Hours are consumed in meetings, discussion, reviewing articles, writing, typing, editing, proofreading, layout, and distribution. Even though pedagogically we advocate "Less is More" in our personal and political lives, we do the opposite. For those most involved, it has become a sort of combination personal support network, education study circle, and political action group. We also had to raise our own money to keep the effort alive.

THE STRUGGLE FOR A LA ESCUELA FRATNEY

The vacating of the old Fratney School presented us with an exciting possibility to put some of our theories into practice on a school level. Set in one of the few integrated neighborhoods in Milwaukee, the ninety-year-old three-story building had at first been slated to be razed. The old staff and student body of Fratney was to move in April of 1988 to a new school six blocks away that was to house

[1] For a complete recounting of the basal reader struggle see Peterson, B. (1989) "Don't Mourn—Organize": Teachers Take the Offensive Against Basals. *Theory Into Practice, 28*(4) 295–99.

a combined population of able-bodied and disabled students. The soon-to-be emptied school set some of us thinking.

A few teachers and parents who live in Riverwest neighborhood began meeting to discuss how Fratney could become the home of a program which capitalized on the unique features of the neighborhood. One parent said, "We started to dream about a school that would provide the highest quality education for all of our children: black, white, and Hispanic."

We quickly developed a comprehensive proposal for a two-way bilingual, whole language, multicultural, site-based managed, neighborhood specialty school. We call it La Escuela Fratney. A few of us from *Rethinking Schools* helped organize a community-based group called Neighbors for a New Fratney.

The school administration had other dreams, however, which came to be viewed as nightmares by some of the community activists. The administration wanted to turn the empty building into an "Exemplary Teaching Center" with a staff comprised of "master teachers" with master's degrees and at least ten years teaching experience using the techniques of Madeline Hunter. Their job would have been to work with MPS teachers who were having classroom difficulties and were brought in for two and a half week training sessions. Many of the parents questioned whether they wanted their kids taught by a series of bad teachers, and argued that such a center could be established anywhere while the New Fratney proposal could only unfold as envisioned at its present site.

Posters went out on New Year's Day, 1988, and several community meetings were called. We mobilized the community to come out to a public hearing (in the midst of a bitter snowstorm that forced all schools to close the next day) and convinced the school board to consider our proposal seriously. They directed the administration to meet with us and try to come back with a recommendation.

From the beginning the leadership at central office (CO) did not appear to understand our project. The administration put forth a "compromise" proposal to combine the Madeline Hunter–type teacher training program with our project. What we had proposed was, in fact, an opposite of their plan. We proposed a whole language, two-way bilingual model with cooperative learning, in a school that was organized and governed by a site-based management council of teachers and parents. What they wanted was a top-down model for a teacher training school, organized and run by the central office. As we sat negotiating with the central office leadership in the superintendent's conference room, the absurdity of the situation became evident. I pointed out to then Superintendent Faison that there was an inherent contradiction between having a school run by the staff development academy and a school run by a local group of teachers and parents. Moreover, the central office's proposal for the exemplary teacher center had not mentioned the word "parents" once. "Wait," responded one top CO official, "While it's true we didn't mention parents once in our proposal, your proposal didn't mention central office." (Actually, ours did.)

The representatives of Neighbors for a New Fratney left that meeting almost in shock. There was a bizarre failure to understand our proposal, but worse yet there was an atmosphere of fear that pervaded the meeting. The CO staff only spoke after raising their hands and being recognized by then-Superintendent Faison, and then only in a rather timid fashion. More frightening was that after the meeting, three staff members came up to us in the hall and, while glancing back over their shoulders, urged us not to compromise. They thought our proposal was sound and should be left intact, but they said they couldn't say anything out of fear of repercussions.

We stuck to our position and continued to mobilize our community. The school board passed our proposal and established the first city-wide speciality school with neighborhood preference. They also directed the central office to cooperate with Neighbors for a New Fratney. We recognize that part of the reason we were successful was the political context in which we found ourselves. The school board had, a few months earlier, publicly gone on record in favor of site-based management. Members of the black community were demanding an independent school district, charging (among other things) that the bureaucracy was incapable of listening to parents. School board members had, through our previous efforts in *Rethinking Schools,* become aware of the benefits of a whole language teaching approach.

Despite the explicit order by the school board to cooperate with our group, a couple of weeks passed with no meeting or contact from the central office. Finally, we heard through a mole that an important meeting to plan Fratney was to take place the next day at 11:00 A.M. and though uninvited, we asked a parent to attend. Because the parent had no idea where the meeting was to be held, she waited five minutes after the meeting was scheduled to begin, and then approached the secretary of the administrator in charge and asked to be taken to the meeting. The secretary, who did not know this parent had not been invited, escorted her into a room of open-mouthed surprised administrators. At that time a joint meeting was set up to start the planning.

But the administration continued to stall, ignore, and even sabotage the efforts of our group. For example, in order to deal with the fact that union seniority might permit teachers who were not in agreement with the concept to teach at the school, we proposed that all teachers be given a one-page explanation of the program when staff openings were announced. The Milwaukee Teachers' Education Association agreed, as did lower level administrators, but someone in power decided against it and it was never done.

The community had called for a nationwide search for a principal. The administration refused, and then proceeded to stall, not hiring anyone. Finally, only a month before the school was to open, and in opposition to what a parent interview committee had recommended, the administration recommended the appointment of a woman with only suburban experience who was bilingual—but in English and German, not English and Spanish. This was seen as a direct affront to the community and once again the community mobilized in opposition to the appointment. Holding picket signs bearing slogans such as "Remember Gallaudet" in reference to a not unsimilar struggle at the College for the Deaf in Washington, D.C., dozens of parents came to school board meetings. Bowing to pressure and publicity, a newly hired superintendent, Robert S. Peterkin from Cambridge, Massachusetts, recognized the problems with central office's action and rejected the recommendation. He hired an interim principal acceptable to the community and promised that a national search would take place in the ensuing year.

Three teachers wrote a draft curriculum at the central office, which houses 240 administrators, in late June and July. We were informed that we would also have to order *everything* for the new school in a two-week time period so materials would be in place for the beginning of school—without administrative help. It was a difficult four weeks working at central office among people who had bitterly opposed our plan. One of the teachers involved remarked at the time that working on the Fratney project at central office was like three peace activists working in the Pentagon.

When we returned in mid-August to begin the process of readying the school, we found that necessary renovation construction had only just begun and that the school building still needed to be cleaned from the previous spring. Curiously, nothing that we had ordered had yet arrived at the school. We started calling the vendors and they told us they had no records of our orders. Upon further investigation (and much to our horror), we discovered that although the requisition forms had been signed on July 18th (or before) by a deputy superintendent, the forms had sat on a shelf in the purchasing division the following month because the department did not have an authorization card with the deputy superintendent's signature. The forms, we learned, had not been sent out until the afternoon of August 15—a full month after we had completed them. The error was particularly annoying because many books and materials had disappeared when the school closed. Our bilingual program necessitated new materials and the few library books that remained at Fratney were in boxes because of the delayed renovation of the library. We started school with virtually no materials. At the time we figured, "Well, at least we ordered a high quality Xerox machine so that we can rely on that for the first few weeks of school." We called to check on that order. It had never been placed. Somehow it had been lost, too.

At that point we had another one of our philosophical discussions. Was this all happening because of sabotage, incompetence, or benign neglect? To this day, we do not know.

Needless to say, we could not sit back and wait. To make a long story a bit shorter, we stormed back up to the central office. Fortunately for us, this time we had gained an ally—actually two; the new superintendent and his assistant, Dr. Deborah McGriff. We called up Dr. McGriff, explained that we had an emergency on our hands, and within an hour we were sitting in her office. We closed the door and told her the story from the beginning, listing seventeen different ways we felt our efforts were being sabotaged or ignored. She responded, "This is going to stop now." She instructed top officials to arrange a meeting with the deputy superintendents and to meet with us the next day. We were extremely skeptical and were ready to go to the press to tell our story. We had even discussed the feasibility of occupying the school.

But at the meeting the next day, we were truly astounded. We felt that we had been beamed to another planet. We laid out our problems and our immediate needs. In every case but one, the administration agreed to act immediately. Our orders would be filled. The Xerox machine was to be delivered the next morning. Our budgetary problems had been relieved. We walked out of there, one week before school was to start, feeling that now—finally—we could direct our energies and attention to the business of creating the new program at La Escuela Fratney. Unfortunately, of course, the consequence of the many months of inaction and poor planning were acutely felt throughout the first year.

But the problems had a positive effect, too. It brought us together as a unit—parents and teachers—and together we survived the first year. In 1989 our elementary school had a population of three hundred students who are thirty-nine percent Hispanic, forty-two percent African-American, and the rest "other"; seventy-nine percent of them are eligible for free lunch. We are attempting to build our school around the following principles:

- A two-way bilingual program in which native Spanish and English speakers are in the same classrooms.
- A multicultural curriculum which draws on our diverse community and also has an explicitly antiracist component to it. We believe children should be taught to be antiracist.
- A whole language and a natural approach to learning first and second languages. Children, we believe, learn to listen, speak, read, and write by listening, speaking, reading, and writing.
- Cooperative learning, where children are taught how to work together and have an environment which fosters such values.
- Democratic discipline, where limits are set, but where children have a voice and are expected to develop self-discipline.
- A thematic approach, in which teachers and parents choose schoolwide themes through which we attempt to interconnect and weave all the curricular areas.
- School-based management, in which a council of parents and staff members make all the major decisions for the school.

The first year was a difficult year. We learned that you can't jump-start a school.[2]

LESSONS FROM THE YEARS OF STRUGGLE

In conclusion I offer five thoughts.

First, people can change city hall, or in our case, the central office of a large bureaucratic school system. We need much less griping and cynicism and much more critique and organizing. There is absolutely no reason for major educational decisions to continue to be made by bureaucrats who are removed from the everyday issues of schools, and many of whom have been out of the classroom for decades. We allegedly live in a democracy and I say it's time we all start acting as if we live in one. In fact, that should be a major goal of teaching—to teach our students what

[2] For more details on the content of the curricular program at La Escuela Fratney see Peterson, B. (1993) Creating a School that Honors the Traditions of a Culturally Diverse Student Body: La Escuela Fratney, in *Public Schools that Work: Creating Community*, Smith, G. A. ed, NY: Routledge. pp 45–67 and Peterson, B. (1995) La Escuela Fratney: A Journey Toward Democracy, in *Democratic Schools*, Apple, M. W. and J. A. Beane, eds., Alexandria, Virginia: ASCD.

some have called civic courage—the capacity and will to act in spite of the difficulties and obstacles we face.

A second lesson is that for educational reform to be successful, it must be rooted in individual schools and classrooms. Teachers and parents must be involved in shaping the reform. Some call this teacher empowerment. That's fine, but it should be empowerment of not just the teacher's union, or of a few lead teachers, but of all classroom teachers working directly with parents.

A third lesson is that teaching is political. Just as the problems of schools must be linked to the problems of society in our organizing, so too must our teaching be linked to the inequities in society. While I have not dealt with classroom practice, I am convinced that as we move from traditionally unequal classrooms, we should recognize the *political* nature of any and all teaching and unapologetically foster antiracist sentiments and social responsibility within our students.

The fourth lesson is the necessity for structural change. The numerous problems we faced in the Fratney project demonstrate that the will and desire for change must include, but go beyond, change in governance. Structures must be created which promote classroom collaboration and teacher-generated curriculum and assessment. Time must be set aside for classroom teachers to reflect, and respect must be given so that our profession receives what it deserves. We don't need the business model that speaks of efficient hierarchies and higher productivity. We need a radical participatory democratic model that involves parents, teachers, and principals as educational partners, taking both the power and the responsibility for quality and humane education.

But there is one final lesson I must speak of as I reflect upon years of being an active fighter for educational change. We need to look beyond city limits or state lines and recognize that if we are going to solve some of our problems, we are going to need many more resources. People speak of urban children being "at risk"— but in one sense this is just another form of blaming the victim. I believe it is time this country declares educational systems in all our major urban centers and in many rural areas to be "at risk." The military budget must be cut dramatically and social service spending, particularly for education and for children, must be increased. We need a national school reconstruction fund to rebuild inner-city schools and to create a new teacher corps. The Marshall Plan committee, of which I was a member, estimated that to reduce class size to eighteen in grades K–3, to twenty in grades 4–8, and to twenty-five in grades 9–12, we would need to build $232 million worth of new schools and pay $63 million to new teachers. This is equivalent to ten hours of spending for the U.S. military budget.

A drastic change in our military budget is needed for an even more fundamental reason. We need to radically improve the life chances of our young people. Without jobs or the hope of jobs, without decent housing, health care, or recreation and cultural opportunities, there is no reason for our young people to stay in school. And they don't. Why stay in school only to find unemployment or a minimum-wage job when dropping out can lead to the possibility of making lots of money through dealing drugs? The life chances of our young people directly affect the quality of life in our schools—and the current military budget is having disastrous effects on the life chances of our youth.

I realize, of course, that money is never enough. New money without major restructuring of schools will not deliver the changes we so desperately need. Both are needed: radical restructuring and increased resources.

I think one of the biggest problems in America today—and it is a direct result of the institutions that most of us work in—is the sad fact that people don't know their history. I don't mean dates and places. I mean key concepts like "peace" and "people are the makers of history." We as conscious beings should be the subject of history—the actors—not objects of history being acted on. To those who say it would be impossible to transform our public school systems into truly humane and quality places, or to the many more skeptics who write off such things as transforming our national priorities as nothing more than a romantic hope, I say look at our history.

I ask, would it take more effort than the members of the abolitionist movement put in as they successfully fought to end the scourge of slavery in this country? Would it take more work than the people in the suffragist movement contributed as they successfully fought to win the right for women to vote? Or of those in the labor movement who won union rights, social security, and medicare? Or of those in the peace movement that finally ended the war in Vietnam?

As far as I know, we only travel on this planet for a short period of time. I find it wholly obscene that during my short stay here, the incredible resources of this rich nation should be wasted on death and destruction while children suffer, go hungry, and lose their spirit to live constructively in our society. I believe that we have an opportunity to radically improve our school systems. But I strongly feel such an improvement will have to come in the context of a broader social movement—a rainbow coalition—in which the host of related social problems are addressed head on. What we need to do now— if we care about the future of this planet and our children—is to organize. In the words of that great American, Frederick Douglass:

> Those who profess to favor freedom, and yet deprecate agitation are men who want crops without plowing up the ground. They want rain without thunder and lightning.
>
> They want the ocean without the awful roar of its many waters. This struggle may be a moral one; or it may be a physical one; or it may be both moral and physical. But it must be a struggle. Power concedes nothing without a demand. It never did, and it never will.

Good luck to us all.

For more information on Rethinking Schools *or La Escuela Fratney contact the author at* Rethinking Schools, *1001 E. Keefe Avenue, Milwaukee, WI 53212. 414/964-9646.*

E-mail: REPMilw@AOL.com.

This is an edited version of the keynote address given in June 1989 at the Democracy and Education Conference in Athens, Ohio, sponsored by the Institute for Democracy in Education.

14. A Vision in Two Languages: Reflections on a Two-Way Bilingual Program

RITA TENORIO

In June of 1989 when the last students said goodbye to their teachers and friends for the summer, La Escuela Fratney had reached a milestone—we had completed our first year. More accurately, we had survived our first year and all the difficulties it presented. It was a time for congratulations and celebration; it was a time for reflection and planning for year two. I felt the greatest successes came in the building of our "identity," in the way we became a community of students, staff, and parents. It was essential that we strengthen our program to ensure the quality of instruction for this new community.

Our program is designed to focus on several important components: multicultural education, a whole language approach to literacy, cooperative learning, and school-based management. Other schools in Milwaukee are also dealing with one or more of these areas, but what makes our school unique is the addition of a dual language program, a "two-way" bilingual component that is the only one of its kind in Wisconsin.

La Escuela Fratney is one of fifteen Milwaukee Public Schools with a bilingual program. In our city, the struggles of the Hispanic community to ensure quality education for its children took the form of parents, teachers, students, and community members demanding bilingual programs that would meet the academic needs of the students. The school board and the state legislature made the commitment to bilingual education in the early 1970s. Because the Hispanic community continues to advocate for quality, Milwaukee has gained a reputation as having one of the best bilingual programs in the country. MPS has a "developmental" program, a Spanish maintenance program in which both the first and second languages of the students are valued and nurtured from kindergarten through twelfth grade. Becoming bilingual and biliterate is the primary focus. Students learn English during classroom instruction and with English as a Second Language (ESL) teachers. Yet, one of the greatest strengths of the program is that the students' native language is developed too. Cultural pride is an important goal of the program. The bilingual schools serve approximately two thousand students in Milwaukee, and are located in several parts of the city. While all of them are under the "bilingual department" umbrella, each has its own individual character and strengths based on the school population, curriculum focus, and local emphasis.

TWO-WAY BILINGUAL EDUCATION

La Escuela Fratney was opened in 1988 as the result of an unusual effort by the community that surrounds the school. Faced with the opportunity to build curriculum from scratch, the parents, teachers, and community members who made up "Neighbors for a New Fratney" decided they wanted to design a bilingual program that would build on the strengths of the local multicultural community. We wanted all the classrooms and students to be involved in the bilingual program in order to avoid separating the language groups and to give meaning and purpose to the acquisition of two languages.

Recent research on second language acquisition confirms that children can excel in two languages and that they benefit from early exposure to the second language. Over time, cognitive abilities are strengthened as a result of learning another language. It is no wonder that parents in middle- and upper-class communities value second language acquisition for their children. Foreign language has held high prestige in these communities for a very long time and "immersion" programs for English-speaking students are very popular. The research also points to the importance of developing a child's native language first. It has been shown that students' abilities in the second language can actually surpass those of the native speaker if they have a rich understanding of their first language. Concepts and skills that are acquired in the child's first language are easily transferred to the child's second language.

The "two-way" model dispels the notion of bilingual education as a remedial or compensatory program. It builds on the research and promotes the desirability of bilingualism for all students, both English- and Spanish-speaking.

The two-way model does this by striving for a fifty-fifty balance of native English- and Spanish-speakers in each classroom. All students are learning a second language. Both languages are valued equally and all students receive instruction for significant amounts of time in each language. The focus of instruction is primarily academic; students are gaining knowledge in many subjects in two languages. Language is a vehicle for instruction, not simply an end in itself. I am not "teaching Spanish," but rather teaching kindergarten "in Spanish." In the native Spanish-speakers I see better growth this year in their literacy skills. Their self-esteem is enhanced as they become the language resources for the English speakers. The Spanish-speakers can "read" a Big Book to the whole group. They beam with pride as they stand up to tell a story, or share a book they've written in the writing center. Because Spanish is "equal" to English in school, there is more emphasis on developing the language, and the native speakers have benefited.

As we watch them interact with each other, I feel that they are gaining a sensitivity to the process of learning a second language. They have learned to be patient with each other's mistakes and take great pleasure in coming to their teacher with the exciting news that "Reinaldo said good morning. He spoke English!" Once children are familiar with the words for common classroom objects and phrases used in daily routines, they know that I will expect them to use those words and phrases. While they know that I really do understand their comment or question in English, they also know that I will only accept words in Spanish at certain times. If they forget or "get stuck," there is always someone else, one of their peers, who is ready to be their resource. We try to stress that they can help each other, rely on each other, and that each student, black, white, and Hispanic, has something important to give to the group in his or her language.

PARENTS RESPOND

Now that we've reached the end of our second year, it's time again to celebrate and reflect. As teachers, Betsy and I have seen the successes. The growth of the students in both their first and second languages has shown us that implementing this model was a good idea. Beyond ourselves, though, we needed to hear the responses of the parents, and so an after-school meeting was scheduled to listen to their feedback and concerns. Almost thirty people attended, and the positive response to this year's instruction was overwhelming. The same parents who in August were concerned that their child would be receiving only "half as much" instruction were now testifying that their child had gained a great deal of knowledge in two languages. The children were not "losing" their academics while learning a second language. As one parent stated, "He's picking up things in English that I thought would take a lot longer. It's carrying over into his reading. I think he's learned a whole lot this year!"

Many parents felt that it was "good that they hear things in both English and Spanish." The children were developing interest in other languages, too. Parents were happy that their children had the opportunity to learn from two teachers and experience two styles of teaching. They saw their children learning to be flexible and comfortable in different situations.

Both English- and Spanish-speaking parents commented that they now saw the advantages of separating and putting equal emphasis on both languages. One Spanish-speaking mother spoke of how her son now sees Spanish as being "validated" and not just something that she and his grandmother feel is important. School becomes more connected to home. One parent said that "Children see the advantage of being bilingual at an early age."

Parents also raised concerns. What about the different personalities of the students—those who are not so anxious to use the second language? How long will it take for the children to be really bilingual? How can I help my child in the second language when I don't know it? They raise concerns about reading, being "immersed" in the second language, and planning time for teachers. The biggest concern that afternoon, though, was "Will the program model continue for them next year?" The strong consensus was that it should.

CHALLENGES AHEAD

Next year, the staff at La Escuela Fratney will take on the challenge of expanding the "two environment" model to the other grade levels. We must strive to provide the best environment—one that fosters growth in two languages, that builds the self-esteem of all children, and stretches them academically as well. Some issues will be ever present: how to provide planning time and in-service for teachers, how to best teach reading and writing in two languages, how to recruit and maintain a school population that reflects the fifty-fifty language balance.

There are other issues, though, that will challenge us even more—questions we must raise if we are really to provide a program that reflects the vision we hold. Will the "reliance" that this year's kindergartners of many cultures have on each other carry over into the next grade and beyond? How can we help them to continue to see each others' strengths, here at school and in their own communities as well? What structures, what vehicles can we as educators put in place to promote a multicultural experience that goes beyond the end of the school day?

While we may have a balance of language at school, the reality in our society is that in the minds of many people Spanish is certainly not equal to English. Can we help our students to understand why that is and challenge them to reconsider that perception? We must also challenge our own perceptions that reflect a bias toward English. For example, parents and teachers will express their concern about the length of time English-speakers are immersed in Spanish. Parents raised concerns about how much Spanish the children would be comfortable with in the program. Teachers feel unsure about "keeping" the children in Spanish all day. Yet our sensitivity doesn't always extend to what the Spanish-speakers are experiencing in the English environment. Maybe because English is the dominant language, we somehow feel that the Spanish-speaking students will cope more easily and adjust more quickly. Yet, anyone who has been immersed in a foreign language knows the difficulty that both language groups face. As teachers, we must strive to lessen the anxiety for all students.

The true test of our vision will come as these children grow. Success will be evident when the learning that takes place at school begins to connect with what goes on at home. We'll see it when students are eager to carry their projects home to share and when parents feel welcome and eager to be at school to share in their child's experience here. La Escuela Fratney is breaking new ground. Children, parents, and educators of many cultures and two language groups are offering an exciting vision of bilingual, multicultural education. In this vision bilingualism is an advantage, a strength, and all students can benefit from learning in two languages.

15. Nobody Mean More to Me Than You[1] and the Future Life of Willie Jordan

JUNE JORDAN

Black English is not exactly a linguistic buffalo; as children, most of the thirty-five million Afro-Americans living here depend on this language for our discovery of the world. But then we approach our maturity inside a larger social body that will not support our efforts to become anything other than the clones of those who are neither our mothers nor our fathers. We begin to grow up in a house where every true mirror shows us the face of somebody who does not belong there, whose walk and whose talk will never look or sound "right," because that house was meant to shelter a family that is alien and hostile to us. As we learn our way around this environment, either we hide our original word habits, or we completely surrender our own voice, hoping to please those who will never respect anyone different from themselves: Black English is not exactly a linguistic buffalo, but we should understand its status as an endangered species, as a perishing, irreplaceable system of community intelligence, or we should expect its extinction, and, along with that, the extinguishing of much that constitutes our own proud, and singular, identity.

What we casually call "English," less and less defers to England and its "gentlemen." "English" is no longer a specific matter of geography or an element of class privilege; more than thirty-three countries use this tool as a means of "intranational communication."[2] Countries as disparate as Zimbabwe and Malaysia, or Israel

[1] Black English aphorisms crafted by Monica Morris, a Junior at S.U.N.Y., Stony Brook, October, 1984.
[2] *English is Spreading, But What Is English*. A presentation by Professor S. N. Sridhar, Department of Linguistics, S.U.N.Y., Stony Brook, April 9, 1985: Dean's Convocation Among the Disciplines.

and Uganda, use it as their non-native currency of convenience. Obviously, this tool, this "English," cannot function inside thirty-three discrete societies on the basis of rules and values absolutely determined somewhere else, in a thirty-fourth other country, for example.

In addition to that staggering congeries of non-native users of English, there are five countries, or 333,746,000 people, for whom this thing called "English" serves as a native tongue.[3] Approximately ten percent of these native speakers of "English" are Afro-American citizens of the U.S.A. I cite these numbers and varieties of human beings dependent on "English" in order, quickly, to suggest how strange and how tenuous is any concept of "standard English." Obviously, numerous forms of English now operate inside a natural, an uncontrollable, continuum of development. I would suppose "the standard" for English in Malaysia is not the same as "the standard" in Zimbabwe. I know that standard forms of English for Black people in this country do not copy that of Whites. And, in fact, the structural differences between these two kinds of English have intensified, becoming more Black, or less White, despite the expected homogenizing effects of television[4] and other mass media.

Nonetheless, White standards of English persist, supreme and unquestioned, in these United States. Despite our multilingual population, and despite the deepening Black and White cleavage within that conglomerate, White standards control our official and popular judgments of verbal proficiency and correct, or incorrect, language skills, including speech. In contrast to India, where at least fourteen languages coexist as legitimate Indian languages, in contrast to Nicaragua, where all citizens are legally entitled to formal school instruction in their regional or tribal languages, compulsory education in America compels accommodation to exclusively White forms of "English." White English, in America, is "Standard English."

[3] *English Is Spreading.*
[4] *New York Times*, March 15, 1985, Section One, p. 14: Report on Study by Linguists at the University of Pennsylvania.

This story begins two years ago. I was teaching a new course, "In Search of the Invisible Black Woman," and my rather large class seemed evenly divided among young Black women and men. Five or six White students also sat in attendance. With unexpected speed and enthusiasm we had moved through historical narratives of the nineteenth century to literature by and about Black women, in the twentieth. I had assigned the first forty pages of Alice Walker's *The Color Purple*, and I came, eagerly, to class that morning:

"So!" I exclaimed, aloud. "What did you think? How did you like it?"

The students studied their hands, or the floor. There was no response. The tense, resistant feeling in the room fairly astounded me.

At last, one student, a young woman still not meeting my eyes, muttered something in my direction:

"What did you say?" I prompted her.

"Why she have them talk so funny. It don't sound right."

"You mean the language?"

Another student lifted his head: "It don't look right, neither. I couldn't hardly read it."

At this, several students dumped on the book. Just about unanimously, their criticisms targeted the language. I listened to what they wanted to say and silently marvelled at the similarities between their casual speech patterns and Alice Walker's written version of black English.

But I decided against pointing to these identical traits of syntax; I wanted not to make them self-conscious about their own spoken language—not while they clearly felt it was "wrong." Instead I decided to swallow my astonishment. Here was a negative Black reaction to a prize-winning accomplishment of Black literature that White readers across the country had selected as a best-seller. Black rejection was aimed at the one irreducibly black element of Walker's work: the language—Celie's Black English. I wrote the opening lines of *The Color Purple* on the blackboard and asked the students to help me translate these sentences into Standard English:

You better not never tell nobody but God. It'd kill your mammy.

Dear God,

I am fourteen years old. I have always been a good girl. Maybe you can give me a sign letting me know what is happening to me.

Last spring after Little Lucious come I heard them fussing. He was pulling on her arm. She say It too soon, Fonso, I aint well. Finally he leave her alone. A week go by, he pulling on her arm again. She say, Naw, I ain't gonna. Can't you see I'm already half dead, an all of these chilren.[5]

Our process of translation exploded with hilarity and even hysterical, shocked laughter: The Black writer, Alice Walker, knew what she was doing! If rudimentary criteria for good fiction include the manipulation of language so that the syntax and diction of sentences will tell you the identity of speakers, the probable age and sex and class of speakers, and even the locale—urban/rural/southern/western—then Walker had written, perfectly. This is the translation into standard English that our class produced:

Absolutely, one should never confide in anybody besides God. Your secrets could prove devastating to your mother.

Dear God,

I am fourteen years old. I have always been good. But now, could you help me to understand what is happening to me?

Last spring, after my little brother, Lucious, was born, I heard my parents fighting. My father kept pulling at my mother's arm. But she told him, "It's too soon for sex, Alfonso. I am still not feeling well." Finally, my father left her alone. A week went by, and then he began bothering my mother, again: Pulling her arm. She told him, "No, I won't! Can't you see I'm already exhausted from all of these children?"

(Our favorite line was "It's too soon for sex, Alfonso.")

Once we could stop laughing, once we could stop our exponentially wild improvisations on the theme of Translated Black English, the students pushed to explain their own negative first

---

[5] Alice Walker, *The Color Purple* (New York: Harcourt Brace Jovanovich, 1982), p. 11.

reactions to their spoken language on the printed page. I thought it was probably akin to the shock of seeing yourself in a photograph for the first time. Most of the students had never before seen a written facsimile of the way they talk. None of the students had ever learned how to read and write their own verbal system of communication: Black English. Alternatively, this fact began to baffle or else bemuse and then infuriate my students. Why not? Was it too late? Could they learn how to do it, now? And, ultimately, the final test question, the one testing my sincerity: Could I teach them? Because I had never taught anyone Black English and, as far as I knew, no one, anywhere in the United States, had ever offered such a course, the best I could say was "I'll try."

He looked like a wrestler.

He sat dead center in the packed room and, every time our eyes met, he quickly nodded his head as though anxious to reassure, and encourage me.

Short, with strikingly broad shoulders and long arms, he spoke with a surprisingly high, soft voice that matched the soft bright movement of his eyes. His name was Willie Jordan. He would have seemed even more unlikely in the context of Contemporary Women's Poetry, except that ten or twelve other Black men were taking the course, as well. Still, Willie was conspicuous. His extreme fitness, the muscular density of his presence underscored the riveted, gentle attention that he gave to anything anyone said. Generally, he did not join the loud and rowdy dialogue flying back and forth, but there could be no doubt about his interest in our discussions. And, when he stood to present an argument he'd prepared, overnight, that nervous smile of his vanished and an irregular stammering replaced it, as he spoke with visceral sincerity, word by word.

That was how I met Willie Jordan. It was in between "In Search of the Invisible Black Women" and "The Art of Black English." I was waiting for departmental approval and I supposed that Willie might be, so to speak, killing time until he, too, could study Black English. But Willie really did want to explore contemporary women's poetry and, to that end, volunteered for extra research and never missed a class.

Towards the end of that semester, Willie approached me for an independent study project on South Africa. It would commence the next semester. I thought Willie's writing needed the kind of improvement only intense practice will yield. I knew his intelligence was outstanding. But he'd wholeheartedly opted for "Standard English" at a rather late age, and the results were stilted and frequently polysyllabic, simply for the sake of having more syllables. Willie's unnatural formality of language seemed to me consistent with the formality of his research into South African apartheid. As he projected his studies, he would have little time, indeed, for newspapers. Instead, more than ninety percent of his research would mean saturation in strictly historical, if not archival, material. I was certainly interested. It would be tricky to guide him into a more confident and spontaneous relationship both with language and apartheid. It was going to be wonderful to see what happened when he could catch up with himself, entirely, and talk back to the world.

September, 1984: breezy fall weather and much excitement! My class, "The Art of Black English," was full to the limit of the fire laws. And in independent study, Willie Jordan showed up weekly, fifteen minutes early for each of our sessions. I was pretty happy to be teaching, altogether!

I remember an early class when a young brother, replete with his ever-present porkpie hat, raised his hand and then told us that most of what he'd heard was "all right" except it was "too clean." "The brothers on the street," he continued, "they mix it up more. Like 'fuck' and 'motherfuck.' Or like 'shit.'" He waited. I waited. Then all of us laughed a good while, and we got into a brawl about "correct" and "realistic" Black English that led to Rule 1.

Rule 1: *Black English is about a whole lot more than mothafuckin.*

As a criterion, we decided, "realistic" could take you anywhere you want to go. Artful places. Angry places. Eloquent and sweetalkin places. Polemical places. Church. And the local Bar & Grill. We were checking out a language, not a mood or a scene or one guy's forgettable mouthing off.

It was hard. For most of the students, learning Black English required a fallback to patterns and rhythms of speech that many of their parents had beaten out of them. I mean beaten. And, in a majority of cases, correct Black English could be achieved only by striving for *incorrect* Standard English, something they were still pushing at, quite uncertainly. This state of affairs led to Rule 2.

Rule 2: *If it's wrong in Standard English it's probably right in Black English, or, at least, you're hot.*

It was hard. Roommates and family members ridiculed their studies, or remained incredulous, "You *studying* that shit? At school?" But we were beginning to feel the companionship of pioneers. And we decided that we needed another rule that would establish each one of us as equally important to our success. This was Rule 3.

Rule 3: *If it don't sound like something that come out somebody mouth then it don't sound right. If it don't sound right then it ain't hardly right. Period.*

This rule produced two weeks of composition in which the students agonizingly tried to spell the sound of the Black English sentence they wanted to convey. But Black English is, preeminently, an oral/spoken means of communication. *And spelling don't talk.* So we needed Rule 4.

Rule 4: *Forget about the spelling. Let the syntax carry you.*

Once we arrived at Rule 4 we started to fly, because syntax, the structure of an idea, leads you to the world view of the speaker and reveals her values. The syntax of a sentence equals the structure of your consciousness. If we insisted that the language of Black English adheres to a distinctive Black syntax, then we were postulating a profound difference between White and Black people, *per se*. Was it a difference to prize or to obliterate?

There are three qualities of Black English—the presence of life, voice, and clarity—that intensify to a distinctive Black value system that we became excited about and self-consciously tried to maintain:

1. Black English has been produced by a pretechnocratic, if not antitechnological, culture. More, our culture has been constantly threatened by annihilation or, at least, the swallowed blurring of assimilation. Therefore, our language is a system constructed by people constantly needing to insist that we exist, that we are present. Our language devolves from a culture that abhors all abstraction, or anything tending to obscure or delete the fact of the human being who is here and now—the truth of the person who is speaking or listening. Consequently, *there is no passive voice construction possible in Black English.* For example, you cannot say, "Black English is being eliminated." You must say, instead, "White people eliminating Black English." The assumption of the presence of life governs all of Black English. Therefore, overwhelmingly, *all action takes place in the language of the present indicative.* And every sentence assumes the living and active participation of at least two human beings, the speaker and the listener.

2. A primary consequence of the person-centered values of Black English is the delivery of voice. If you speak or write Black English, your ideas will necessarily possess that otherwise elusive attribute, *voice*.

3. One main benefit following from the person-centered values of Black English is that of *clarity*. If your idea, your sentence, assumes the presence of at least two living and active people, you will make it understandable, because the motivation behind every sentence is the wish to say something real to somebody real.

As the weeks piled up, translation from Standard English into Black English or vice versa occupied a hefty part of our course work.

Standard English (hereafter S.E.): "In considering the idea of studying Black English those questioned suggested—"

(What's the subject? Where's the person? Is anybody alive in here, in that idea?)

Black English (hereafter B.E.): "I been asking people what you think about somebody studying Black English and they answer me like this."

But there were interesting limits. You cannot "translate" instances of Standard English preoccupied with abstraction or with nothing/nobody evidently alive, into Black English. That would warp the language into uses antithetical to the guiding perspective of its community of users. Rather you must first change those standard English sentences, themselves, into ideas consistent with the person-centered assumptions of Black English.

Guidelines for Black English

1. Minimal number of words for every idea: this is the source for the aphoristic and/or poetic force of the language; eliminate every possible word.
2. Clarity: if the sentence is not clear it's not Black English.
3. Eliminate use of the verb *to be* whenever possible. This leads to the deployment of more descriptive and, therefore, more precise verbs.
4. Use *be* or *been* only when you want to describe a chronic, ongoing state of things.
   He *be* at the office, by 9. (He is always at the office by 9.)
   He *been* with her since forever.
5. Zero copula: always eliminate the verb *to be* whenever it would combine with another verb, in Standard English.
   S.E.: She is going out with him.
   B.E.: She going out with him.
6. Eliminate *do* as in:
   S.E.: What do you think? What do you want?
   B.E.: What you think? What you want?
   Rules number 3, 4, 5, and 6 provide for the use of the minimal number of verbs per idea and, therefore, greater accuracy in the choice of verb.
7. In general, if you wish to say something really positive, try to formulate the idea using emphatic negative structure.

S.E.: He's fabulous.

B.E: He bad.

8. Use double or triple negatives for dramatic emphasis.

S.E.: Tina Turner sings out of this world.

B.E.: Ain nobody sing like Tina.

9. Never use the *-ed* suffix to indicate the past tense of a verb.

S.E.: She closed the door.

B.E.: She close the door. Or, she have close the door.

10. Regardless of intentional verb time, only use the third person singular, present indicative, for use of the verb *to have,* as an auxiliary.

S.E.: He had his wallet then he lost it.

B.E.: He have him wallet then he lose it.

S.E.: We had seen that movie.

B.E.: We seen that movie. Or, we have see that movie.

11. Observe a minimal inflection of verbs. Particularly, never change from the first person singular forms to the third person singular.

S.E.: Present tense forms: He goes to the store.

B.E.: He go to the store.

S.E.: Past tense forms: He went to the store.

B.E.: He go to the store. Or, he gone to the store. Or, he been to the store.

12. The possessive case scarcely ever appears in black English. Never use an apostrophe ('s) construction. If you wander into a possessive case component of an idea, then keep it logically consistent: *ours, his, theirs, mines.* But, most likely, if you bump into such a component, you have wandered outside the underlying world view of black English.

S.E.: He will take their car tomorrow.

B.E.: He taking they car tomorrow.

13. Plurality—logical consistency, continued—if the modifier indicates plurality then the noun remains in the singular case.

S.E.: He ate twelve doughnuts.

B.E.: He eat twelve doughnut.

S.E.: She has many books.

B.E.: She have many book.

14. Listen for, or invent, special Black English forms of the past tense, such as: "He losted it. That what she felted." If they are clear and readily understood, then use them.

15. Do not hesitate to play with words, sometimes inventing them: e.g. "astropotomous" means huge like a hippo plus astronomical and, therefore, signifies real big.

16. In black English, unless you keenly want to underscore the past tense nature of an action, stay in the present tense and rely on the overall context of your ideas for the conveyance of time and sequence.

17. Never use the suffix -*ly* form of an adverb in Black English.

S.E.: The rain came down rather quickly.

B.E.: The rain come down pretty quick.

18. Never use the indefinite article *an* in Black English.

S.E.: He wanted to ride an elephant.

B.E.: He wanted to ride him a elephant.

19. Invariant syntax: in correct Black English it is possible to formulate an imperative, an interrogative, and a simple declarative idea with the same syntax:

B.E.: You going to the store?

You going to the store.

You going to the store!

Where was Willie Jordan? We'd reached the mid-term of the semester. Students had formulated Black English guidelines, by consensus, and they were now writing with remarkable beauty, purpose, and enjoyment:

I am hardly speakin for everybody but myself so understan that.—Kim Parks

Samples from student writings:

Janie have a great big ole hole inside her. Tea Cake the only thing that fit that hole . . .

That pear tree beautiful to Janie, especial when bees fiddlin with the blossomin pear there growing large and lovely. But personal speakin, the

love she get from starin at that tree ain the love what starin back at her in them relationship.
(Monica Morris)

Love a big theme in, *They Eye Was Watching God*. Love show people new corners inside theyself. It pull out good stuff and stuff back bad stuff . . . Joe worship the doing uh his own hand and need other people to worship him too. But he ain't think about Janie that she a person and ought to live like anybody common do. Queen life not for Janie.
(Monica Morris)

In both life and writin, Black womens have varietous experience of love that be cold like a iceberg or fiery like a inferno. Passion got for the other partner involve, man or women, seem as shallow, ankle-deep water or the most profoundest abyss.
(Constance Evans)

Family love another bond that ain't never break under no pressure.
(Constance Evans)

You know it really cold/When the friend you/Always get out the fire/Act like they don't know you/When you in the heat.
(Constance Evans)

Big classroom discussion bout love at this time. I never take no class where us have any long arguin for and against for two or three day. New to me and great. I find the class time talkin a million time more interestin than detail bout the book.
(Kathy Esseks)

As these examples suggest, Black English no longer limited the students, in any way. In fact, one of them, Philip Garfield, would shortly "translate" a pivotal scene from Ibsen's *A Doll's House* as his final term paper:

Nora: I didn't gived no shit. I thinked you a asshole back then, too, you make it so hard for me save mines husband life.

Krogstad: Girl, it clear you ain't any idea what you done. You done exact what I once done, and I losed my reputation over it.

Nora: You asks me believe you once act brave save you wife life?

Krogstad: Law care less why you done it.

Nora: Law must suck.

(187)

Krogstad: Suck or no, if I wants, judge screw you wid dis paper.

Nora: No way, man.
(Philip Garfield)

But where was Willie? Compulsively punctual and always thoroughly prepared with neat typed compositions, he had disappeared. He failed to show up for our regularly scheduled
conference, and I recieved neither a note nor a phone call of explanation. A whole week went by. I wondered if Willie had finally
been captured by the extremely current happenings in South
Africa: passage of a new constitution that did not enfranchise the
Black majority, and militant Black South African reaction to that
affront. I wondered if he'd been hurt, somewhere. I wondered if
the serious workload of weekly readings and writings had over-
whelmed him and changed his mind about independent study.
Where was Willie Jordan?

One week after the first conference that Willie missed, he
called: "Hello, Professor Jordan? This is Willie. I'm sorry I wasn't
there last week. But something has come up and I'm pretty upset.
I'm sorry but I really can't deal right now."

I asked Willie to drop by my office and just let me see that he
was okay. He agreed to do that. When I saw him I knew something hideous had happened. Something had hurt him and scared
him to the marrow. He was all agitated and stammering and terse
and incoherent. At last, his sadly jumbled account let me surmise,
as follows: Brooklyn police had murdered his unarmed, twenty-
five-year-old brother, Reggie Jordan. Neither Willie nor his elderly
parents knew what to do about it. Nobody from the press was
interested. His folks had no money. Police ran his family around
and around, to no point. And Reggie was really dead. And Willie
wanted to fight, but he felt helpless.

With Willie's permission I began to try to secure legal counsel
for the Jordan family. Unfortunately, Black victims of police violence are truly numerous, while the resources available to prose-
cute their killers are truly scarce. A friend of mine at the Center for

Constitutional Rights estimated that just the preparatory costs for bringing the cops into court normally approaches $180,000. Unless the execution of Reggie Jordan became a major community cause for organizing and protest, his murder would simply become a statistical item.

Again, with Willie's permission, I contacted every newspaper and media person I could think of. But the Bastone feature article in *The Village Voice* was the only result from that canvassing.

Again, with Willie's permission, I presented the case to my class in Black English. We had talked about the politics of language. We had talked about love and sex and child abuse and men and women. But the murder of Reggie Jordan broke like a hurricane across the room.

There are few "issues" as endemic to Black life as police violence. Most of the students knew and respected and liked Jordan. Many of them came from the very neighborhood where the murder had occurred. All of the students had known somebody close to them who had been killed by police, or had known frightening moments of gratuitous confrontation with the cops. They wanted to do everything at once to avenge death. Number One: They decided to compose a personal statement of condolence to Willie Jordan and his family, written in black English. Number Two: They decided to compose individual messages to the police, in black English. These should be prefaced by an explanatory paragraph composed by the entire group. Number Three: These individual messages, with their lead paragraph, should be sent to *Newsday*.

The morning after we agreed on these objectives, one of the young women students appeared with an unidentified visitor, who sat through the class, smiling in a peculiar, comfortable way.

Now we had to make more tactical decisions. Because we wanted the messages published, and because we thought it imperative that our outrage be known by the police, the tactical question was this: should the opening, group paragraph be written in Black English or Standard English?

I have seldom been privy to a discussion with so much heart at the dead heat of it. I will never forget the eloquence, the sudden haltings of speech, the fierce struggle against tears, the furious throwaway, and useless explosions that this question elicited.

That one question contained several others, each of them extraordinarily painful to even contemplate. How best to serve the memory of Reggie Jordan? Should we use the language of the killer—Standard English—in order to make our ideas acceptable to those controlling the killers? But wouldn't what we had to say be rejected, summarily, if we said it in our own language, the language of the victim, Reggie Jordan? But if we sought to express ourselves by abandoning our language wouldn't that mean our suicide on top of Reggie's murder? But if we expressed ourselves in our own language wouldn't that be suicidal to the wish to communicate with those who, evidently, did not give a damn about us/Reggie/police violence in the black community?

At the end of one of the longest, most difficult hours of my own life, the students voted, unanimously, to preface their individual messages with a paragraph composed in the language of Reggie Jordan. *"At least we don't give up nothing else. At least we stick to the truth: Be who we been. And stay all the way with Reggie."*

It was heartbreaking to proceed, from that point. Everyone in the room realized that our decision in favor of Black English had doomed our writings, even as the distinctive reality of our Black lives always has doomed our efforts to "be who we been" in this country.

I went to the blackboard and took down this paragraph dictated by the class:

YOU COPS!

WE THE BROTHER AND SISTER OF WILLIE JORDAN, A FELLOW STONY BROOK STUDENT WHO THE BROTHER OF THE DEAD REGGIE JORDAN. REGGIE, LIKE MANY BROTHER AND SISTER, HE A VICTIM OF BRUTAL RACIST POLICE, OCTOBER 25, 1984. US APPALL, FED UP, BECAUSE THAT ANOTHER SENSELESS DEATH WHAT OCCUR IN OUR COMMUNITY. THIS WHAT WE FEEL, THIS, FROM OUR HEART, FOR WE AIN'T STAYIN' SILENT NO MORE:

With the completion of this introduction, nobody said anything. I asked for comments. At this invitation, the unidentified visitor, a young Black man, ceaselessly smiling, raised his hand. He was, it so happens, a rookie cop. He had just joined the force in September and, he said, he thought he should clarify a few things. So he came forward and sprawled easily into a posture of barroom, or fireside, nostalgia:

"See," Officer Charles enlightened us, "Most times when you out on the street and something come down you do one of two things. Overreact or underreact. Now, if you underreact then you can get yourself kilt. And if you overreact then maybe you kill somebody. Fortunately it's about nine times out of ten and you will overreact. So the brother got kilt. And I'm sorry about that, believe me. But what you have to understand is what kilt him: overreaction. That's all. Now you talk about black people and white police but see, now, I'm a cop myself. And (big smile) I'm black. And just a couple months ago I was on the other side. But it's the same for me. You a cop, you the ultimate authority: the Ultimate Authority. And you [i.c.] on the street, most of the time you can only do one of two things: overreact or underreact. That's all it is with the brother. Overreaction. Didn't have nothing to do with race."

That morning Officer Charles had the good fortune to escape without being boiled alive. But barely. And I remember the pride of his smile when I read about the fate of black policemen and other collaborators, in South Africa. I remember him, and I remember the shock and palpable feeling of shame that filled the room. It was as though that foolish, and deadly, young man had just relieved himself of his foolish, and deadly, explanation, face to face with the grief of Reggie Jordan's father and Reggie Jordan's mother. Class ended quietly. I copied the paragraph from the blackboard, collected the individual messages and left to type them up.

Newsday rejected the piece.

The Village Voice could not find room in their "Letters" section to print the individual messages from the students to the police.

None of the TV news reporters picked up the story.

Nobody raised $180,000 to prosecute the murder of Reggie Jordan.

Reggie Jordan is really dead.

I asked Willie Jordan to write an essay pulling together everything important to him from that semester. He was still deeply beside himself with frustration and amazement and loss. This is what he wrote, unedited, and in its entirety:

Throughout the course of this semester I have been researching the effects of oppression and exploitation along racial lines in South Africa and its neighboring countries. I have become aware of South African police brutalization of native Africans beyond the extent of the law, even though the laws themselves are catalyst affliction upon black men, women and children. Many Africans die each year as a result of the deliberate use of police force to protect the white power structure.

Social control agents in South Africa, such as policemen, are also used to force compliance among citizens through both overt and covert tactics. It is not uncommon to find bold-faced coercion and cold-blooded killings of blacks by South African police for undetermined and/or inadequate reasons. Perhaps the truth is that the only reasons for this heinous treatment of blacks rests in racial differences. We should also understand that what is conveyed through the media is not always accurate and may sometimes be construed as the tip of the iceberg at best.

I recently received a painful reminder that racism, poverty, and the abuse of power are global problems which are by no means unique to South Africa. On October 25, 1984 at approximately 3:00 p.m. my brother, Mr. Reginald Jordan, was shot and killed by two New York City policemen from the 75th precinct in the East New York section of Brooklyn. His life ended at the age of twenty-five. Even up to this current point in time the Police Department has failed to provide my family, which consists of five brothers, eight sisters, and two parents, with a plausible reason for Reggie's death. Out of the many stories that were given to my family by the Police Department, not one of them seems to hold water. In fact, I honestly believe that the Police Department's assessment of my brother's murder is nothing short of ABSOLUTE BULLSHIT, and thus far no evidence had been produced to alter perception of the situation.

Furthermore, I believe that one of three cases may have occurred in this incident. First, Reggie's death may have been the desired outcome of the police officer's action, in which case the killing was premeditated. Or, it was a case of mistaken identity, which clarifies the fact that the two officers who killed my brother and their commanding parties are all grossly incompetent. Or, both of the above cases are correct, i.e., Reggie's murderers intended to kill him and the Police Department behaved insubordinately.

Part of the argument of the officers who shot Reggie was that he had attacked one of them and took his gun. This was their major claim. They also said that only one of them had actually shot Reggie. The facts, however, speak for themselves. According to the Death Certificate and autopsy report, Reggie was shot eight times from point-blank range. The doctor who performed the autopsy told me himself that two bullets entered the side of my brother's head, four bullets were sprayed into his back, and two bullets struck him in the back of his legs. It is obvious that unnecessary force was used by the police and that it is extremely difficult to shoot someone in his back when he is attacking or approaching you.

After experiencing a situation like this and researching South Africa I believe that to a large degree, justice may only exist as rhetoric. I find it difficult to talk of true justice when the oppression of my people both at home and abroad attests to the fact that inequality and injustice are serious problems whereby Blacks and Third World people are perpetually shortchanged by society. Something has to be done about the way in which this world is set up. Although it is a difficult task, we do have the power to make a change.

—Willie J. Jordan Jr.

EGL 487, Section 58, November 14, 1984

It is my privilege to dedicate this to the future life of Willie J. Jordan Jr.

16. The Politics of Teaching Literate Discourse

LISA DELPIT

I have encountered a certain sense of powerlessness and paralysis among many sensitive and well-meaning literacy educators who appear to be caught in the throes of a dilemma. Although their job is to teach literate discourse styles to all of their students, they question whether that is a task they can actually accomplish for poor students and students of color. Furthermore, they question whether they are acting as agents of oppression by insisting that students who are not already a part of the "mainstream" learn that discourse. Does it not smack of racism or classism to demand that these students put aside the language of their homes and communities and adopt a discourse that is not only alien, but that has often been instrumental in furthering their oppression? I hope here to speak to and help dispel that sense of paralysis and powerlessness and suggest a path of commitment and action that not only frees teachers to teach what they know, but to do so in a way that can transform and subsequently liberate their students.

DISCOURSE, LITERACY, AND GEE

This article got its start as I pondered the dilemmas expressed by educators. It continued to evolve when a colleague sent a set of papers to me for comment. The papers, authored by literacy specialist James Paul Gee ("Literacy, Discourse, and Linguistics: Introduction" and "What Is Literacy?"), are the lead articles of a special issue of the *Journal of Education* devoted solely to Gee's work. The papers brought to mind many of the perspectives of the educators I describe. My colleague, an academic with an interest in literacy issues in communities of color, was disturbed by much of what she read in the articles and wanted a second opinion.

As I first read the far-reaching, politically sensitive articles, I found that I agreed with much that Gee wrote, as I have with much of his previous work. He argues that literacy is much more than reading and writing, but rather that it is part of a larger political entity. This larger entity he calls a discourse, construed as something of an "identity kit," that is, ways of "saying-writing-doing-being-valuing-believing," examples of which might be the discourse of lawyers, the discourse of academics, or the discourse of men. He adds that one never learns simply to read or write, but to read and write within some larger discourse, and therefore within some larger set of values and beliefs.

Gee maintains that there are primary discourses, those learned in the home, and secondary discourses, which are attached to institutions or groups one might later encounter. He also argues that all discourses are not equal in status, that some are socially dominant—carrying with them social power and access to economic success—and some nondominant. The status of individuals born into a particular discourse tends to be maintained because primary discourses are related to secondary discourses of similar status in our society (for example, the middle-class home discourse to school discourse, or the working-class African-American home discourse to the black church discourse). Status is also maintained because dominant groups in a society apply frequent "tests" of fluency in the dominant discourses, often focused on its most superficial aspects—grammar, style, mechanics—so as to exclude from full participation those who are not born to positions of power.

These arguments resonate in many ways with what I also believe to be true. However, as I reread and pondered the articles, I began to get a sense of my colleague's discomfort. I also began to understand how that discomfort related to some concerns I have about the perspectives of educators who sincerely hope to help educate poor children and children of color to become successful and literate, but who find themselves paralyzed by their own conception of the task.

There are two aspects of Gee's arguments which I find problematic. First is Gee's notion that people who have not been born into dominant discourses will find it exceedingly difficult, if not impossible, to acquire such a discourse. He argues strongly that discourses cannot be "overtly" taught, particularly in a classroom, but can only be acquired by enculturation in the home or by "apprenticeship" into social practices. Those who wish to gain access to the goods and status connected to a dominant discourse must have access to the social practices related to that discourse. That is, to learn the "rules" required for admission into a particular dominant discourse, individuals must already have access to the social institutions connected to that discourse—if you're not already in, don't expect to get in.

This argument is one of the issues that concerned my colleague. As she put it, Gee's argument suggests a dangerous kind of determinism as flagrant as that espoused by the geneticists: instead of being locked into "your place" by your genes, you are now locked hopelessly into a lower-class status by your discourse. Clearly, such a stance can leave a teacher feeling powerless to effect change, and a student feeling hopeless that change can occur.

The second aspect of Gee's work that I find troubling suggests that an individual who is born into one discourse with one set of values may experience major conflicts when attempting to acquire another discourse with another set of values. Gee defines this as especially pertinent to "women and minorities," who, when they seek to acquire status discourses, may be faced with adopting values that deny their primary identities. When teachers believe that this acceptance of self-deprecatory values is *inevitable* in order for people of color to acquire status discourses, then their sense of justice and fair play might hinder their teaching these discourses.

If teachers were to adopt both of these premises suggested by Gee's work, not only would they view the acquisition of a new discourse in a classroom impossible to achieve, but they might also view the goal of acquiring such a discourse questionable at best. The sensitive teacher might well conclude that even to try to teach a dominant discourse to students who are members of a nondominant oppressed group would be to oppress them further. And this potential conclusion concerns me. While I do agree that discourses may embody conflicting values, I also believe there are many individuals who have faced and overcome the problems that such a conflict might cause. I hope to provide another perspective on both of these premises.

OVERCOMING OBSTACLES TO ACQUISITION

One remedy to the paralysis suffered by many teachers is to bring to the fore stories of the real people whose histories directly challenge unproductive beliefs. Mike Rose has done a poignantly convincing job of detailing the role of committed teachers in his own journey toward accessing literate discourse, and his own role as a teacher of disenfranchised veterans who desperately needed the kind of explicit and focused instruction Rose was able to provide in order to "make it" in an alien academic setting. But there are many stories not yet documented which exemplify similar journeys, supported by similar teaching.

A friend and colleague who teaches in a college of education at a major Midwestern university, told me of one of her graduate students whom we'll call Marge. Marge received a special fellowship funded by a private foundation designed to increase the numbers of faculty holding doctorates at black colleges. She applied to the doctoral program at my friend's university and traveled to the institution to take a few classes while awaiting the decision. Apparently, the admissions committee did not quite know what to do with her, for here was someone who was already on campus with a fellowship, but who, based on GRE scores and writing samples, they determined was not capable of doing doctoral-level work. Finally, the committee agreed to admit Marge into the master's program, even though she already held a master's degree. Marge accepted the offer. My friend—we'll call her Susan—got to know Marge when the department head asked her to "work with" the new student who was considered "at risk" of not successfully completing the degree.

Susan began a program to help Marge learn how to cope with

the academic setting. Susan recognized early on that Marge was very talented but that she did not understand how to maneuver her way through academic writing, reading, and talking. In their first encounters, Susan and Marge discussed the comments instructors had written on Marge's papers, and how the next paper might incorporate the professor's concerns. The next summer Susan had Marge write weekly synopses of articles related to educational issues. When they met, Marge talked through her ideas while Susan took notes. Together they translated the ideas into the "discourse of teacher education." Marge then rewrote the papers referring to their conversations and Susan's extensive written comments.

Susan continued to work with Marge, both in and out of the classroom, during the following year. By the end of that year, Marge's instructors began telling Susan that Marge was a real star, that she had written the best papers in their classes. When faculty got funding for various projects, she became one of the most sought-after research assistants in the college. And when she applied for entry into the doctoral program the next fall, even though her GRE scores were still low, she was accepted with no hesitation. Her work now includes research and writing that challenge dominant attitudes about the potential of poor children to achieve.

The stories of two successful African-American men also challenge the belief that literate discourses cannot be acquired in classroom settings, and highlight the significance of teachers in transforming students' futures. Clarence Cunningham, now a vice chancellor at the largest historically black institution in the United States, grew up in a painfully poor community in rural Illinois. He attended an all African-American elementary school in the 1930s in a community where the parents of most of the children never even considered attending high school. There is a school picture hanging in his den of a ragtag group of about thirty-five children. As he shows me that picture, he talks about the one boy who grew up to be a principal in Philadelphia, one who is now a vice president of a major computer company, one who was recently elected attorney general of Chicago, another who is a vice president of Harris Bank in Chicago, another who was the first black pilot hired by a major airline. He points to a little girl who is now an administrator, another who is a union leader. Almost all of the children in the photo eventually left their home community, and almost all achieved impressive goals in life.

Another colleague and friend, Bill Trent, a professor and researcher at a major research university, told me of growing up in the 1940s and 1950s in inner-city Richmond, Virginia, "the capital of the Confederacy." His father, a cook, earned an eighth-grade education by going to night school. His mother, a domestic, had a third-grade education. Neither he nor his classmates had aspirations beyond their immediate environment. Yet, many of these students completed college, and almost all were successful, many notable. Among them are teachers, ministers, an electronics wizard, state officials, career army officers, tennis ace Arthur Ashe, and the brothers Max and Randall Robinson, the national newscaster and the director of Trans-Africa, respectively.

How do these men explain the transformations that occurred in their own and their classmates' lives? Both attribute their ability to transcend the circumstances into which they were born directly to their teachers. First, their teachers successfully taught what Gee calls the "superficial features" of middle-class discourse—grammar, style, mechanics—features that Gee claims are particularly resistant to classroom instruction. And the students successfully learned them.

These teachers also successfully taught the more subtle aspects of dominant discourse. According to both Trent and Cunningham, their teachers insisted that students be able to speak and write eloquently, maintain neatness, think carefully, exude character, and conduct themselves with decorum. They even found ways to mediate class differences by attending to the hygiene of students who needed such attention—washing faces, cutting fingernails, and handing out deodorant.

Perhaps more significant than what they taught is what they believed. As Trent says, "They held visions of us that we could not imagine for ourselves. And they held those visions even when they themselves were denied entry into the larger white world. They were determined that, despite all odds, we would achieve." In an era of overt racism when much was denied to African-Americans, the message drilled into students was "the one thing people can't take away from you is what's between your ears." The teachers of both men insisted that they must achieve because "you must do twice as well as white people to be considered half as good."

As Cunningham says, "Those teachers pushed us, they wouldn't let us fail. They'd say, 'The world is tough out there, and you have to be tougher.'" Trent recalls that growing up in the "inner-city," he had no conception of life beyond high school, but his high school teachers helped him to envision one. While he happily maintained a C average, putting all of his energy into playing football, he experienced a turning point one day when his coach called him inside in the middle of a practice. There, while he was still suited up for football, all of his teachers gathered to explain to him that if he thought he could continue making Cs and stay on the team he had another thing coming. They were there to tell him that if he did not get his act together and make the grades they knew he was capable of, then his football career would be over.

Like similar teachers chronicled elsewhere, these teachers put in overtime to ensure that the students were able to live up to their expectations. They set high standards and then carefully and explicitly instructed students in how to meet them. "You can and will do well," they insisted, as they taught at break times, after school, and on weekends to ensure that their students met their expectations. All of these teachers were able to teach, in class-rooms, the rules for dominant discourses, allowing students to succeed in mainstream America who were not only born outside of the realms of power and status, but who had no access to status institutions. These teachers were not themselves a part of the power elite, not members of dominant discourses. Yet they were able to provide the keys for their students' entry into the larger world, never knowing if the doors would ever swing open to allow them in.

The renowned African-American sociologist E. Franklin Frazier also successfully acquired a discourse into which he was not born. Born in poverty to unschooled parents, Frazier learned to want to learn from his teachers and from his self-taught father. He learned his lessons so well that his achievements provided what must be the ultimate proof of the ability to acquire a secondary dominant discourse, no matter what one's beginnings. After Frazier completed his master's degree at Clark University, he went on to challenge many aspects of the white-dominated oppressive system of segregation. Ironically, at the time Frazier graduated from Clark, he received a reference from its president, G. Stanley Hall, who gave Frazier what he must have thought was the highest praise possible in a predominantly white university in 1920. "Mr. Frazier . . . seems to me to be quite gentlemanly and *mentally white."* What better evidence of Frazier's having successfully acquired the dominant discourse of academe?

These stories are of commitment and transformation. They show how people, given the proper support, can "make it" in culturally alien environments. They make clear that standardized test scores have little to say about one's actual ability. And they demonstrate that supporting students' transformations demands an extraordinary amount of time and commitment, but that teachers *can* make a difference if they are willing to make that commitment.

Despite the difficulty entailed in the process, almost any African-American or other disenfranchised individual who has become "successful" has done so by acquiring a discourse other than the one into which he or she was born. And almost all can attribute that acquisition to what happened as a result of the work of one or more committed teachers.

ACQUISITION AND TRANSFORMATION

But the issue is not only whether students can learn a dominant secondary discourse in the classroom. Perhaps the more significant issue is, should they attempt to do so? Gee contends that for those who have been barred from the mainstream, "acquisition of many mainstream Discourses . . . involves active complicity with the values that conflict with one's home and community-based Discourses." There can be no doubt that in many classrooms students of color do reject literacy, for they feel that literate discourses reject them. Keith Gilyard, in his jolting autobiographical study of language competence, graphically details his attempt to achieve in schools that denied the very existence of his community reality:

> I was torn between institutions, between value systems. At times the tug of school was greater, therefore the 90.2 average. On the other occasions the streets were a more powerful lure, thus the heroin and the 40 in English and a brief visit to the Adolescent Remand Shelter. I . . . saw no middle ground or more accurately, no total ground on which anomalies like me could gather. I tried to be a hip schoolboy, but it was impossible to achieve that persona. In the group I most loved, to be fully hip meant to repudiate a school system in which African-American consciousness was undervalued or ignored; in which, in spite of the many nightmares around us, I was urged to keep my mind on the Dream, to play the fortunate token, to keep my head straight down and "make it." And I pumped more and more dope into my arms. It was a nearly fatal response, but an almost inevitable one.

Herb Kohl writes powerfully about individuals, young and old, who choose to "not-learn" what is expected of them rather than to learn that which denies them their sense of who they are:

> Not-learning tends to take place when someone has to deal with unavoidable challenges to her or his personal and family loyalties, integrity, and identity. In such situations there are forced choices and no apparent middle ground. To agree to learn from a stranger who does not respect your integrity causes a major loss of self. The only alternative is to not-learn and reject the stranger's world.

I have met many radical or progressive teachers of literacy who attempt to resolve the problem of students who choose to "not-learn" by essentially deciding to "not-teach." They appear to believe that to remain true to their ideology, their role must be to empower and politicize their most disenfranchised students by refusing to teach what Gee calls the superficial features (grammar, form, style, and so forth) of dominant discourses. Believing themselves to be contributing to their students' liberation by de-emphasizing dominant discourses, they instead seek to develop literacy *solely* within the language and style of the students' home discourse.

Feminist writer bell hooks writes of one of the consequences of this teaching methodology. During much of her postsecondary school career she was the only black student in her writing courses. Whenever she would write a poem in black Southern dialect, the teachers and fellow students would praise her for using her "true authentic voice" and encourage her to write more in this voice. hooks writes of her frustration with these teachers who, like the teachers I describe, did not recognize the need for African-American students to have access to many voices and who maintained their stance even when adult students or the parents of younger students demanded that they do otherwise.

I am reminded of one educator of adult African-American veterans who insisted that her students needed to develop their "own voices" by developing "fluency" in their home language. Her students vociferously objected, demanding that they be taught grammar, punctuation, and "standard English." The teacher insisted that such a mode of study was "oppressive." The students continued venting their objections in loud and certain tones. When asked why she thought her students had not developed "voice" when they were using their voices to loudly express their displeasure, she responded that it was "because of who they are," that is, apparently because they were working-class, black, and disagreed with her. Another educator of adults told me that she based her teaching on liberating principles. She voiced her anger with her mostly poor, working-class students because they rejected her pedagogy and "refused to be liberated." There are many such stories to recount.

There are several reasons why students and parents of color take a position that differs from the well-intentioned position of the teachers I have described. First, they know that members of society need access to dominant discourses to (legally) have access to economic power. Second, they know that such discourses can be and have been acquired in classrooms because they know individuals who have done so. And third, and most significant to the point I wish to make now, they know that individuals have the ability to transform dominant discourses for liberatory purposes—to engage in what Henry Louis Gates calls "changing the joke and slipping the yoke," that is, using European philosophical and critical standards to challenge the tenets of European belief systems.

bell hooks speaks of her black women teachers in the segregated South as being the model from which she acquired both access to dominant discourses and a sense of the validity of the primary discourse of working-class African-American people. From their instruction, she learned that black poets were capable of speaking in many voices, that the Dunbar who wrote in dialect was as valid as the Dunbar who wrote sonnets. She also learned from these women that she was capable of not only participating in the mainstream, but redirecting its currents: "Their work was truly education for critical consciousness. . . . They were the teachers who conceptualized oppositional world views, who taught us young black women to exult and glory in the power and beauty of our intellect. They offered to us a legacy of liberatory pedagogy that demanded active resistance and rebellion against sexism and racism."

Carter G. Woodson called for similar pedagogy almost seventy years ago. He extolled teachers in his 1933 *Mis-Education of the Negro* to teach African-American students not only the language and canon of the European "mainstream," but to teach as well the life, history, language, philosophy, and literature of their own people. Only this kind of education, he argued, would prepare an educated class which would serve the needs of the African-American community.

Acquiring the ability to function in a dominant discourse need not mean that one must reject one's home identity and values, for discourses are not static, but are shaped, however reluctantly, by those who participate within them and by the form of their participation. Many who have played significant roles in fighting for the liberation of people of color have done so through the language of dominant discourses, from Frederick Douglass to Ida B. Wells, to Mary McCloud Bethune, to Martin Luther King, to Malcolm X. As did bell hooks' teachers, today's teachers can help economically disenfranchised students and students of color, both to master the dominant discourses and to transform them. How is the teacher to accomplish this? I suggest several possibilities.

What can teachers do? First, teachers must acknowledge and validate students' home language without using it to limit students' potential. Students' home discourses are vital to their perception of self and sense of community connectedness. One Native American college student I know says he cannot write in standard English when he writes about his village "because that's about me!" Then he must use his own "village English" or his voice rings hollow even to himself. June Jordan has written a powerful essay about teaching a course in Black English and the class's decision to write a letter of protest in that language when the brother of one of the students was killed by police. The point must not be to eliminate students' home languages, but rather to add other voices and discourses to their repertoires. As bell hooks and Henry Gates have poignantly reminded us, racism and oppression must be fought on as many fronts and in as many voices as we can muster.

Second, teachers must recognize the conflict Gee details between students' home discourses and the discourse of school. They must understand that students who appear to be unable to learn are in many instances choosing to "not-learn" as Kohl puts it, choosing to maintain their sense of identity in the face of what they perceive as a painful choice between allegiance to "them" or "us." The teacher, however, can reduce this sense of choice by transforming the new discourse so that it contains within it a place for the students' selves. To do so, they must saturate the dominant discourse with new meanings, must wrest from it a place for the glorification of their students and their forbears.

An interesting historical example is documented by James

Anderson. Anderson writes of Richard Wright, an African-American educator in the post-Reconstruction era, who found a way through the study of the "classical" curriculum to claim a place of intellectual respect for himself and his people. When examined by the U.S. Senate Committee on Education and Labor, one senator questioned Wright about the comparative inferiority and superiority of the races. Wright replied:

> It is generally admitted that religion has been a great means of human development and progress, and I think that about all the great religions which have blessed this world have come from the colored races—all . . . I believe, too, that our methods of alphabetic writing all came from the colored race, and I think the majority of the sciences in their origin have come from the colored races. . . . Now I take the testimony of those people who know, and who, I feel are capable of instructing me on this point, and I find them saying that the Egyptians were actually wooly-haired negroes. In Humboldt's *Cosmos* (Vol. 2, p.531) you will find that testimony, and Humboldt, I presume, is a pretty good authority. The same thing is stated in Herodotus, and in a number of other authors with whom you gentlemen are doubtless familiar. Now if that is true, the idea that the negro race is inherently inferior, seems to me to be at least a little limping.

Noted educator Jaime Escalante prepared poor Latino students to pass the tests for advanced calculus when everyone else thought they would do well to master fractions. To do so, he also transformed a discourse by placing his students and their ancestors firmly within its boundaries. In a line from the movie chronicling his success, *Stand and Deliver,* he entreated his students, "You *have* to learn math. The Mayans discovered zero. Math is in your blood!"

And this is also what those who create what has been called "Afrocentric" curricula do. They too seek to illuminate for students (and their teachers) a world in which people with brown and black skin have achieved greatness and have developed a large part of what is considered the great classical tradition. They also seek to teach students about those who have taken the language born in Europe and transformed it into an emancipatory tool for those facing oppression in the "new world." In the mouths and pens of Bill

Trent, Clarence Cunningham, bell hooks, Henry Louis Gates, Paul Lawrence Dunbar, and countless others the "language of the master" has been used for liberatory ends. Students can learn of that rich legacy, and they can also learn that they are its inheritors and rightful heirs.

A final role that teachers can take is to acknowledge the unfair "discourse-stacking" that our society engages in. They can discuss openly the injustices of allowing certain people to succeed, based not upon merit but upon which family they were born into, upon which discourse they had access to as children. The students, of course, already know this, but the open acknowledgment of it in the very institution that facilitates the sorting process is liberating in itself. In short, teachers must allow discussions of oppression to become a part of language and literature instruction. Only after acknowledging the inequity of the system can the teacher's stance then be "Let me show you how to cheat!" And of course, to cheat is to learn the discourse which would otherwise be used to exclude them from participating in and transforming the mainstream. This is what many black teachers of the segregated South intended when they, like the teachers of Bill Trent and Clarence Cunningham, told their students that they *had* to "do better than those white kids." We can again let our students know that they can resist a system that seeks to limit them to the bottom rung of the social and economic ladder.

Gee may not agree with my analysis of his work, for, in truth, his writings are so multifaceted as not to be easily reduced to simplistic positions. But that is not the issue. The point is that some aspects of his work can be disturbing for the African-American reader, and reinforcing for those who choose—wrongly, but for "right" reasons—not to educate black and poor children.

Individuals *can* learn the "superficial features" of dominant discourses, as well as their more subtle aspects. Such acquisition can provide a way both to turn the sorting system on its head and to make available one more voice for resisting and reshaping an oppressive system. This is the alternative perspective I want to give to teachers of poor children and children of color, and this is the perspective I hope will end the paralysis and set teachers free to teach, and thereby to liberate. When teachers are committed to teaching all students, and when they understand that through their teaching change *can* occur, then the chance for transformation is great.

City Teachers

PART III

You may write me down in history
With your bitter, twisted lies,
You may trod me in the very dirt
But still, like dust, I'll rise.
—MAYA ANGELOU

Chance has never yet satisfied
hope of a suffereing people. Action,
self-reliance, the vision of self and the
future have been the only means by
which the oppressed have seen and
realized the light of their own fredom.
Up, up, you mighty race! You can
accomplish what you will.
—MARCUS GARVEY

One feels his two-ness—an
American, a Negro, two souls, two
thoughts, two unreconciled
strivings; two warring ideals in one
dark body, whose dogged strength
alone keeps it from being torn asunder.
—W. E. B. DUBOIS

The so called modern education,
with all its defects, however, does
others so much more good than it
does the Negro because it has been
worked out in conformity to the
needs of those who have enslaved and
oppressed weaker peoples.
—CARTER G. WOODSON

Urban Pedagogy

Is there a distinctly urban pedagogy?

In the front row of a celebrity press conference announcing a major grant to the Chicago school reform effort sat five young men: Cornell Faust, Antwoine Conaway, Kelly Floyd, Derrhun Whitten, and Darnell Faust. Wearing starter jackets and gold chains with elaborate designs etched into their short-cropped hair, they draped their long bodies casually over the folding chairs. City kids. "I'll bet that's Farragut's fabulous five," whispered a reporter. "They're a cinch to be state basketball champs this year."

When the young men were introduced fifteen minutes later, and stood with awkward smiles and waves, there was an audible gasp throughout the auditorium, followed by sustained applause—these were state champions all right, 1994 Illinois state chess champions from Orr High School. Orr is a Chicago Public School, eighty-five percent low-income, ninety-five percent African-American. The chess team defeated New Trier High School from the wealthy gold coast suburbs to advance to the nationals, where they came in second by half a point to New York's famous Peter Stuyvesant High School. Something in the contrast between the stereotype of young black men and the actual accomplishment of these students made the applause warmer and more moving.

The chess program at Orr began in 1986 under the leadership of math teacher Tom Larson. "I love chess," Larson said, "And I believe in these kids. I thought chess could be a way to get them to sit still and begin using their thinking skills. So far it's worked." Larson is a big bearded man on a mission. "My job is to guide them to independence, to guide them through the process of maturing . . . I'm trying to build the dream. Faith, hope, and love."

Tom Larson has qualities all good teachers need: a passion for something (in his case, chess, but it could as easily be literature, music, art, politics, geometry, history, algebra, quilts, or quarks), and an unshakable belief in the capacities of his students. In other words, he loves the kids and he's engaged in life. He brings to his teaching a passion for the world and an abiding regard for his students. Faith, hope, and love.

The city is a place, a big and growing place. On September 20, 1994, the Chicago *Tribune* wire service reported that according to a World Bank Study, the world's big cities together are growing by a million people a week. Within a decade, the study predicts, more than half the earth's people will live in cities. It is a geographic location for billions.

But the city is more than geography. It is bright lights, big chances, a place for new experiences and bold experiments. It is also a metaphor for corruption and degeneracy. And increasingly it is a code for the poor, the nonwhite, the immigrant, the economically marginal. The city as seething.

The problem for teachers is to figure out what and how much to take into account when inventing teaching in city schools. There is the danger of not taking enough into account—poverty is significant for kids who are unable to acquire the basic sustenance for a healthy life; race matters in a society that structures rewards and privileges in part on the hierarchies of color and background. Hungry children can't learn; hurt children can't learn; frightened or distraught children can't learn; upset children can't learn. There is a lot that city teachers need to take into account.

On the other hand, there is the danger of taking too much into account or of making stereotypical generalizations about children and their families that can destroy teaching efforts. For example, when a group of new city teachers met for orientation with their principal, he was kind enough, and complimentary: "I'm so glad you will be with us for the coming year," he began. "You're just what we need—energetic, fresh, filled with youthful idealism." When anyone applauds youthful idealism, duck! He went on to explain to them that even though they thought these kids would become great students under their tutelage, they had to understand the real world. "These kids come from homes where there is too much noise and chaos," he explained. "Just learning to listen is hard enough. Don't expect them to be good readers."

In a single gesture, this principal lowered expectations, encouraged teachers to teach less, and reduced the power of the curriculum—all in a benevolent-sounding talk to new teachers about the "real" world of city kids. He based his advice on assumptions about families he didn't know in any sustained or personal or intimate way. And his beneficence would have a terrible impact on the kids.

For teachers "being nice" can lead to teaching less. "I don't ask much of April," says her teacher. "She's probably got a tough life." Probably? What's the evidence? Be careful. This is no help to April. Caring for kids' lives—*really* caring for them—involves understanding and nurturing them in the present, and also seeing to their futures. It involves knowing them well, knowing their strengths and capacities and abilities. Teachers need to know the world well enough to help kids envision and nurture a future, and they must know kids well enough to know what it will take to advance learning. Families can be important allies and informants in serious attempts to teach—and families must be approached with respect and a sense of solidarity if they are to be a source of knowledge and assistance. No teacher is truly student-centered who is not at the same time family-centered.

Doris Lessing grew up in rural Africa in a strict, highly regimented family. She was not a happy child, and yet by the age of twelve she knew "how to set a hen, look after chickens and rabbits, worm dogs and cats, pan for gold, take samples from reefs, cook, sew, use the milk separator and churn butter, go down a mine shaft in a bucket, make cream cheese and ginger beer, paint stencilled patterns on materials, make paper mache, walk on stilts . . . drive the car, shoot pigeons and guinea-fowl for the pot, preserve eggs—and a lot else . . ."

And so in spite of living in a society she describes as stingy and cold-hearted, and a family that was cruel and abusive, Lessing says of her long list of knowledge and experience at twelve, "That is real happiness, a child's happiness: being enabled to do and to make, above all to know you are contributing . . . you are valuable and valued."

This lesson from rural Africa has application to urban America. "Being enabled to do and to make"—to find opportunities in our schools for every youngster to create meaning, to construct projects, to invent products, to leave a mark. Every child needs something important to strive for, real work to do, something to belong to and care about. A good school—or a good classroom—provides multiple entry points for students to do and to make, and there is evidence of doing and making in the halls, on the walls, throughout the space.

"To know you are contributing . . . you are valuable and valued"—once again, the message that this place is incomplete without you, cannot function fully without your effort, is not whole until your piece is added.

An urban pedagogy must be built on the strengths of the city, the hope and the promise of city kids and families, on the capacities of city teachers. We must create an enjoyable teaching experience and a classroom life that teachers want to be a part of. The classroom cannot be a place where teachers bite their lips, hold their breath, and endure. Rather, urban classrooms must be places where teachers can pursue their ideas, explore their interests, follow their passions—and be engaged with students in living lives of purpose. This, as opposed to some phony stance of unquestioned authority, is the essence of teacher professionalism.

This is not simple. It requires attention, effort, intelligence. It takes enormous commitments of time and energy. And it takes focus—focus on the child first of all, focus on the student as a learner, focus on the strengths and assets youngsters bring with them to school, and focus on our shared world.

"What do you need to know and experience? Why?" These are good questions to invite into your school or classroom. Embedded in these questions are a wide range of other questions: "Who are you? What do you know? What is the nature of the society we share and the world we inhabit? What is required of each of us practically, politically, ethically, socially?" In order to answer—collectively or individually—the question "What do you need to know and experience?" we are pushed to focus on children as dynamic, diverse, unique, whole, and real. And we are pushed to know more about an infinitely interesting and ever expanding world. We cannot simply close our doors or put our heads in the sand—we must engage, interact, be involved.

Education is not a commodity, like a car, to be bought and sold. Education is never neutral; it is always toward something, toward some changed condition or situation, or toward maintaining things just as they are. Good city teachers start with the lived experiences of youngsters, with how they think of themselves and their lives, and take as a fundamental stance, "You can change your life." There are, of course, skills needed to change lives, and those skills include the capacity to read the word. But perhaps more fundamental, youngsters need sustained opportunities and open invitations to make sense of the fabric of their lives or, as Paulo Freire puts it, to read the *world*. Students don't simply learn to read and write as a repetitive, meaningless skill; they read and write to make sense of what's happening to them, to join with, participate, and overcome when necessary.

In a sense the basic curriculum becomes an engagement with the question of what ought to be. Education for a free people is education designed to understand the world as it is, honestly and fully, to act responsibly upon that world, and, where appropriate, to transform that world. This means that education for a free people is education that encourages people to be subjects, not objects, actors *in* history not victims *of* history. It is education that encourages people in the process of becoming more human, in the vocation of thoughtfulness and care. There is an urgency to this kind of teaching in our precious and precarious cities today.

And not just in our cities. The broad outlines of what is described here could productively inform teaching from the gold coast suburbs to the red hills of Georgia or the rich farmlands of the prairies. Every community faces problems of alienation, disconnection, meaninglessness; every young person deserves a chance to make and remake, to become valued and valuable. The city is the place where these contradictions appear with fire and intensity.

During the historic "Freedom Summer" of 1964, when volunteers poured into Mississippi to fight for civil rights, register voters, and participate in the movement, hundreds of "freedom schools" were organized to teach basic skills to the victims of racism so that they could register and vote, and in the process to transform the social order of the south. The schools were vital centers of learning, and explicitly political settings. As Charlie Cobb, an activist with the Student Nonviolent Coordinating Committee, wrote, the freedom schools would draw "the link between a rotting shack and a rotting America."

The curriculum of the "freedom schools" points, again, to the ways learning to read the word can link powerfully to reading the world. Teachers in these schools were advised that while every student would be different, all would likely bear the scars of a racist system—cynicism, distrust, lack of intellectual preparation. But students would have important strengths to build upon as well, notably experience and knowledge of how to survive under the intense pressure of poverty, discrimination, and injustice. As with many of our kids today, the scars of distrust and poor preparation are plainly visible, but so are the strengths of knowledge and experience concerning survival on some complex and sometimes mean streets. The curriculum of the freedom schools included a basic set of questions: 1) Why are we (teachers and students) in freedom schools? 2) What is the Freedom Movement? 3) What alternatives does the Freedom Movement offer us? Secondary questions included: 1) What does the majority culture have that we want? 2) What does the majority culture have that we don't want? 3) What do we have that we want to keep?

In the first unit teachers tell students that they are there to learn alongside their students, that they will investigate important questions together, and that they will help each other find their way. The initial investigation is into the state of their schools, and a comparison with what more privileged students enjoy. What kind of school do you attend? What is its physical condition? How old is it? Do you have a library? A science lab? What foreign languages are taught there? What do you learn about citizenship? How many graduates go on to higher education? And on and on.

Later questions include: What do people learn in school besides reading, writing, and arithmetic? Do schools teach you things you think are untrue? At one point teachers are encouraged to pass out copies of the Pledge of Allegiance, and to engage students in a serious analysis of it. Does America mean everything it says? How do you know? What is the evidence? Later the Bill of Rights is analyzed in the same withering detail.

Once again, there are lessons from the countryside that might expand our sense of what city schools and urban pedagogy might be today. Think of serious, engaging questions to focus your teaching: What are the unemployment trends in the neighborhood? How does it compare to twenty years ago? What happened to make it so? What could change it?

The celebrated children's book author Maurice Sendak and the dark cartoonist Art Speigelman highlight the inner life of children in a dialogue in the *New Yorker* about art. When Speigelman says, "I wanna protect my kids!" Sendak responds, "Art—you can't protect kids . . . they know everything! I'll give you an example . . . My friend lost his wife recently, and right at the funeral his little girl said, 'Why don't you marry miss so-and-so?' He looked at her as if she were a witch. But she was just being a real kid, with desperate day-to-day needs that had to be met no matter what. People say, 'Oh, Mr. Sendak, I wish I were in touch with my childhood self, like you!' As if it were all quaint and succulent, like Peter Pan . . . I say, 'You are in touch, lady—you're mean to your kids, you treat your husband like shit, you lie, you're selfish . . . That *is* your childhood self!' In reality, childhood is deep and rich. It's vital, mysterious, and profound. I remember my own childhood vividly . . . I knew terrible things . . . But I knew I mustn't let adults *know* I knew . . . It would scare them."

We would do well to remember this: childhood is deep and rich, vital, mysterious, and profound. What kids know can be scary, but denying them voice, denying their experiences and their sense-making, will undermine their capacities to learn, and withhold an education of value and power to them. If we offer ourselves as teachers to the city's young, we will need to step forward with appreciation, respect, and a little awe.

17. A Talk to Teachers

JAMES BALDWIN

Let's begin by saying that we are living through a very dangerous time. Everyone in this room is in one way or another aware of that. We are in a revolutionary situation, no matter how unpopular that word has become in this country. The society in which we live is desperately menaced, not by Khrushchev, but from within. So any citizen of this country who figures himself as responsible—and particularly those of you who deal with the minds and hearts of young people—must be prepared to "go for broke." Or to put it another way, you must understand that in the attempt to correct so many generations of bad faith and cruelty, when it is operating not only in the classroom but in society, you will meet the most fantastic, the most brutal, and the most determined resistance. There is no point in pretending that this won't happen.

Since I am talking to schoolteachers and I am not a teacher myself, and in some ways am fairly easily intimidated, I beg you to let me leave that and go back to what I think to be the entire purpose of education in the first place. It would seem to me that when a child is born, if I'm the child's parent, it is my obligation and my high duty to civilize that child. Man is a social animal. He cannot exist without a society. A society, in turn, depends on certain things which everyone within that society takes for granted. Now, the crucial paradox which confronts us here is that the whole process of education occurs within a social framework and is designed to perpetuate the aims of society. Thus, for example, the boys and girls who were born during the era of the Third Reich, when educated to the purposes of the Third Reich, became barbarians. The paradox of education is precisely this—that as one begins to become conscious one begins to examine the society in which he is being educated. The purpose of education, finally, is to create in a person the ability to look at the world for himself, to make his own decisions, to say to himself this is black or this is white, to decide for himself whether there is a God in heaven or not. To ask questions of the universe, and then learn to live with those questions, is the way he achieves his own identity. But no society is really anxious to have that kind of person around. What societies really, ideally, want is a citizenry which will simply obey the rules of society. If a society succeeds in this, that society is about to perish. The obligation of anyone who thinks of himself as responsible is to examine society and try to change it and to fight it—at no matter what risk. This is the only hope society has. This is the only way societies change.

Now, if what I have tried to sketch has any validity, it becomes thoroughly clear, at least to me, that any Negro who is born in this country and undergoes the American educational system runs the risk of becoming schizophrenic. On the one hand he is born in the shadow of the stars and stripes and he is assured it represents a nation which has never lost a war. He pledges allegiance to that flag which guarantees "liberty and justice for all." He is part of a country in which anyone can become president, and so forth. But on the other hand he is also assured by his country and his countrymen that he has never contributed anything to civilization— that his past is nothing more than a record of humiliations gladly endured. He is assured by the republic that he, his father, his mother, and his ancestors were happy, shiftless, watermelon-eating darkies who loved Mr. Charlie and Miss Ann, that the value he has as a black man is proven by one thing only—his devotion to white people. If you think I am exaggerating, examine the myths which proliferate in this country about Negroes.

All this enters the child's consciousness much sooner than we as adults would like to think it does. As adults, we are easily fooled because we are so anxious to be fooled. But children are very different. Children, not yet aware that it is dangerous to look too deeply at anything, look at everything, look at each other, and draw their own conclusions. They don't have the vocabulary to express what they see, and we, their elders, know how to intimidate them very easily and very soon. But a black child, looking at the world around him, though he cannot know quite what to make of it, is aware that there is a reason why his mother works so hard, why his father is always on edge. He is aware that there is some reason why, if he sits down in the front of the bus, his father or mother slaps him and drags him to the back of the bus. He is aware that there is some terrible weight on his parents' shoulders which menaces him. And it isn't long—in fact it begins when he is in school—before he discovers the shape of his oppression.

Let us say that the child is seven years old and I am his father, and I decide to take him to the zoo, or to Madison Square Garden, or to the U.N. Building or to any of the tremendous monuments we find all over New York. We get into a bus and we go from where I live on 131st Street and Seventh Avenue downtown through the park and we get into New York City, which is not Harlem. Now, where the boy lives—even if it is a housing project—is in an undesirable neighborhood. If he lives in one of those housing projects of which everyone in New York is so proud, he has at the front door, if not closer, the pimps, the whores, the junkies—in a word, the danger of life in the ghetto. And the child knows this, though he doesn't know why.

I still remember my first sight of New York. It was really another city when I was born—where I was born. We looked down over the Park Avenue streetcar tracks. It was Park Avenue, but I didn't know what Park Avenue meant *downtown*. The Park Avenue I grew up on, which is still standing, is dark and dirty. No one would dream of opening a Tiffany's on that Park Avenue, and when you go downtown you discover that you are literally in the white world. It is rich—or at least it looks rich. It is clean—because they collect garbage downtown. There are doormen. People walk about as though they owned where they are—and indeed they do. And it's a great shock. It's very hard to relate yourself to this. You don't know what it means. You know—you know instinctively—that none of this is for you. You know this before you are told. And who is it for and who is paying for it? And why isn't it for you?

Later on when you become a grocery boy or messenger and you try to enter one of those buildings a man says, "Go to the back door." Still later, if you happen by some odd chance to have a friend in one of those buildings, the man says, "Where's your package?" Now this by no means is the core of the matter. What I'm trying to get at is that by this time the Negro child has had, effectively, almost all the doors of opportunity slammed in his face, and there are very few things he can do about it. He can more or less accept it with an absolutely inarticulate and dangerous rage inside—all the more dangerous because it is never expressed. It is precisely those silent people whom white people see every day of their lives—I mean your porter and your maid, who never say anything more than "Yes, Sir" and "No, Ma'am." They will tell you it's raining if that is what you want to hear, and they will tell you the sun is shining if that is what you want to hear. They really hate you—really hate you because in their eyes (and they're right) you stand between them and life. I want to come back to that in a moment. It is the most sinister of the facts, I think, which we now face.

There is something else the Negro child can do, too. Every street boy—and I was a street boy, so I know—looking at the society which has produced him, looking at the standards of that society which are not honored by anybody, looking at your churches and the government and the politicians, understands that this structure is operated for someone else's benefit—not for his. And there's no reason in it for him. If he is really cunning, really ruthless, really strong—and many of us are—he becomes a kind of criminal. He becomes a kind of criminal because that's the only way he can live. Harlem and every ghetto in this city—every ghetto in this country—is full of people who live outside the law. They wouldn't dream of calling a policeman. They wouldn't, for a moment, listen to any of those professions of which we are so proud on the Fourth of July. They have turned away from this country forever and totally. They live by their wits and really long to see the day when the entire structure comes down.

The point of all this is that black men were brought here as a source of cheap labor. They were indispensable to the economy. In order to justify the fact that men were treated as though they were animals, the white republic had to brainwash itself into believing that they were, indeed, animals and *deserved* to be treated like animals. Therefore it is almost impossible for any Negro child to discover anything about his actual history. The reason is that this "animal," once he suspects his own worth, once he starts believing that he is a man, has begun to attack the entire power structure. This is why America has spent such a long time keeping the Negro in his place. What I am trying to suggest to you is that it was not an accident, it was not an act of God, it was not done by well–meaning people muddling into something which they didn't understand. It was a deliberate policy hammered into place in order to make money from black flesh. And now, in 1963, because we have never faced this fact, we are in intolerable trouble.

The Reconstruction, as I read the evidence, was a bargain between the North and South to this effect: "We've liberated them from the land—and delivered them to the bosses." When we left Mississippi to come North we did not come to freedom. We came to the bottom of the labor market, and we are still there. Even the Depression of the 1930s failed to make a dent in Negroes' relationship to white workers in the labor unions. Even today, so brainwashed is this republic that people seriously ask in what they suppose to be good faith, "What does the Negro want?" I've heard a great many asinine questions in my life, but that is perhaps the most asinine and perhaps the most insulting. But the point here is that people who ask that question, thinking that they ask it in good faith, are really the victims of this conspiracy to make Negroes believe they are less than human.

In order for me to live, I decided very early that some mistake had been made somewhere. I was not a "nigger" even though you called me one. But if I was a "nigger" in your eyes, there was something about you—there was something you needed. I had to realize when I was very young that I was none of those things I was told I was. I was not, for example, happy. I never touched a watermelon for all kinds of reasons that had been invented by white people, and I knew enough about life by this time to understand that whatever you invent, whatever you project, is you! So where we are now is that a whole country of people believe I'm a "nigger," and I *don't*, and the battle's on! Because if I am not what

I've been told I am, then it means that you're not what you thought you were *either!* And that is the crisis.

It is not really a "Negro revolution" that is upsetting the country. What is upsetting the country is a sense of its own identity. If, for example, one managed to change the curriculum in all the schools so that Negroes learned more about themselves and their real contributions to this culture, you would be liberating not only Negroes, you'd be liberating white people who know nothing about their own history. And the reason is that if you are compelled to lie about one aspect of anybody's history, you must lie about it all. If you have to lie about my real role here, if you have to pretend that I hoed all that cotton just because I loved you, then you have done something to yourself. You are mad.

Now let's go back a minute. I talked earlier about those silent people—the porter and the maid—who, as I said, don't look up at the sky if you ask them if it is raining, but look into your face. My ancestors and I were very well trained. We understood very early that this was not a Christian nation. It didn't matter what you said or how often you went to church. My father and my mother and my grandfather and my grandmother knew that Christians didn't act this way. It was as simple as that. And if that was so there was no point in dealing with white people in terms of their own moral professions, for they were not going to honor them. What one did was to turn away, smiling all the time, and tell white people what they wanted to hear. But people always accuse you of reckless talk when you say this.

All this means that there are in this country tremendous reservoirs of bitterness which have never been able to find an outlet, but may find an outlet soon. It means that well-meaning white liberals place themselves in great danger when they try to deal with Negroes as though they were missionaries. It means, in brief, that a great price is demanded to liberate all those silent people so that they can breathe for the first time and *tell* you what they think of you. And a price is demanded to liberate all those white children— some of them near forty—who have never grown up, and who never will grow up, because they have no sense of their identity.

What passes for identity in America is a series of myths about one's heroic ancestors. It's astounding to me, for example, that so many people really appear to believe that the country was founded by a band of heroes who wanted to be free. That happens not to be true. What happened was that some people left Europe because they couldn't stay there any longer and had to go someplace else to make it. That's all. They were hungry, they were poor, they were convicts. Those who were making it in England, for example, did not get on the *Mayflower*. That's how the country was settled. Not by Gary Cooper. Yet we have a whole race of people, a whole republic, who believe the myths to the point where even today they select political representatives, as far as I can tell, by how closely they resemble Gary Cooper. Now this is dangerously infantile, and it shows in every level of national life. When I was living in Europe, for example, one of the worst revelations to me was the way Americans walked around Europe buying this and buying that and insulting everybody—not even out of malice, just because they didn't know any better. Well, that is the way they have always treated me. They weren't cruel, they just didn't know you were alive. They didn't know you had any feelings.

What I am trying to suggest here is that in the doing of all this for one hundred years or more, it is the American white man who has long since lost his grip on reality. In some peculiar way, having created this myth about Negroes, and the myth about his own history, he created myths about the world so that, for example, he was astounded that some people could prefer Castro, astounded that there are people in the world who don't go into hiding when they hear the word "Communism," astounded that Communism is one of the realities of the twentieth century which we will not overcome by pretending that it does not exist. The political level in this country now, on the part of people who should know better, is abysmal.

The Bible says somewhere that where there is no vision the people perish. I don't think anyone can doubt that in this country today we are menaced—intolerably menaced—by a lack of vision.

It is inconceivable that a sovereign people should continue, as we do so abjectly, to say, "I can't do anything about it. It's the government." The government is the creation of the people. It is responsible to the people. And the people are responsible for it. No American has the right to allow the present government to say, when Negro children are being bombed and hosed and shot and beaten all over the Deep South, that there is nothing we can do about it. There must have been a day in this country's life when the bombing of the children in Sunday School would have created a public uproar and endangered the life of a Governor Wallace. It happened here and there was no public uproar.

I began by saying that one of the paradoxes of education was that precisely at the point when you begin to develop a conscience, you must find yourself at war with your society. It is your responsibility to change society if you think of yourself as an educated person. And on the basis of the evidence—the moral and political evidence—one is compelled to say that this is a backward society. Now if I were a teacher in this school, or any Negro school, and I was dealing with Negro children, who were in my care only a few hours of every day and would then return to their homes and to the streets, children who have an apprehension of their future which with every hour grows grimmer and darker, I would try to teach them—I would try to make them know—that those streets, those houses, those dangers, those agonies by which they are surrounded, are criminal. I would try to make each child know that these things are the result of a criminal conspiracy to destroy him. I would teach him that if he intends to get to be a man, he must at once decide that he is stronger than this conspiracy and that he must never make his peace with it. And that one of his weapons for refusing to make his peace with it and for destroying it depends on what he decides he is worth. I would teach him that there are currently very few standards in this country which are worth a man's respect. That it is up to him to begin to change these standards for the sake of the life and the health of the country. I would suggest to him that the popular culture—as represented, for example, on television and in comic books and in movies—is based on fantasies created by very ill people, and he must be aware that these are fantasies that have nothing to do with reality. I would teach him that the press he reads is not as free as it says it is—and that he can do something about that, too. I would try to make him know that just as American history is longer, larger, more various, more beautiful, and more terrible than anything anyone has ever said about it, so is the world larger, more daring, more beautiful, and more terrible, but principally larger— and that it belongs to him. I would teach him that he doesn't have to be bound by the expediencies of any given administration, any given policy, any given morality; that he has the right and the necessity to examine everything. I would try to show him that one has not learned anything about Castro when one says, "He is a Communist." This is a way of his learning something about Castro, something about Cuba, something, in time, about the world. I would suggest to him that he is living, at the moment, in an enormous province. America is not the world and if America is going to become a nation, she must find a way—and this child must help her to find a way to use the tremendous energy which this child represents. If this country does not find a way to use that energy, it will be destroyed by that energy.

18. A Teacher Ain't Nothin' But a Hero: Teachers and Teaching in Film

WILLIAM AYERS

Curled up in a well-worn seat in a large dark theater, wrapped around a box of stale popcorn, and illuminated by the eerie flicker of moving pictures across a silver screen, I search in shadows for images of teachers and teaching. This is a private screening, a lonely marathon of movie madness, and my mind and body begin to ache. But I am an explorer, I remind myself, and even bruised or battered I must go on. *Blackboard Jungle* blinks off and *Stand and Deliver* starts to roll.

I feel punchy, and I begin to wonder what a visitor from outer space would conclude if the dozen or so films I subject myself to were her only point of reference. Without experience or memory, prior knowledge or teacher autobiography, this visitor would be in an interesting position to help me get beyond my own distorting spaces, to read what the moviemakers—these "writers with light"—make of teaching, to see what is actually there.

What *is* actually there? The movies tell us, to begin with, that schools and teachers are in the business of saving children—saving them from their families, saving them from the purveyors of drugs and violence who are taking over our cities, saving them from themselves, their own pursuits and purposes. The problem is that most teachers are simply not up to the challenge. They are slugs: cynical, inept, backward, naive, hopeless. The occasional good teacher is a saint—he is anointed. His job—and it's always *his* job because the saint-teachers, and most every other teacher in the movies is a man—is straightforward: he must separate the salvageable students from those who are beyond redemption and he must win them over to a better life, all the while doing battle with his idiot colleagues, the dull-witted administration, and the dangerously backward parents. He is a solitary hero. The saint-teacher's task is urgent because he must figure out who can be saved before it's too late, before the chosen few are sucked irredeemably back into the sewers of their own circumstances. Giving up on some kids is okay, according to the movies, but the bad teachers have already given up on *all* the kids. That's their sin.

These themes are articulated in a particularly loud voice in Richard Brooks' 1955 classic, *Blackboard Jungle,* a film that manages to exploit perfectly the tinny patriotism and surface smugness of its era while reflecting, and in a sense prefiguring, the underground conflicts and tensions about to burst to the surface. *Blackboard Jungle* says it all—beginning with its title it taps into deep racial stereotypes and captures the sense of civilization doing battle with savagery, of white chalk scraping along a black surface. It plays excitedly to all the received wisdom of teaching and schooling, as well as to the wider fears—racial, sexual—of a precarious middle class. Its portrait of the idealistic teacher struggling to save the delinquent boy with a good heart is imprinted on our collective consciousness—it is a major myth. Much of our cultural common sense, as well as every popular film since, is in some way derivative. The fact that the police were called in to control violence in theaters across the country when it opened (a first), set a pattern that has also become a cliche.

Blackboard Jungle opens with a straight-laced if disingenuous apology read against a military drumbeat:

> We in the United States are fortunate to have a school system that is a tribute to our communities and to our faith in American youth.
>
> Today we are concerned with juvenile delinquency—its causes—and its effects. We are especially concerned when this delinquency boils over into our schools.
>
> The scenes and incidents depicted here are fictional.
>
> However, we believe that public awareness is a first step toward a remedy for any problem.
>
> It is in this spirit and with this faith that *Blackboard Jungle* was produced.

But the filmmakers don't mean it. The moment passes and we are thrust into an urban schoolyard where tough-looking youngsters jitterbug and jostle one another to the pounding rhythm of Bill Haley and the Comets' "Rock Around the Clock." It is sexual and chaotic, and the audience is whiplashed, threatened.

Enter Richard Dadier (Glenn Ford), wide-eyed, shy, a young Korean War vet looking for a teaching job. Dadier, to his delight and surprise, is hired quickly, but he turns to the harsh and aloof principal with "just one question—the discipline problem . . ." His voice trails off uncertainly, but the response is loud and clear: "There is no discipline problem—not as long as I'm principal." The Joe Clark bit feels false; we are not reassured.

The principal's bravado is mimicked and mocked by the teachers: "There's no discipline problem at Alcatraz either"; "You can't teach a disorderly mob"; "They hire fools like us with college degrees to sit on that garbage can and keep them in school so women for a few hours a day can walk around the city without being attacked." Dadier is awed, but he can't resist the rookie's question: "These kids . . . they can't *all* be that bad . . . ?"

Oh no? Opening day is anarchy. The new teachers sit blinking at the barbarians, while the tough assistant principal snarls and cracks the whip. The auditorium pulsates—kids fighting and pushing one another, smoking, and shouting. It is a mob scene. When the innocent Miss Hammond is introduced the crowd goes wild, and with the camera playing on her ass, everyone leers. The film is ambivalent about the attack that follows: she really shouldn't dress that way, it says, look that way, but at the same time these boys are clearly animals—can't they draw the line between wolf-whistles and rape? All of Mr. Dadier's students shun him for his heroism in saving Miss Hammond and capturing her attacker.

Mr. Dadier struggles on. He means well, of course, and he cares. Within a certain framework he even tries. He shows his students a cartoon to accompany his homily on thinking for themselves; he encourages them to see the importance of English if they want to become "a carpenter or a mechanic." He encourages Gregory Miller (Sidney Poitier), the good delinquent ("a little smarter, a little brighter"), to play piano and to sing in the Christmas show. This is, of course, all part of the Hollywood dream: blacks sing and dance, aspirations for working-class youth are appropriately low, and white liberals are loved for their good intentions. There is no hint that the problems facing these young people include structures of privilege and disadvantage, social class, racism, or the existence of two societies, separate and unequal. In fact, Mr. Dadier tells Miller to get the chip off his shoulder, that racism is "not a good excuse" for failure—"Dr. Ralph Bunche proved that." 1955!

Here is short list of what Mr. Dadier endures: he is mugged and badly cut in an alley by a group of delinquents, his best friend on the faculty has his priceless collection of jazz records smashed up by the kids, he and his pregnant wife are almost killed by youngsters who are drag racing, he is accused of racial prejudice after attempting to teach the ignorance of "name-calling," his wife goes into labor prematurely as a result of anonymous notes and phone calls indicating that Miss Hammond and Dadier are having an affair. Dadier bends, but he never breaks—he perseveres. At his lowest point (with a new job offer in hand) his wife reminds him that "Kids are people . . . Most people are worthwhile; we all need the same things: patience, love, understanding." Her list is missing, of course, other possibilities: justice, power, collective solutions.

Mr. Dadier is wide-eyed much of the time, unable to believe the depths to which humanity can sink. About to give up, he revisits his old professor and seeks advice. It is pure corn: with the "Star-Spangled Banner" playing in the background Dadier watches well-mannered students attending well-run classrooms, and he questions how he can teach "kids who don't want to learn," have "IQs of sixty-six" and "act like wild animals." The sage old man reminds him that most people want to be creative, and that Dadier is called to "sculpt minds" in a school where he is badly needed.

"For every school like yours there are hundreds like this. This school could use you; your school needs you." Dadier and the professor join the last lines of the national anthem, and as he prepares to leave, Dadier thanks his mentor: "I think I'll take another crack at my jungle."

Back in the jungle Dadier's efforts are paying off. He works on Miller, urging him to use his influence ("I've been looking at your file, and you're a natural leader") to break the grip of the gangs, and especially the power of the disturbed Artie West (Vic Morrow). When West pulls a knife on Dadier, Miller backs his teacher. The tide turns. One student breaks West's knife while another pulls the American flag from its wall brace and knocks West to the ground. West and his gang are finished. Dadier exhorts the whole class to take them to the principal: "There's no place for these two in our classroom." With the bad delinquents gone, the good delinquents can get on to the serious business of learning: copying sentences from the board and so on. Miller gets the last word: "Everyone learns something in school—even the teacher."

Fast-forward to 1984. The corny sincerity and idealized chivalry of 1955 yield to a kind of hip idealism, but the messages are intact. Take the question of women. In glaring contradiction with reality, teachers in the movies are men. The occasional woman teacher is a prop—something to look at or rescue. "Bright kid; great ass"— thus the sensitive Alex Jerrel (Nick Nolte) describes one of his favorite former students (Jobeth Williams) in Arther Hiller's starstudded *Teachers*. The student is grown up now, and being a modern woman she's got it all—a law degree and a great ass. The line back to *Blackboard Jungle* is direct: the lawyer's name is also Miss Hammond, only this time the hero-teacher can go ahead and fall for her, they can hop in bed, and together they can fight for school reform; the hero again rescues a woman in distress, only this time it is a student (Laura Dern) suffering abuse from a teacher, and the rescue involves a trip to the abortion clinic. The more things change, the more they stay the same.

Or take the question of barbarians at the gate. *Teachers* opens with cops literally unlocking gates and unruly kids swarming into school. Once again, chaos. The principal hides in his office, teachers (one of whom is the school psychologist) go nuts fighting each other over the mimeograph machine, one child sits bleeding in the office waiting for someone to call an ambulance, the union rep is making some inane point to his colleagues about the school board wanting teachers to report at 7:35 and the necessity of holding out until 7:38, and the assistant principal (Judd Hirsch), desperate for substitutes, tells his secretary to "scrape the bottom of the barrel."

Alex's phone rings. He stirs slowly, hungover and partied out, picks up the receiver, and is summoned to school. The woman he is sleeping with is incensed to discover that he's only a teacher, and dresses hurriedly. This is apparently Alex's life: drinking, carousing, losing women (in one drunken scene he tells a friend that his wife left him because she wanted more than a teacher can provide—"food, clothing, shelter"), and dragging himself to school.

Alex battles a rogue's gallery in the school; a frightened principal, a union hack, incompetent colleagues and mindless bureaucrats, one teacher called "Ditto" who passes out worksheets and sleeps behind his newspaper (he dies one day and no one notices), another who appears as a popular and creative history teacher but in fact has recently escaped from a mental hospital, and an old friend (Hirsch) who once shared Alex's zeal but burned out long ago ("We are not the bad guys; we do good with what we got"). As in *Blackboard Jungle* where there is "no home life, no church life [and] gangs are taking the place of parents," Alex must do hand-to-hand combat with the putatively pathological parents. At one point he explodes, "The parents and the system so fucked up this kid that I don't think I can ever reach him," and at another he asks a mother, "Don't you care about your son's education?" She replies, "Isn't that your job, Mr. Jerrell?" Alex's project is Eddie (Ralph Maccio), the bad kid who will come around in spite of the lure of the streets and his parents' indifference, in spite of the official judgment that he's a lost cause. Only Alex cares, and when he's called crazy he responds, "I can't help it, I'm a teacher."

(233)

Connections, connections. *Lean on Me,* the 1987 film that made Joe Clark, the baseball-bat-toting, bullhorn-exhorting real-life principal of Eastside High in Patterson, New Jersey the most famous principal in the world, opens to the pounding hard-rock rhythms of Guns 'n Roses' "Welcome to the Jungle." Again the montage of open drug deals, teachers being assaulted, a woman's clothes being ripped from her body. Again the barbarians at the gate. Again our hero saving the kids from their parents ("Why don't you get off welfare? Why don't you help your kids with their homework?"). And again Morgan Freeman—in *Teachers* he was a toady lawyer for the superintendent; here he is the strutting St. Joe.

Joe Clark harangues, batters, and bullies everyone around him, but for a purpose. Clark cares in his megalomaniacal way. He tells the kids that the larger society believes they are failures—"a bunch of niggers and spicks and poor white trash"—but that society is wrong. "You are not inferior," he insists, and this is his appeal. When Joe Clark says, "If you do not succeed in life I don't want you to blame your parents, I don't want you to blame the white man, I want you to blame yourselves," it resonates quite the opposite from Richard Dadier's anemic invocation of Ralph Bunche. One hopes at this point that Clark is going to organize the youngsters to overthrow the system that perpetuates their oppression, or that he will at least find some way to unleash their energy and intelligence; alas, he urges them to do a better job on the standardized tests.

Clark begins his tenure with the famous event that framed his career. He assembles "every hoodlum, drug dealer, and miscreant" on the stage of the auditorium, and in front of the whole school expels the bunch. "These people are incorrigible," he shouts above the din. "You are all expurgated, you are dismissed, you are out of here forever." He turns then to the remaining students: "Next time it may be you." It's dramatic—an attention-getter—but the drama is repeated one way or another in every popular film on teaching.

Joe Clark is at war—"a war to save 2,700 other students." He's in the trenches, on the front lines, fighting mano a mano to save the good ones—he doesn't want to hear about the miscreants. Let them go to hell; let the liberals bleed for them. The film ends with his vindication—the school retains its accreditation because the kids pass the basic skills test. But since it is dubbed "A True Story," it might be fair to peek outside the movie for just a moment. In the real Eastside High test scores are in the basement, half of the kids drop out before graduation, and hundreds more are pushed out by the principal. Clark apparently believes in some of the kids, but there really are a bunch who are trash. And he's the judge. Say it ain't so, Joe.

Stand and Deliver is "based on a true story" too, this time the story of Jaime Escalante (Edward James Olmos), the renowned math teacher from Garfield High School in Los Angeles. Escalante battles the ghetto, the gangs, the low expectations. He teaches pride— we get glimpses of a Che Guevara mural and of graffiti proclaiming "Not a Minority," and we hear him tell his students that "your ancestors, the Mayans, contemplated zero—math is in your blood." He also teaches *ganas*—desire. "You already have two strikes," he says. "Your name and your complexion . . . Math is the great equalizer . . . I don't want to hear your problems. If you have *ganas* you can succeed."

Escalante chases the bad delinquents away, humiliates them, drives them from his class. Angel (Lou Diamond Phillips) is the good delinquent to be saved. Escalante gives him a set of books to keep at home so his gang-banger pals won't know he's studying. Angel cares for his sick grandmother who has no idea of the importance of school to him. Other parents are worse; one student has to stop studying when her mother comes home from work, another is pulled from school to become a waitress in the family-owned restaurant, a third is told by her mom that "guys don't like it if you're too smart."

Escalante fights the parents' ignorance and he aims to turn the school around. His strategy is "to start at the top." (Perhaps the trickle-down theme of social improvement is one reason the Reagan-Bush administrations embraced this film so wholeheartedly.)

He wants to teach AP calculus. The principal laughs and the chair of the math department scoffs, "Our kids can't handle calculus." But they can, and they do, and Escalante practically kills himself making it true.

Unlike Joe Clark, whose wife divorced him, Escalante's obsession is dutifully tolerated at home. Escalante works sixty hours a week, teaches ESL at night, never takes a vacation. Like all the saint-teachers he has no life—he is never learning something new, coaching Little League, making art, pursuing political projects. He doesn't need to reflect or consider or weigh or wonder—he's living an irrational life with a powerful pull. He is sacrificing himself for his students alone. Whereas Clark casts himself as crucified for his commitment, Escalante is downed by a heart attack only to rise again on behalf of inspiring his students to win in their confrontation with the test. Jesus Christ with a punch.

In Pat Conroy the "Christ Complex" is fully realized. Based on *The Water is Wide*, the movie *Conrack* (directed by Martin Ritt in 1974) is billed as another "true story," this time an account of Conroy's one-year sojourn as a teacher on the sea islands off South Carolina in 1969. It is, of course, true in the same sense that *Lean on Me* or *Stand and Deliver* is true—a few ready-made verities, a handful of simple formulas, a couple of slogans thrown out and passed along. It is a comfortable kind of truth, a painless and uncomplicated romance, an easy belief.

The film opens with the humane and gentle Pat Conroy (Jon Voight) waking up in his comfortable and vital home, feeding his fish, birds, and plants, gathering his belongings to venture across the wide water to awaken his black brethren on an isolated island off the coast. As the titles roll, they too awaken, but in poverty, simplicity, suspicion, and backwardness. But Conroy is coming: he is the missionary, full of light and love.

False prophets are everywhere. The white superintendent, Mr. Skeffington (Hume Cronyn) who "never accepted Appomattox" preaches that the important things are "order, control, obedience," and urges Conroy to beat the children: "Just milkin' the rat." "Mad

Billy" (Paul Winfield) raves about the dangers of white folks. And the dreadful principal, Mrs. Scott, tells Conroy, "You're in a snake-pit, son. Treat your babies tough. Step on them. I know colored people better than you." But of course she doesn't. Later she tells him she's "making 'em tough, because it is tough. What do you know about it? You got that thin white skin. I don't have your advantages."

Conroy believes he has a direct line to the light, and he's not listening to blasphemy. He knows better. "We're off the old plantation, Mrs. Scott," he tells her, all shiny and smiling, a model for Bill Clinton, Al Gore, and the "New South" to come. "And I'll be damned if you're gonna turn me into an overseer." True enough, the plantation days *are* gone, and instead of overseers the field is crowded with self-righteous, self-important, self-anointed professional saints. Pat Conroy, sugary and sweet, is the model.

Professionals—saints and otherwise—need clients. In fact professionals turn us into clients—we become defined by our weaknesses, our deficits, our shortcomings. Lawyers litigate, doctors heal, therapists feel for us. In education we create deficiencies with dangerous generalizations, and then compete for resources based on our deprived and degraded condition. The object of everyone's ministrations has no name, simply a condition.

In *Conrack* only Conroy has a name, and no one is smart enough to even get it right. Mrs. Scott calls him "Mr. Patroy" throughout, and the kids slaughter his name consistently calling him "Conrack."

If the indistinguishable mass of youngsters have any name at all, it is Ignorance. Conroy initially asks the kids what country they live in. Blank stares. "Come on, gang. What's the name of this little red, white, and blue country of ours? Land of the free and home of the brave?" Nothing. "Honey," he turns to one of the girls. "How much is two and two?" There is nothing there. Conroy's heart is breaking as the scene fades.

Here is some of what the kids living on this island don't know: they don't know how to cook or make biscuits, they don't know how to play games of any kind, they don't know how to differentiate foxfire from baby's breath from Queen Anne's lace, they don't know how to build a fire or camp out or sing. They've never been in a boat or in the water. It's amazing they can even get up in the morning, they are that backward.

It never occurs to Conroy, of course, to find out if they have their own names for Queen Anne's lace, or for their own island. He knows best. And so instead of assuming an intelligence in youngsters, instead of investigating and questioning as a step toward authentic teaching, he launches a campaign of cultural literacy that would make Allan Bloom proud. Who's the home run king? Babe Ruth. Who led the barbarian hordes? Attila the Hun. And so on.

From *Blackboard Jungle* to *Stand and Deliver,* teacher films are entirely comfortable with a specific common stance on teaching. This stance includes the wisdom that teaching can occur only after discipline is established, that teaching proceeds in stages: first, get order, then, deliver the curriculum. The curriculum is assumed to be stable and good—it is immutable and unproblematic; it is disconnected (but important) bits and pieces of information. The movies assume that anyone with any sense would agree, and so they toss off the familiar phrases, and we can add ones of our own: don't turn your back on the class; don't smile until Christmas; if you can't control them you can't teach them; establish authority early; survival in the trenches requires good classroom control. And so on. Everyone believes it—experienced teachers mimic it—and so beginning teachers grasp for anything that will help them with "classroom management," the assumed first principle of teaching.

The only problem with this prime piece of received wisdom is that it is not true. In fact real learning requires assertion, not obedience; action, not passivity. It is an intimate act, an ambiguous and unpredictable act. It is deeply human. Teaching demands some connection between the knowledge, experiences, and aspirations of students, and deeper and wider ways of knowing. Teaching is intellectual work—puzzling and difficult—and at its heart it is ethical work. It is idiosyncratic, improvisational, and most of all, relational. All attempts to reduce teaching and learning to a formula, to something easily predicted, degrade it immeasurably.

Concerns about classroom management must be reconsidered in light of concerns about curriculum—about what knowledge and experiences are of most value—as well as concerns about students' hopes and dreams. This is a complex process and it involves learning how to see beyond the blizzard of labels and stereotypes, and how to embrace students as dynamic beings and fellow creatures. It requires building bridges from the known to the not-yet-known. And it demands liberating schooling from its single-minded obsession with control, obedience, hierarchy and everyone's place in it. Alas, the movies are of no help in this regard. On the contrary, the ready-made cliches and empty repetitions feed our collective powerlessness, manage our mindless acquiescence.

Common sense can be more dogmatic than any political party, more totalizing than any religious sect—it is insistent in its resistance to contradiction or even complexity. It wants to be taken on faith—there isn't room for either reflection or objection. Take it or leave it. Films on teaching fall into step—they are all about common sense and they immunize against a language of possibility.

Becoming an outstanding teacher is exceedingly difficult work. The first step is a commitment to teach all children, regardless of condition or circumstance. Movie-star teachers make no such commitment. They are invested in some youngster or another and willing to drive away many more. A second step is to find common cause with youngsters, their families, and their communities. Again, movie teachers despise families and can barely tolerate communities. The common wisdom is that children of the poor are lost in islands of nothingness, and that school will lead them into the human family. In many real-life schools nothing about the presence of poor youngsters, and especially African-American youngsters, is considered valuable or important—it is always a problem, an encumbrance, a deficit, an obstacle. Contempt, fear, and condescension are not a strong foundation for real teaching.

Real teachers need to question the common sense, break the rules, become political and activist in concert with kids. This is true heroism, an authentic act of courage. We need to take seriously the experiences of youngsters, their sense-making, their knowledge, and their dreams—and particularly we must interrogate the structures that kids are rejecting. In other words, we must assume an intelligence in youngsters, assume that they are acting sensibly and making meaning in situations that are difficult and often dreadful, and certainly not of their own making. In finding common cause with youngsters, we may also find there our own salvation as teachers.

19. The Tree of Knowledge

GLORIA LADSON-BILLINGS

Patricia Hilliard's teaching is a model of the kind of teaching that sees knowledge as an evolutionary process. Her classroom is large and painted bright yellow and filled with evidence of student work throughout. All kinds of containers—plastic sandwich bags, plastic bowls, baskets, and boxes—hold learning objects, papers, magazines, and student folders. The classroom is filled with books, many that have an African or African-American emphasis, such as *The Boy Who Didn't Believe in Spring*, by Lucille Clifton (1973), *Daydreamers*, by Eloise Greenfield (1981), and *Bringing the Rain to Kapiti Plain* (1981). Large photos above the bulletin board show such African-American and Latino personalities as Nikki Giovanni, Jesse Jackson, and Cesar Chávez. The students sit in groups of four or five while working and are permitted to chat with one another in conversational tones.

Every student in Hilliard's classroom is an author. During my classroom visits they were eager to share their latest "publications." Although she is a fan of the process-writing approach advocated by the Bay Area Writing Project . . . Hilliard is wary of an approach that fails to make students cognizant of the power of language and of the language of power. The process-writing approach encourages teachers and students to view writing as an ongoing process, wherein multiple drafts are written and content is valued more than writing conventions. Thus, in a first draft, students' errors in spelling, syntax, and sentence construction are not of primary import. Rather, in subsequent drafts, students are expected to improve both the form and the substance of their writing:

> I get so sick and tired of people trying to tell me that my children don't need to use any language other than the one they come to school with. Then those same people turn right around and judge the children negatively because of the way they express themselves. My job is to make sure that they can use *both* languages, that they understand that their language is valid but that the demands placed upon them by others mean

that they will constantly have to prove their worth. We spend a lot of time talking about language, what it means, how you can use it, and how it can be used against you.

Hilliard knows how fond her students are of the rap music and hip-hop culture that pervades the radio waves and other popular media. In an attempt to help them become more at ease with standard forms of English, Hilliard asked them to vote on their favorite song. It was no surprise to her that many students selected a rap song by local hero and superstar M.C. Hammer.

I was really happy that the kids picked Hammer because some of the others are pretty rough. You know, songs filled with obscenities and negative images of women. At least I could work with some of Hammer's stuff. (She laughs.)

Hilliard copied the words of the song and distributed the text to the students the next day. The students tittered with excitement at seeing in print a song they often sang. Several began to recite it. Hilliard called for the students' attention and asked for volunteers to pronounce the rap. Three boys' hands shot up. Hilliard asked them to come to the front of the room to perform the song.

The three "rap artists" came to the front without their photocopied texts. After a brief discussion about how to begin, they "sang" (actually recited) the song, to the delight of the other students, many of whom were mouthing the words along with them. At the end of their performance there was thunderous applause from the class and the teacher alike. Hilliard thanked the boys for their willingness to share their talents. She explained that although she was their teacher and a college graduate, there was much about the song that she did not understand. She asked if the students would be willing to help her. Several laughed but all seemed willing to share their knowledge. Hilliard placed a transparency of the lyrics on the overhead projector. She had double-spaced the copy so that she could write between the lines. She explained to the students that they would be doing what interpreters do when they translate from one language into another.

Line by line the students went through the rap lyrics and

explained what they meant. Hilliard carefully transferred their informal words into a more standard form. From time to time she placed words in a vocabulary list. Although she did not ask them to, most of the students copied Hilliard's version to their own papers. After the class, Hilliard explained her goals for this activity:

> We'll continue doing this kind of thing all year long. I want the children to see that they have some valuable knowledge to contribute. I don't want them to be ashamed of what they know but I also want them to know and be comfortable with what school and the rest of the society requires. When I put it in the context of "translation" they get excited. They see it is possible to go from one to the other. It's not that they are not familiar with standard English . . . they hear standard English all the time on TV. It's certainly what I use in the classroom. But there is rarely any connection made between the way they speak and standard English. I think that when they can see the connections and know that they can make the shifts, they become better at both. They're bilingual!

This notion of speakers of African-American language as bilingual is a decidedly different perspective. . . . By believing her students to be capable and knowledgeable, Hilliard reinforces this belief and her high expectations for the students. The language they bring with them serves as a tool that helps them with additional language learning, just as speakers of standard English use English to help them acquire new languages.

In Ann Lewis's sixth-grade class, knowledge construction is a full-time activity. Ann paid close attention to the debate about the state's new history and social science curricula. One area of contention, the diluting of multicultural issues and concerns, was of special interest to Lewis. Because the state curricula would determine which books were available to teachers, she knew that she and her students could not rely on these books alone and would have to develop their own social studies program. She decided to analyze one of the questions that emerged from the curriculum debate with her students: Were the ancient Egyptians black?

On a large piece of paper, Lewis wrote out the question. She divided the paper into two sections. On one side she wrote, "Disconfirming Evidence." On the other side she wrote, "Confirming

Evidence." The titles were consistent with her practice of using sophisticated vocabulary with her students.

She explained to the students that they would be conducting research in order to answer the question of the ancient Egyptians' race.

Lewis: Why would we care whether or not the Egyptians were black?

First student: Because then we could prove that black people did great things.

Lewis: But can't we already prove that black people did great things? Don't we already know about a lot of black people who have done great things?

Second student: Yeah, but you know how they're always talkin' about great things from Europe and how all these white people did so many great things, but you never hear about great things from Africa. They talk about Egypt but they talk about it like it's not Africa.

Lewis: Why do you think that's so?

Second student: Well, because everybody can see the great things the Egyptians did, like the pyramids, so then if you just talk about Egypt maybe people won't think about it as a part of Africa.

Third student: What does that prove?

Second student: I didn't say it proved anything. I'm just saying that if you make people think of the Egyptians as white then you will think that only white people can make great things.

The discussion continued as many of the students expressed their opinions about ancient Egypt. Some referred to movies they had seen depicting ancient Egyptians as white. Almost all of the students had seen *Cleopatra* and *The Ten Commandments*.

Lewis encouraged the students to raise additional questions, which she wrote on the board. By the end of the discussion, she had a series of student comments and questions that she wanted them to investigate in order to answer the initial question. Next, she asked the students to suggest ways that they could find the answers to these questions. The students suggested library research, interviews of experts, educational films. She asked each team of five or six students (there were five teams in the class) to select a question and discuss how they would divide their work and start their investigation.

The quest to answer the question about the ancient Egyptians' race went on for almost a month. In the second week, one of the teams decided that the class should identify itself as the "Imhotep Project." In the course of its research, this team had discovered Imhotep, the first physician known by name, later elevated to the status of a god.

As a result of this month-long inquiry, Lewis' students probably learned much more than they would have from a textbook lesson about ancient Egypt. And, although they did not settle the question conclusively, they felt that the evidence they assembled supporting the blackness of the ancient Egyptians was more compelling than refuting it.

An interesting point about the students' classroom experience is that, in larger society's debate about multiculturalism, conservative scholars have suggested that knowing the race or ethnicity of historical figures does little to enhance the learning of students of color. (This would probably be true if all teachers did was to recite a laundry list of people of color—tangential to the "real" history.) But by making race problematic, Lewis helped the students understand that knowledge is not something hidden in a book. Rather than require the students to remember and recite some predetermined facts about ancient Egypt, she led them on an adventure toward answering a question that is important to students of color.

In the course of that quest, the students learned many other things about the ancient civilization. They learned why it was regarded as a great civilization. They raised their own questions about ancient Egypt. They confronted contradictory information and learned that even the experts disagreed sometimes.

A hallmark of the culturally relevant notion of knowledge is that it is something that each student brings to the classroom. Students are not seen as empty vessels to be filled by all-knowing teachers. What they know is acknowledged, valued, and incorporated into the classroom.

Pauline Dupree recognizes the link between verbal ability and cognition. Rather than concern herself solely with the form of students' language, she is interested in the meaning and sense of their words.

> Our children are very verbal and very bright. They can really get going on a topic and make you think about it in so many different ways.

Gertrude Winston expresses frustration at the limits of standardized testing in measuring student knowledge accurately. Rather than being concerned about memorization of trivial or out-of-context information, she acknowledges the complexity of students' knowledge. This sensitivity to their knowledge and skills reflects her belief system and can be seen in the high expectations she holds for her students.

> Nobody ever really measures what the children really know. They have knowledge and skills that don't show up on standardized tests—important knowledge and skills, the kind of stuff that can mean the difference between life and death.

Ann Lewis's words are filled with anger about the ultimate future of the students in the district. Seeing extremely bright elementary school children fail in high school fires her political consciousness; she has seen for herself that the students are capable.

> I've worked with children in this school who were geniuses. I mean it, geniuses, minds so quick you wouldn't believe, able to conceptualize in ways far beyond college professors I've had. I just can't reconcile their intelligence with what happens to them in high school (where there is a seventy percent drop-out rate of students from this district).

For Lewis, the students' performance in school is less related to their family structure, their income, or their race, than it is to their ability to receive quality education. However, she has enough political savvy to know that the combination of student status and race with structural inequalities can mean educational failure. She believes that teachers should play an intervening role between the students' lives and the society.

Like Ann Lewis, Patricia Hilliard recognizes the powerful negative impact poor schooling has on students like hers. She is able to identify their intellectual strengths and motivations while simultaneously recognizing the ways that much of their schooling has served to demotivate them.

> I've taught all kinds of kids, rich ones, poor ones, white ones, black ones. Some of the smartest youngsters I've worked with have been right here in this community, but a lot of the time they don't believe in themselves. School saps the life out of them. You want to see intelligence walking around on two legs? Just go into a kindergarten class. They come to school with fresh faces, full of wonder. But by third grade you can see how badly school has beaten them down. You can really see it in the boys. I sometimes ask myself just what it is we're doing to these children.

Elizabeth Harris's spiritual and religious convictions demand that she see every child's potential. Her concern with fairness and justice is rooted in her Christianity. For her, working with the children is a "holy" responsibility and her adherence to the golden rule is unwavering.

> God's little flowers, that's what I call them. Every one a little different but every one so sweet. And just like a garden, the classroom has got to be a place that nurtures them. They don't all need the same thing. One might need a little more sunlight, another a little fertilizer. Some might need a little pruning (she laughs) and some might need to roam free. They're just so precious and it breaks my heart to see the hurtful way they are treated. Some teachers think they are hard because they live tough lives but they are just as fragile as hothouse orchids.

Margaret Rossi's broader social analysis is reflected in her dialectical relationship with her students. Rossi understands that her future is inextricably linked with that of her students. By ensuring their success, she reasons, she ensures her own. Perhaps her training as a nun gave her an ethical perspective grounded in religious practice like that of Elizabeth Harris.

> I can't think of anything any one of my students could do to keep me from teaching them. If more teachers understood the connections between themselves and their students they might feel this same way. These children are the future. There is no way for me to have a secure future if they don't have one. It's going to take three of them to support one of me

in my retirement years. They have to be capable of assuming highly skilled positions. They have the brain power, but they need the opportunity. The society can't keep saying, "I'm sorry but there's no place for you." I'm amazed that we don't see more rage among African-Americans.

These teachers' belief in the knowledge their students bring to school is quite different from the view of African-American students revealed by a set of comments I collected in a predominantly white school district.

How can I hook these unmotivated, uninterested, low-achieving African-American children who have no vision of a future in the world of employment? These children are usually from poor, disadvantaged families on welfare assistance.

A lot of African-American children come from homes with little structure, discipline, and value for education. The deck is already stacked against them.

Most of the black students come from this neighborhood. It has a very poor reputation and a history of problems. What insights do you have about dealing with students from this neighborhood?

These students generally lack that "spark" for learning because of all these environmental factors—parental neglect, abuse . . . I'm not just referring to one or two kids in my room but close to fifty percent of my classroom.

We need help accepting black children's differences which are so drastically different from the white upper-class students who also attend this school.

Although these statements represent a cross section of teacher responses, I do not believe they are atypical. After conducting scores of teacher workshops and teacher education classes throughout the country, I have heard similar beliefs expressed. In the case of these teachers' statements, I have the added advantage of knowing the community (and the community members) that they are discussing. The teachers and I read the students' circumstances very differently. The teachers seem to see only deficit and need. I admire the resilience and strength of the students who continue to come to school and participate, even when their intellect and culture are regularly questioned.

These kinds of statements underscore the deep ideological biases and lack of expectations for success for African-American students that exist for too many teachers. As a researcher I am cynical about the potential for change. But as an African-American parent I am desperate for change. I cling to the possibilities held forth by culturally relevant teaching.

CULTURALLY RELEVANT TEACHING VIEWS KNOWLEDGE CRITICALLY

Ann Lewis's Imhotep Project is a good example of the kind of teaching that views knowledge critically. An example from Julia Devereaux's class also illustrates this view.

Devereaux resembles a perpetual-motion machine and her class reflects her "busy-ness." An early morning visitor sees students going about various management tasks. One is taking the roll, another collecting lunch money, still another collecting permission slips for an upcoming field trip. Once the late bell rings, Devereaux forces herself to sit down and then asks rhetorically, "What should we do today?"

On one particular day, when the students had finished reading a Greek myth about a princess, Devereaux asked, "How would you describe the princess?" Her question was designed to elicit responses about the princess' character, but the first student to respond began with a physical description. "She was beautiful, with long blond hair," said the student. Nowhere in the story was there a description that matched this response. "What makes you say that?" Devereaux asked. "Because that's the way princesses always are," the student replied. "I don't have long blond hair and neither does anyone else in here. Does that mean that none of us could be a princess?" Devereaux asked. The student and several others seemed resigned to the fact that that was the case. Devereaux feigned disbelief that they were unaware of black princesses.

Slowly, without fanfare, Devereaux walked to her bookshelf and selected a book, John Steptoe's *Mufaro's Beautiful Daughters* (1987) about two African sisters, one good and one evil. After reading the fourth graders the book, Devereaux asked how many students still believed that a princess had to have long blond hair. No one raised a hand.

In our discussion after class, Devereaux told me that she had not intended to read that book.

> I just couldn't believe that in this day and age our children still believe that white skin and long blond hair is the standard of beauty. When that child said that I thought I would have a stroke. It just goes to show you how powerful the things they see and hear are. People think we're nit-picking when we talk about needing materials that include people who resemble the students. I realize we were reading a Greek myth, and that's a whole other story, but the students have got to be able to ask, "Is this the truth? Whose reality is this?"

Devereaux's spontaneous dismay about the students' images of princesses is the kind of reaction that teachers must have in order to respond critically to the content students are presented in the classroom. The ability to create knowledge works in conjunction with the ability (and the need) to be critical of content.

Margaret Rossi learned a way to help her students develop their critical capacity from a lesson she read about in the radical education newspaper, *Rethinking Schools*. One afternoon, just before the social studies period, Rossi sent one of her students on an errand to the teacher next door. While the student was gone, Rossi sat at her desk. When she returned, Rossi exclaimed, "Look at all this great stuff *I discovered* in this desk *I discovered!*" Rossi began raving over the pencils, books, and other personal effects in the student's desk, which she now claimed as her own. "Uh-un, Ms. Rossi. You know you wrong!" the student exclaimed, her hands on her hips. The rest of the class laughed uproariously as Rossi and the student argued back and forth about the ownership of the desk. Finally, Rossi gave up the desk and went to the chalk board where she wrote the word "discover."

In the subsequent discussion, the students contended that a person could not be said to have "discovered" something that belonged to others. At this point, Rossi asked the students to turn to a section of their social studies textbook (which bore the copyright date 1977) entitled, "The Age of Discovery." Rossi posed a series of questions about the European explorers. Her students also raised questions. Gradually, their textbook took on a less authoritative aura. Rossi seemed pleased with the way the lesson developed.

> I didn't ask LaShondra to act out that scene about my discovering her desk, but she was wonderful. I had read about a teacher who did something similar with high school students in Oregon and I knew that my students could handle this. Last year in fifth grade most of them learned the Columbus "mantra" so I wanted them to really think about this idea of "discovery" as we study world history. My kids are naturally skeptical because their lives don't match what they see on TV or in their textbooks. I have to work to make sure they understand that it's okay for them to challenge what's in the book. It should be simple for them, but like kids everywhere they want to accept the book as gospel. Now they know that that will never do. (She laughs.)

The ability to examine critically and challenge knowledge is not a mere classroom exercise. By drawing on the perspectives of critical theorists, culturally relevant teaching attempts to make knowledge problematic. Students are challenged to view education (and knowledge) as a vehicle for emancipation, to understand the significance of their cultures, and to recognize the power of language. As a matter of course, culturally relevant teaching makes a link between classroom experiences and the students' everyday lives. These connections are made in spirited discussions and classroom interactions. Teachers are not afraid to assume oppositional viewpoints to foster the students' confidence in challenging what may be inaccurate or problematic.

By explicitly laying the ground rules for debate and creating a psychologically safe place, this kind of teaching allows students to express themselves in a variety of forms (for example, in their conversation, in their writing, in their art). By owning the form of expression, students become enthusiastic participants in classroom discourse and activities. This spiritedness is reflected in the next characteristic of the culturally relevant concept of knowledge.

CULTURALLY RELEVANT TEACHING
IS PASSIONATE ABOUT KNOWLEDGE

For several years I served on university panels for education candidates. Because of the renewed popularity of teaching as a career and because of the reputation of our teacher education program and its small size, we received applications from many more than we had spaces for. We decided that each candidate should come in for an interview. Although the interviews rarely excluded a candidate who met the admissions requirements, they sometimes served to improve the chances of a student who seemed marginal on paper. Generally the interviews confirmed what was already evident in a candidate's file.

One of the first questions asked of each candidate was "Why do you want to be a teacher?" A stock answer for prospective elementary teachers was, "I just love kids." It also was not unusual to hear someone say something to the effect that she (and it was almost always a woman who applied to the elementary education program) "got along better with kids than with adults." Along with my fellow teacher education professionals, I believe that caring about youngsters is an important prerequisite for a teaching career. However, after a couple of years of hearing, "I just love kids," we began to respond, "Yes, but why do you want to *teach?*" We suggested to candidates that they could choose many careers other than teaching and still "be with kids." We suggested such professions as pediatrics or pediatric nursing, library science, recreation, or social work.

Most of the candidates were at a loss when asked to explain further why they wanted to teach. Some commented that they had loved school or that they were from a family of teachers. I cannot recall a single one who talked about loving intellectual activity or who spoke of knowledge as empowering. Of course, this may have been a function of their youth and inexperience. However, a colleague who had taught many of the prospective students in the college of arts and sciences remarked, "The very students who hate learning and intellectual rigor seem to be ones who decided they want to teach . . ."

A search for important ideas and the construction of knowledge fuels the excitement and enthusiasm that exemplify culturally relevant teaching. For example, instead of concentrating on memorizing facts, such as the names of their U.S. senators and representatives, students are encouraged to think about the ways that these officials function in relation to their constituents. Thus the teachers help the students conceive of analogies that make this relationship understandable. In one instance, Rossi talked to the students about the governing structure of a Baptist church, with the pastor as president, the deacons as senators, and the trustees as representatives. Within a few minutes, students were able to demonstrate a rudimentary knowledge of how the two houses of Congress work. The important idea was that in a bicameral legislative body, the two houses are chosen differently, have different functions, and wield different power. Just knowing the names of congresspeople does not imply creating knowledge.

CULTURALLY RELEVANT TEACHING HELPS STUDENTS DEVELOP NECESSARY SKILLS

By building bridges or a scaffolding that meets students where they are (intellectually and functionally), culturally relevant teaching helps them to be where they need to be to participate fully and meaningfully in the construction of knowledge. In contrast, assimilationist teaching assumes that students come to class with certain skills and suggests that it is impossible to teach those who are not at a certain skill level.

As one teacher noted, "There is a curious phenomena occurring in schools today. Teachers expect students to come to school reading and they resent those children who don't. If that's the case, what do they need a teacher for?"

Margaret Rossi's thinking about her students' abilities is a good example of the bridge-building quality in action. Despite the mandated curriculum, Rossi regularly challenges her sixth-grade students with algebra. Although many have been previously unsuccessful in mathematics, Rossi takes an approach that says they can and will learn the sophisticated mathematical ideas and concepts of algebra. Rather than select the top students to participate, Rossi expects the entire class to develop competency in algebra—both problem-solving and problem-posing abilities. Even James, a student whom previous teachers have described as special-education material, is included in these sessions.

Rather than place James in a special group or attempt "to keep him busy" with sheets of drill (and kill) problems, Rossi works hard to build on the skills he already has and helps him make connections to the new learning. By providing him with a few structural clues, she builds his confidence, allowing him the psychological freedom to solve some problems and raise questions. His inclusion in the sessions also means that students with more advanced skills have the opportunity to act as teachers without regarding him as capable of only "baby work."

Gertrude Winston also builds bridges and scaffolding for her students. However, she gets the help of parents and other adults as she does so. The following example is representative of Winston's shared-responsibility strategy:

Like most ten-year-olds in the United States, Winston's fifth-graders cannot imagine life without television. This semester, Winston uses their natural curiosity about how things were "way back when" to look at leisure time during the late 1700s and early 1800s. One of the participatory activities she offers is a quilting bee.

Winston calls upon parents and grandparents to come demonstrate their skills with needle and thread to help make the class quilt; even small children are allowed. The quilting bee becomes an intergenerational affair.

Winston points out that in the past older siblings were regularly asked to care for younger ones. She also helps her students make connections between quilting and the kind of crafts that African slaves brought with them to this country.

On the day of the quilting bee, Winston's class looks very different. The students' tables are pushed to one side of the room, and their chairs are arranged in a big circle around the room. Winston wants to create a feeling of a big family, where everyone can see everyone else and talk not only to the people seated near them but also across the circle. Adults bring covered dishes to share. Students take turns watching the younger children. Some parents come only for an hour or two because of other commitments. Some who can't come were asked to send along a special dish or eventually do some of the finishing work on the quilt (such as hemming or ironing). Finally, never one to waste a resource, Winston has her students identify a charity or a needy family to which the finished quilt will be donated.

Several reading and writing activities are associated with the quilting bee; overall, the activity helps the students to use and improve the skills they had and to learn new ones. One student's journal reads:

> No wonder the people of old times didn't need no TV. They were so busy with their work that they didn't have no time to just sit and watch a TV. If you wanted to make a quilt you could have a lot of people over and talk and visit and eat. It's like having a party but you get your work done. My Auntie did something like that when she moved to a new house. Our hole (sic) family was there to help her clean and paint. We had a lot of food and we got the work done fast because we had a lot of help.

This journal entry demonstrates the ways that Winston's integrative and communal approach fosters basic skills like literacy. And by situating the learning in a context that includes the families and even serves the community in a small way, she makes a strong connection between knowledge and power.

CULTURALLY RELEVANT TEACHING SEES EXCELLENCE AS A COMPLEX STANDARD THAT TAKES STUDENT DIVERSITY AND INDIVIDUAL DIFFERENCES INTO ACCOUNT

Each of the classrooms I studied were examples of this characteristic. However, for the purpose of explanation I will focus on those of Pauline Dupree and Peggy Valentine.

Dupree's classroom structure might cause the casual observer to dismiss her teaching as too regimented, too authoritarian. After ongoing and in-depth observations, however, the reason her style can be considered culturally relevant becomes apparent. Always on the lookout for ways to recognize and affirm student accomplishments, Dupree distinguishes between acknowledging student effort and rewarding substandard performance:

> I don't believe in telling students that they are doing well when they aren't. Some teachers come into this district and think they're doing the children a favor by sticking a star on everything. They don't care that they're rewarding mediocrity. But in doing so, they're really just setting the kids up for failure because somewhere down the road they're going to learn that that A really was a C or a D.
>
> What I try to do is find those things the children really are good at and acknowledge them in the classroom. That means knowing about their sports and church activities. If someone is on a championship team, we try to get the coach to come in and talk about that person's contribution. I have had coaches, ministers, Scout leaders, family members—you name it—in here to tell the class about the excellence of the class members.

Dupree's in-class recognition of out-of-class excellence encourages the students to conceive of excellence broadly. It also begins to create a stronger connection between home and school. Once students see that Dupree makes a fuss about the things they enjoy, they seek similar recognition in the classroom.

Valentine's approach to acknowledge a broad range of student excellence involves the students in making the assessment. Each week during a class meeting the students nominate classmates for excellence in a variety of areas, both academic and social. Each nomination is supported by evidence. To ensure that the nominations are sincere, Valentine asks students to substantiate them orally. For example, "I nominate Tyrell for an excellence award because he helped me with my math this week." Other members of the class are encouraged to question the nomination. Valentine allows extracurricular activities as a basis for nomination but pushes students to think about classroom and school-related deeds by reminding them that the nominations have a better chance of success when others can verify them. After the nominations have been made, the students vote. Valentine rewards the winner with a small prize or privilege: gift certificates for the local fast food outlet, extended recess time, or exemptions from particular assignments, for example.

In addition to the weekly excellence awards, Valentine has her students participate in an "internship program." She pairs students with workers in the local school such as the janitor, a secretary, the library aide, cafeteria workers, and teachers' aides, so that they get a brief opportunity to learn about the value of work. According to Valentine:

> Fewer and fewer of our students understand the value of work or see work as a productive and satisfying activity. Too many of the teenagers won't take jobs in fast food stores because they don't pay much and because their friends would tease them. Because you can make easy money on the street, kids think anybody who takes a job at a fast food place is a fool. With the internship I'm just trying to get the kids to see that we work for more than just money. We work because our work means something to us.

Thus culturally relevant teaching recognizes the need for students to experience excellence without deceiving them about their own academic achievement. Rewarding students for a whole array of activities ensures that they understand that hard and fast rules do not exist for determining excellence. It also underscores the students' understanding that the teacher has high expectations for each of them.

20. Getting to Know You Culturally

YOLANDA SIMMONS AND PAT BEARDEN

Yolanda Simmons and Pat Bearden are sisters who teach in two different Chicago schools. They have designed a multicultural cross-disciplinary unit that they conduct in similar ways for three different audiences—Pat's third-graders, Yolanda's high-schoolers, and groups of teachers in in-service programs. The students at all three levels find it involving and rewarding. The biggest difference in the activity between the three groups is simply the time allotment—high-schoolers work longer on the whole project than either the younger kids or the adults. Here is the activity as it plays out in a high school classroom.

Day One. Students choose partners and conduct three-minute interviews with one another, taking notes on the following questions:

- Where were you born?
- Who were you named after, and what does your name mean?
- Where do your ancestors come from within the United States? Where do they come from outside the United States?
- Have you or anyone in your family researched your family history?

While the students are working, Simmons circulates around the room taking Polaroid pictures of each kid. She also makes sure she has a bit of information of her own about at least one student. Students then take a minute or two to review and select from their notes, in preparation for oral presentations.

Next, each student introduces his or her partner "culturally." Simmons provides a model by doing the first introduction, giving some of the information briefly:

> This is John. He was born here in Chicago on the South Side, and he was named after his great uncle. His family comes from Macon, Georgia, where he used to visit every summer when he was small. He loved his grandmother's cooking, but hated the farm work he had to do. He doesn't know anything about where his family came from before that, but he wishes he did. Mee-ee-eet John Coleman!

Everyone applauds. As the introductions proceed, Simmons records the place-of-family-origin information in two columns—origins inside the United States and origins outside the United States—using newsprint paper on the wall.

Day Two. The students complete and edit one-page written versions of their interviews, with space left on each page for a photograph. These are pasted on, and someone with artistic talent is drafted to make a cover. Overnight, Yolanda photocopies the interviews to produce a class book, and everyone receives a copy the next day. The kids immediately check their own photographs and moan that they don't do the owner justice. But they save and browse through this information about their peers for weeks.

Day Three. The students come in to class to find newsprint sheets taped to the walls, with the headings, "English," "Language Arts," "Math," "Social Studies," Science," "Phys. Ed.," plus a few blank sheets. Students are told to gather next to the sheets according to their strongest categories—often "Dance," "Music," and "Home Economics/Foods." Their task is now to brainstorm and list questions for researching information about some of the locations on the "Origins" chart for their chosen subject area. The students especially warm to this work, no doubt because it offers a rare opportunity to share in control of the curriculum. Simmons remarks that no subject area seems to go without a few devotees in each class. Some typical questions the kids put on their charts:

- English—Who were some famous authors from this place, and what did they write?
- Language Arts—What are some slang terms teenagers use in this area?
- Social Studies—What is the student drop-out rate in this city?

- Science—What are some of the diseases that occur specially in this area, and what are their causes?
- Math—What are the population statistics, comparisons among them, and trends, for various ethnic groups in this area?

Days Four and Five. These are spent in the library. Each group chooses one of the research questions listed on their chart (the charts are brought to the library before hand and hung up so the students can consult them), and looks for answers to that question for each place of family origin in the United States, in their particular group. The kids work on their research with help from Simmons and the librarian. Yolanda has been delighted to see even the low-achieving students working intently in their groups, and skipping lunch to continue their search.

Day Six. The students bring in their research reports and each group compiles an information book on their subject area. These books are kept as references in the classroom, reading material that the students can study on other occasions when they do reading of their own choice.

Days Seven and Eight. Each group gives an oral report to the class, sharing some of the knowledge they've gained on their particular aspect of the locations of the family origins.

Day Nine. At the end—and also at various points all along—the students "debrief" their research work in short discussion sessions. Among the important questions Yolanda poses are "How do you feel when you were doing_____?" and "Why do you think we included that step?" The students especially enjoy this reflecting, and find the latter question most thought-provoking. Such reflection adds to students' sense of ownership of the curriculum because they are asked to evaluate it. It also strengthens their learning by making them aware of the processes they've learned that lead to success in school. Many go on to write up their thoughts on these reflection questions as extra work on their own.

Clearly, this unit of study starts students thinking about multicultural issues, but it also does much more. It integrates all of the subject areas of school, and applies them to topics of real interest

in the students' lives. It involves interviewing; writing; researching; working individually, in pairs, and small groups; and giving
oral reports to the whole class. It honors students' own knowledge
and backgrounds, but also helps them discover much that they did
not know about their own past, in aspect of geography and history
that are actually quite traditional academically. It builds a classroom rapport that helps the students become a serious community
of learners as well as a class that achieves a level of inter-group
understanding that is sorely needed in many locales. It requires an
extended piece of time—two weeks—but provides a powerful
springboard to many other social studies topics, either in traditional areas or further afield.

21. A Day in the Life of a Developmentally Appropriate Whole Language Kindergarten

LYNN CHERKASKY-DAVIS

Lynn Cherkasky-Davis teaches in the Foundations School in Chicago, a school that sits in the middle of an extremely poor neighborhood. A visitor knows when he or she is approaching Lynn's room because the kids' work spills out the door and down the hallway. A metal cabinet full of narrow drawers with a child's name on each serves as the class mail system. A huge bulletin board is encrusted with materials—not the usual neat rows of kids' essays or drawings, because that couldn't possibly hold it all. Instead, there are ceiling-to-floor charts listing books the class has read in two categories, "real" and "make believe." A "brick wall" of reading is made up of colored squares stating, "This brick wall is under construction. Hopefully it will take a lifetime to complete. Welcome to our community of readers." One section holds letters from parents, the mayor, visiting teachers, letters from the kids to visitors, and "letters to an absent teacher." Several projects hang in thick clusters, each grouped together on a ring. One is a science project, "Fish or Not Fish," with a news article about whales and dolphins, and the kids' own research on sea animals. Another, on math, includes a read-aloud book, *Fruit Salad,* plus charts and graphs comparing the numbers of each kind of fruit the children brought in to *make* fruit salad. A book on a particular theme—*In My Bed*—is grouped with kids' versions of similar stories and maps of their bedrooms. But there's plenty more going on *in* the room, as Lynn will tell you.

The children enter the classroom for family-style breakfast at 8:45 after they "sign in" outside the door, thereby taking their own attendance. The first day of school the children may draw their "portrait" as a signature, or may choose a color and shape to use as theirs until they are able to sign their names or parts thereof. From the first day, children use writing for authentic purposes, never for isolated tasks. We sign up for photographs, learning centers, literature preferences, activity helpers, field trip participation, etc.

Following breakfast the children blend into the rest of the classroom for family reading. Children may read alone, in pairs, or in small groups. Volunteer parents, a part-time teacher aide, and I read with the kids. We listen to them picture read, approximate read, or actually read—whatever stage they're at. Children may listen to literature tapes while following along in books, read from charts, content area books, Big Books, literature sets, song books, poetry, library books (with their mandatory library cards), magazines, literature from home, and/or materials written by other children (or themselves). Our reading period illustrates the cooperative and collaborative nature of the classroom. The students are comfortable risk-takers who, without hesitation or embarrassment, will simply tell you what they can't read or need help on. But they don't stop there, because they've learned how to gather context clues and continue on with their story. While this myriad of reading activities goes on, I am a participant as well as evaluator, making note of further instruction particular children need.

Calendar activity comes next, and we address many content areas: math, language arts, science, and social studies. We tally, seriate, categorize, classify, write, pattern, order, and rhyme, as well as develop number, pattern, place value, and time sense. We classify the days as rainy, sunny, windy, etc., count them up, discuss the groupings, and so on. The children take the lunch tally and record the day's weather. They are empowered to do all "housekeeping business," following patterns set by children before them.

Several times throughout the day I read to the children. The books are alternately of my choosing (on a theme or particular subject matter) and the children's. Discussion follows. Another reading activity is "author's circle." When a student has gone through all the writing process steps and a work is ready for publication, he or she comes to "author's circle." Today Shanika read a book she wrote. The class was interested in her title page and how she produced the book as well as the story and illustrations. Shanika explained her writing process clearly, and her sequencing of information. She called for questions and comments when she finished "reading" her story, and the children eagerly verbalized their thoughts and feelings.

The rest of our day is spent in a literate, "hands on," problem-solving environment. The children circulate to various learning centers—some of their own choosing, some as a result of teacher and child evaluation. Teacher planning underlies all the activities, but they are all child-centered, and the children construct their own knowledge. The classroom is set up to provide opportunities for children to explore, discover, experiment, and create their own sense of their kindergarten world and tasks.

Let's tour the classroom to view some of these activities as they're organized in thematic centers. We have a home and family center where children role-play, write shopping lists (while consulting peers and other class resources for color sequencing and correct spellings) and family stories. I am consulted as a last resource. Today I observed Daniel trying to figure out how to spell "hamburger." He asked a peer who replied, "I don't know. Research it in our 'Food text set.'" Not finding it there, Daniel flipped through previous lunch menus, looking for "H" and "A," two letters he was sure about. He found "Ha" and knew it was the word he was looking for. Daniel has been encouraged to be self-sufficient, self-directed, and resourceful. He could construct what was unfamiliar from the familiar.

Continuing the tour, we find the science center filled with things to manipulate and experiences to create and re-create. In the transportation center, children can build "cities" in conjunction with the construction site adjacent to it. They map their designs, post signs, and write speeding tickets. They may also explore various means of travel and building.

Around the corner from the manipulative shelves and math materials are art materials, musical instruments, and easels in the Fine Arts center. Back to back are the writing table and publishing and bookbinding cart. At the typewriter and resource desk (the only desk in the classroom), the kids experiment with reading and writing connections. Here they keep writing portfolios and "works in progress," and conduct conferences with peers. These are but a few of the learning centers the children can work at.

What ties all these centers together are books, books, books and writing, writing, writing! Out in the hallway you will find the kids' mailboxes. Children write to each other, to me, parents, the principal, volunteers, upper graders, and anyone else. Today two children wrote to a publisher, explaining that the tape for Goldilocks does not match the words in the book in two places. In the mailboxes one will find some of the letters and stories written in full sentences with just about perfect spelling. Others combine functional spelling, letter strings, recognizable words, and pictures. Some may be pictures only, but interestingly each is addressed, dated, and signed by its author in clear letters.

On the walls around the room, the writing the children do fills so much space that we're continually in trouble with the fire marshall. One chart shows how each child is progressing with various tasks surrounding the bedtime story parents are expected to read to them each week. In another area, pocket folders hold projects kids have done as part of their "Book-of-the-Month" Club. Each kid has a folder with his or her name and picture, and a list of the books selected. Charts list things in various categories—"Films we have seen," titles of books about families, books about food, etc. Another display lists various items, one hundred of which children brought for counting—one hundred noodles, one hundred beans, etc. This leaves room for others and allows us to unroll them when we need to take a look at them.

Looking around my class today I saw that Lakita and Jinae were busy in the writing center. Jinae had written a story, and Lakita was her peer reviewer (yes, even in kindergarten!). She posed such questions as, "Did you leave spaces between words? What kind of letter must your sentence begin with? Check your punctuation. You need to research the spelling of that word." (The children follow my style of integrating phonics instruction into reading and writing.) With that, Jinae got up from the writing table and went to the housekeeping/grocery store area where she thumbed through menus, recipe cards, shopping lists, books, magazines, and the class lunch menu to figure out the spelling of the word in question. She committed the word to memory but knew that it needed an "s" at the end to make it plural. This she double-checked with her peer reviewer. (The previous phonics lesson of "More Than One" had not been an isolated lesson but was a natural part of a story we wrote as a class. The plural "s" was introduced during the story where it was needed. Thereafter, it will be pointed out often in books we read. All letters and sounds are learned in this context of real literature.)

When Jinae's writing process was completed, another classmate was summoned to do final editing. This kindergarten child followed a checklist the class devised earlier in the year. "Do the illustrations match the print? Are the pages numbered and ordered? Is it ready to be bound?" At this point Jinae signed up for a writing conference with me during the next learning center time, to fine-tune her work and decide on the binding (as it is a multiple page story). She will then go to the publishing center, and with the help of a parent volunteer, bind her work. After completion, Jinae is ready for Author's Chair. Anyone who collaborated on the story will join in.

My eyes scanned the room. Donald was in the math center making three-dimensional patterns and recording them. He was using Unifix cubes, chips, and colored toothpicks. Another student was checking him. Donald put his findings in his math journal and went on to seek out the books in our class library that will reinforce his patterning (although books, like writing materials, abound at all learning centers). Donald has integrated math and readings. I noted this behavior in my anecdotal records. That, with his recordings, will go into his evaluation portfolio. Using this and my "kid watching" guide, we will evaluate his progress, needs, and desires.

Moving about this small room, which has no front or back but is fluid in its space, I discovered several children moving ahead with what had begun, earlier in the week, as a teacher-directed whole class activity on categorization. The kids often take off with such activities and go as far as they are presently able. Today Antione, Octavius, and Carla had taken books out of the classroom library and were categorizing them by "books about school," "books about home," or "books about food." They went one step further and noted that some books fit into more than one category and some fit into none. Carla wandered off to the Bean Bag to read one of the books about food she thought looked interesting. She then decided to make a "text set" with other books on cooking and placed them in the kitchen area. Meanwhile, the two boys continued to list the books in their appropriate categories. Octavius called Nicky over to read the list with him. Nicky then decided to categorize his own list. He chose another section of books and classified them according to "real" or "make-believe." He took a survey of classmates to discover and graph how many preferred fact over fiction and vice versa. When I left him, he was graphing learning centers.

Patrice sat in the rocking chair by the post office drafting a letter to her pen pal. She needed to spell "spaghetti." She went to the recipe box and child-written menus in the kitchen/housekeeping area (a popular spot today). She asked her friends for help and seemed satisfied. Seeing that I was busy with another child, she consulted her classmates first. Although she knows she can come to me after she has exhausted all other resources, she did not this time. However, I looked at the letter to her pen pal and saw, "We eight bus spgte pasta." (We ate busghetti, spaghetti, pasta.)

When the second learning center time was over, we used what I had learned from the children during the day for our culminating lesson. We brainstormed a list of food categories: meats, liquids, junk, pasta. Of course, under the pasta category, we listed spaghetti. Several purposes and subject areas were served here: consensus building, reading, writing, speaking, listening, science, nutrition, and setting another research base. This chart will be kept at an appropriate spot in the classroom, available as a resource.

At 2:15 we completed our daily diary. Children got coats and signed out. Patrice quickly went to the "out" mailbox, carefully opened the envelope to her pen pal, and did something to it. The bell rang and she didn't have time to reglue or tape her envelope. I told her I'd do it. Patrice gave me a hug, filled out her exit slip, and ran to meet her auntie.

The children are gone. For the first time since 8:30, it is quiet. I read the student exit slips (I too am a learner!) and review and alter my plans for the rest of the week: 1) Upper Grade Reading Buddies will visit; 2) parent volunteers will transcribe the stories children dictated into the tape recorder; they will illustrate, order, and enumerate pages to ready them for "read-aloud" or publication; 3) children will direct and act out stories they have written for the preschoolers; 4) the class will design covers for books they bind and sell to authors from other classes; 5) favorite literature will be discussed, compared, and contrasted for Book-of-the-Month Club; 6) we will do an author study of Stephen Kellogg; 7) scientific experiments, readings, and recordings regarding plants will take place; 8) we'll begin our study of black authors and illustrators for age-appropriate literature; and 9) a new learning center will be introduced. My lesson plans are a hodgepodge.

There is never enough time. I read Patrice's exit slip. This is her "lesson plan." It says: "Today: I speled my letter write. Tomorrow: I want to write a store book." I read the letter she has written her pen pal before sealing it. It says, "We eight bus, spgte, pasta." as before, but she has crossed it out. (The children do not erase, knowing I like to see the steps in their writing process.) It now says: "We eight spaghetti." No reading series, ditto page, or isolated skill drill would have accomplished this.

Creating a literate, problem-solving, risk-free, higher-level critical thinking, encouraging environment for all twenty-five Patrices, taking into account their individual needs, desires, and learning styles—this is the embodiment of Best Practice in any developmentally appropriate classroom, not just kindergarten but preschool through grade twelve. Best Practice is not vase-filling. Rather, it is fire-lighting.

22. Go Back and Circle the Verbs

JAY REHAK

I work in a great school surrounded by an economically devastated neighborhood, surrounded by a society that can't understand why students don't park their problems at the front door of the school and enter into the wonderful world of knowledge. Society believes my students should be able to separate the reality outside the classroom walls from the reality inside. This intellectual "separation," society assumes, should allow students the opportunity to enter the four walls of compulsory education "equal" to one another.

Because society assumes this separation of inside and outside reality is possible, and because education is one of the few socially acceptable means of escaping poverty, many people can't understand why children in economically distressed areas score so much lower on standardized tests than children from wealthy areas. These men and women, professional and otherwise, are perplexed that the children who have the most to gain by high academic achievement, rarely do so.

Forget race. Forget economic situations. Forget gender. Forget family problems. Forget neighborhood distress.

"If I were in their shoes," these people suggest, "I would work as hard as I could to be at the top of my class. Education would be my solitary ambition. What is the problem with those people?"

Harry Daniels walks in wearing a worn-out yellow windbreaker. Underneath his windbreaker is a T-shirt. On the T-shirt is an advertisement for a local pizzeria. The advertisement is faded and the T-shirt worn thin. It's the middle of December and it's cold in Chicago.

As soon as Harry enters into the classroom, he heads immediately to the radiator and sits on it. He continues to sit on the radiator as many of his classmates come in and join him. He sits there for fifteen minutes until I tell him to take a seat so we can get started.

Now it's against school rules to sit in class with your coat on, but I let Harry slide. A windbreaker isn't a coat. My classroom is warm, but it's not that warm. Come to think of it, it's against school rules to sit on the radiator.

When I first started teaching, I used to get aggravated with the children who came into school during the winter wearing only a T-shirt and coat. It put me in a difficult position. I'm supposed to enforce school policy against wearing coats in the school, but on the other hand, a T-shirt doesn't provide enough warmth for the student wearing it. Since the children knew it was only moderately warm in the classroom, I couldn't understand why they wore T-shirts or short sleeve shirts in the winter. At the end of the day, I used to remind, encourage, and practically beg the children to wear a sweater the next day. Few did.

"What's the problem?" I wondered. I was twelve once. When I was a boy I occasionally forgot to wear my sweater on a cold winter's day. I'd spend the day shivering in the room. No coats allowed. Whose fault was that? By day's end I'd promise myself I'd never do it again. It was a tough lesson to learn, but I finally did it. By my senior year in high school, I rarely left for school completely underdressed.

As a teacher, I have been guided by my own school experiences as I make judgment calls throughout the day. Because my perspective is borne out of that limited experience, I regularly misjudge situations. In Harry's case, it took longer than it should have for me to realize he was wearing the T-shirt because he didn't have a sweater or long sleeve shirt that fit.

So Harry Daniels wears that same yellow windbreaker every day through the winter. The T-shirts change; the advertisements on them occasionally are current. Harry sits at the front of the room because he moves around so much. I've got to keep my eye on him.

He wouldn't hurt anybody—he's a nice guy. He just likes to talk and since he's a very thin boy, his form of self-defense is a very loud threat. Everybody knows he can't carry out any threat he makes, but if he thinks he's been wronged, he'll yell one out just the same. "Stop calling out my momma or I'll hit you in your eye!" is a particular favorite of his.

When I first heard students threatening each other I took it upon myself to get involved. Every threat I heard I perceived as real, and an affront to me because I heard it. It didn't matter that what was said was not directed at me or intended for me to hear. I was insulted. It's the Clint Eastwood/Billy Jack/Superhero in me. Someone would say something to one of the "vulnerable" students, and I would step in and make sure that the aggressor knew who he was up against. Me. Six-foot-three. Two hundred and fifteen pounds of justice. I had an image of myself as "Jesus with a punch." Any vulnerable student was under my protection. "Vulnerable" students came to have a wide range of shapes and forms: short, thin, tall but weak, female, stutterer, slow learner, quick learner, kid with a hygiene problem, a family problem, a social problem, a health problem. Hundreds of variations. In an instant I could work it out, a pecking order in my mind. Every child was vulnerable, especially as he or she related to others in the class, and I was the chief defender.

Each child's vulnerability has led me to a special disdain for classroom violence. When a fight occurs inside my classroom I am annoyed and feel particularly compelled to react. Often, my response is more than is necessary, triggered by my need to make things right as quickly as possible. Additionally, my childhood experiences come into play and often interfere with my ability to make a more reasoned professional response.

As a twelve-year-old boy, I never would think to fight someone in the classroom. If, for some reason, it became necessary to duke it out with someone, the fighting was always reserved for recess or after school. Only the biggest fools dared fight inside a classroom. The nuns would have your parents up to school faster than your friends could pull off your clip-on tie. Then your father'd show up and really get it to turning. No. In my day, fighting was reserved for the playgrounds. And if by chance someone were really getting the worst of it, I would occasionally step in and break it up. We all liked to see fights, but no one really liked to see someone get hurt in a big way. These childhood experiences led me to view classroom fighting twenty years later as a serious breach of etiquette. My thoughts as a twelve-year-old influenced the way I handled fights as a thirty-year-old.

During my first year as a teacher, the two smallest children in the class became involved in a one-sided fistfight. David, the smallest boy in the class, and Chou Minh, who was only slightly taller, got into an argument over a pencil. One thing led to another, and suddenly, David bolted out of his seat, across the room to where Chou Minh was sitting. Chou Minh was a recent Cambodian refugee, and he spoke little English. To my way of thinking, this made him the more vulnerable of the two. Additionally, since David was out of his seat, I immediately made an emotional decision to defend Chou Minh.

David gave Chou Minh one solid punch to the head while Chou Minh sat in his desk stunned. David was about to continue what was to be possibly the greatest physical classroom experience of his life, when I reached the two boys.

I picked David up by his armpits and began my admonition. "You think you're a tough guy, huh? You think you can just get up when you feel like it and hit a man, huh? You think you're such a big man, huh?" (A slip of the tongue, yet arising from some subconscious source. I was often teased for being a clumsy, big kid.)

I continued to carry David across the room, finally depositing him in his seat with a thud. "Now you sit there. Get up again and see what happens. Go ahead. We'll see how tough you are! Now sit down and stay down!"

The class sat momentarily stunned into silence. Then, laughter erupted until I stopped that with a cold stare. David started crying uncontrollably. I stood shaking, angry and embarrassed, saying, "Nobody fights in my classroom. You want to fight, take it outside. Take it into the streets and beat the hell out of each other. That's your business. But here, no fighting. I don't care who you are or what somebody did to you. You've got a problem, you let me know. I'll straighten it out if I can. But in this room, there'll be no more fighting." What could David have been thinking? To fight in full view of the teacher! Did he possibly think he could get away with it? Did he possibly think I would let him fight?

There were two fights on the same day subsequent to my speech to the class following David's and Chou Minh's fight. Despite my warnings, the children knew the safest place to take out their aggressions was here, in front of me.

My experience had taught me to fight on the playground. My experience had taught me that it was wiser to fight outside the view of my teacher than in plain sight. In my present situation, the reality is inverted. The streets are not the safest place to have a fight. It is far safer to have fights within view of the teacher, especially if that teacher speaks harshly but does not hit.

Fortunately, through the years, I have learned to understand when things are real and when they are practice for the real thing. The "real thing" is a fight that actually comes to blows. It happens more than any teacher would like, but it happens in every class. In my class, on average, maybe once every other month.

The degree to which I can separate myself as twelve-year-old boy student from thirty-five-year-old teacher is the degree to which I can effectively control circumstances in my classroom.

This is not to say that my experience as a twelve-year-old are not valuable to my teaching, but it is necessary that I not equate the experience of the twelve-year-olds I teach with those that I remember from my days as a twelve-year-old.

For example, I think again about Harry Daniels. I've been without a coat in the winter. For a day. Yes, I understand what it's like to be cold, I can empathize with Harry on that. I've sat all day in a cold room without a sweater. Yes. But the experience is not the same. Harry's short of winter clothes. I was just a forgetful kid when I didn't wear my sweater. Should Harry take off his coat in class? No. Would it help if Harry wore a sweater in class instead of a windbreaker? Yes. I don't know exactly how Harry feels wearing the same windbreaker every day. Besides cold, I assume Harry wishes he had something else to wear. I'd give Harry one of my sweaters, but it's too big and he'd never wear it. Should Harry wear a sweater far too large for him? It would keep him warmer. Who can say? Can I say? No. Why? Because maybe in Harry's circumstance he'd rather be cold than embarrassed. Let someone in Harry's position give me his or her studied opinion. The best I can do is offer Harry one of my sweaters or with a little luck and resourcefulness come up with one that will fit him. I'm not in Harry's position. I've never been in Harry's position. My experience in that area is limited. It has never happened to me.

That is the critical difference. Sometimes the experiences do run parallel or at least offer insights. Relationships with the opposite sex, desire to please the family, peer group pressures all offer parallels. But they are not the same and today's children in an urban setting should not be presumed to be under the same stresses as I was as a suburban child twenty years ago. It seems simple enough to say the two experiences are different, but that also is not the healthiest response.

What I try to do is take into account my experiences when making daily judgment calls without holding my children up to a standard they should not be measured by. This type of thinking requires that I have some understanding of the limit of my experience.

On a larger scale, when the surrounding circumstances of my children's lives are considered, can I honestly suggest that I have the depth of experience to understand the backgrounds of their lives?

While walking through the school's neighborhood this past year, on my way to the subway, I was attacked from behind by three high school gang-bangers. Their purpose was to rob me. Being hit from behind, I was too stunned to fall down. I retained my balance, rubbing my head while the three young guys stood in front of me.

"Why'd you do that?" I asked, genuinely confused. I had never been jumped from behind before in my life. The idea was outside the range of my experience and virtually outside the range of my fears. I'd always thought getting jumped never happened to big guys.

"We want your money," they said with a laugh.

I hesitated. I felt like I was in a cartoon, these boys waiting patiently, casually humored, for me to understand what it was they wanted, and me just rubbing my head thinking it over. "Your money or your life," I'm thinking. I'm thinking, Clint Eastwood, Billy Jack, Superhero, Jesus with a punch. I wanted to rub my chin as if I didn't want to have to do what I had to do, then start whaling with my fists, fast and furious until I had won the fight. Two of them, yes. Three of them, unlikely. More than three, I could be a dead man. "And if I lose, how do I get home?" I thought. "And if these guys wanted my money so badly, why didn't they just ask me nicely?" Finally, after a suspended moment in time, I said, "No!" and bolted into the middle of Pulaski.

Out of nowhere another guy runs out into the middle of the street wielding a golf club. He's about to hit me over the head when I put my briefcase over my head and yell, "What are you doing, man?" Again, the scope of my experience closed in on me, and it struck me as completely ludicrous that someone I didn't know would whack me over the head with a golf club.

The man did not answer but instead hit me across the thigh with what I believe to be a five iron. Just as I was about to be hit again, and apparently again, one of my students recognized me as the man in the middle of a losing battle. He comes running out on to the street and stops it, insisting that he knows me and that I should not be hit. Everyone backs off, my student walks me to the subway, I arrive home in good enough shape to ride to the hospital. X rays reveal no breaks of the spinal cord, and after a night in the hospital I am released.

Do I know what it's like to live in a tough, gang-infested neighborhood? Of course not. I know what it's like to get roughed up a bit, but I remain a visitor in the community I teach in. I don't know what it's like to live where I teach. I don't know what my students have to do to survive on a daily basis. I do know that I won't ever recommend to my students that they take their fights outside. I know that isn't an acceptable alternative to fighting in school. Maybe me getting roughed up has given me new insights into my children's lives outside of the classroom, but I still don't know what it's like to be in their shoes.

All of this is not to say, "Oh, my poor children! Look what they have to go through to get to school. They don't have to do anything in school because they've already done enough by getting here." No. These kids need to learn and they need to be reinforced in their efforts to learn. They need to have an insight into the small picture and the big picture. They need to be clued in. By me. By their families. By society. I know I want it to happen. I know their families want it to happen. I've already told you what I think society wants.

Over the Christmas holidays, one of my students from the previous year was murdered in a gang related incident. Anthony Young, ostensibly a freshman in high school, was shot six times on December 30th. Because he had been threatened, he spent the last two weeks of his life locked inside his aunt's apartment. The only reason he ventured outside on the last day of his life was that it was his sixteenth birthday. He died two blocks from his aunt's home.

Anthony was in my language arts class for two years. He was a boy with a good heart, but he had no self-control. He absolutely could not or would not sit down and focus on the lesson at hand. I tried for two years to find something that interested him for more than a few minutes. I never found it.

He was a good speaker, in part because he never stopped talking. He had a good sense of what was going on in the world around him, he "knew" the street life a thousand times better than I ever will, but his self-preservation instincts were weak. Thinking about his life from the time that I met him until his death two weeks ago makes me think that he got what he wanted: a quick exit from an unfriendly place.

Anthony was raised by his aunt, his mother being in jail and his father long gone. His aunt had a number of children of her own, and she could not afford to keep Anthony. Consequently, he always came to school in dirty T-shirts and jeans, and he was perpetually hungry.

He needed so much attention I don't think there was any way the schools could have provided him with enough. When he came into my classroom, he needed to have all of the focus. To get it, he would talk loudly, hit the nearest person to him, run around, wear a coat over his head, anything to get and maintain attention.

I always sat him next to me or at my desk. All of my attention might have been enough to have affected him in some slight way, but I couldn't give all of it to him all the time. There were thirty other children in my class.

I never sent him down to the office, but I often sat him outside the classroom, next to the window looking in, when I couldn't get him to let the class have their time to learn.

Other teachers would regularly send him down to the office, where he would sit with the school principal and while away the day. My principal is a good man with a big heart, and he would do his best to counsel Anthony. Although it's impossible to say what Anthony heard, my impression was his mind was made up about this world. He had decided some time before I met him that this life and this society could not hold him to anything. He was a directionless boy who could not grab onto anything that was not immediate.

The closest he ever got to participating in class was on the days he would sit and correct papers for me. He never actually corrected them in the purest sense, but he would put a check mark next to the students' names who had done their homework. This he would do for ten minutes, then get tired and quit.

On one occasion, near Halloween, I remember he was able to sit for about twenty minutes and draw me a spider, but in the end he tore the spider up and went back to looking for everyone's attention. He had artistic skills, and I tried to interest him in drawing, but he couldn't focus on it long enough to get it done.

The school social worker, available to students twice a week, regularly sat and talked with Anthony.

He loved to play basketball, but because he was quick tempered and annoying he did not make the school basketball team. During tryouts he mumbled something after the coach had told the boys to stand quietly. When he was told to leave by the coach, I could see the sadness in his face, as well as a look of resignation. He knew as well as everyone that he'd never make the team. Few students wanted him on their team when sides were drawn up for pick-up games, although he occasionally found his way into one.

When he died I asked my children to write about him. Many said they hardly knew him, but those who did know him said he had a big heart. He just couldn't master the concept of consistent friendship.

I remember dreading to see him walk into my room, but I'd always try to give him a big friendly hello. I did this not so much because I was a nice guy, but because I always hoped that by being nice to him, he would be nice to me. He was nice to me, in a personal sense. Sometimes during my "breaks" I would see him sitting in the office and ask him to take a walk with me. We would walk the halls, and I'd buy him a soft drink from the engineer's office. We would walk and talk, with me asking him what was going on, and him telling me very little. I would then try to give him some friendly advice, usually about strategies to be a good friend. He never said a bad thing about or to me, but as a student, he remained a nightmare.

If I were to vote on a child "most likely to get a bullet" it would have been him. Anthony annoyed so many people. He wouldn't exactly turn on you, he just couldn't help striking out at anything near him. He'd hit students in a playful way that wasn't playful to the child being hit. He'd catch the student off guard with a slap to the back of the head, or he'd walk up to someone's desk and snatch a book and put it on someone else's desk. It was as if he were trying to be funny and failing at it miserably.

Had Anthony lived I don't think he would have been in for much better than what he got. I know the system would not have been kind to him.

A number of boys from last year's class have been arrested and are flirting with serious jail sentences. Some of them have been implicated in Anthony's death. I don't know the extent of the police "investigation" into Anthony's death. Inasmuch as it was a "gang" killing, the police may not be as pressed to find the killers. Chances are Anthony's killing will prompt a reprisal killing.

The talk in school the week we returned from Christmas vacation has been in hushed tones. I mentioned the murder to the class on the Monday I heard about it, we discussed it briefly, and then moved on. On Tuesday when I brought it up again, one of the students in the class, herself a gang-banger, shouted, "Not this again! Why do all you teachers have to bring Anthony up again. Let the dead alone!"

I couldn't leave Anthony's death alone during the week. There was a memorial service for him on Friday night of the first week back. Many students asked if I would attend. I was ambivalent. Although I have been to the funerals of parents I have known, I attended those funerals because I wanted to support the living. I knew Anthony, but he was dead. I didn't know Anthony's aunt. Furthermore, the boys who had attacked me the previous spring would be there, as well as a number of gang members. Rumors floated around the school that the memorial service might not be peaceful. Anthony was to be buried with a gold chain with a UVL pendant attached to it—the UVL representing Anthony's gang. A number of colleagues told me not to go to the funeral. It was no place for a tall white guy. Passions would be running too deeply. I skipped it and instead said prayers for Anthony during my family meal.

I don't want Anthony's death to turn into an anecdote. I don't want it to be a teachable moment. He died and that is a part of my life and experiences. The children I work with have to live with his death, too. I see a number of children going the way of Anthony. I want them to see the bullet before it hits them, but I am afraid the gun has already been fired at some. The bullet hasn't reached them yet, but I see it streaking toward them. Is there any way to stop it?

Society wants a workforce that does what it's told and on time. That's all. Someone will break through and be creative, but the status quo never finds it necessary. Society has what it wants now, and although it can always use a better, faster, more interesting product, it is not necessary that it actually exist. Society just wants to keep things going as they are.

Teaching children to think, absolutely, positively "what-do-you-think, how-could-this-be-better-think," is a threat to the existing order. Any creative idea makes noise. Society doesn't want to hear noises. Society wants it quiet, and with good television reception.

And so as a teacher, when I invite students to think, I am faced with more work than if I just ask them to fill themselves up with what someone else has thought.

I give a lot of assignments that come straight out of the book. And students do them the most quietly. I give these assignments whenever I feel threatened by the noise. When students start "going off" on each other or me.

Kids have to know that society does expect them to jump through a certain number of hoops. That is socio-reality. This society pays people more money when they have a degree, degrees, or academic credentials. More people listen to you. You've proved you've been able to sit down, shut up, and listen to someone else. That's worth money in this society.

But if you are constantly challenging, nobody wants to pay you; they more or less want you to go away. There is a practical side to being a free thinker; free thought costs you in this society. It costs you in dollars. You don't make the money. You only get a bit of peace of mind. Kids have to know that they have the option.

Now as a teacher, I occasionally challenge my students to think on their own. "What would you do if you were me?" Most students respond with suggestions of heavy repression. "Whip kids!", "Beat kids up!", "Kick kids out of school!" When I suggest that they might be the ones who suffer under this type of siege mentality, they say, "We know. That's what we want."

The problem, simply put, is that children, left to their own education, would probably be all right, but society isn't really interested in well-rounded students. Society wants a workforce that does what it's told, and does it on time. It doesn't make a difference if what is being created is worthless—the point is, someone's paying for it, and if you're drawing a check from it, shut up and do it.

So we get an educational policy that teaches children to more or less shut up and do as they're told. This type of instruction makes teaching easier if "resistors" are heavily punished and made to feel like outsiders. The Japanese have a saying, "The nail that sticks out gets pounded down."

Our educational system is designed to promote quiet learning and reward obedience. Above all obedience. And so it is that if a teacher helps students achieve high standardized test scores, but if students are noisy in the hallway, the teacher is rated less than superior.

Now as a teacher, if I work to create free thinkers, there's going to be a lot of noise in the halls. If there's noise in the halls, someone in a position of power is sure to be disappointed, and other quiet classes are sure to be disturbed.

Students need to know that quiet is respected by the culture, but they should learn that it's not only because of the "courtesy" that is implied by not disturbing people, but also they should know that quiet means "all's well" in the society. If it's quiet, people aren't plotting anything. Nothing dangerous can be happening that society can't handle. Because if all is quiet, you must be working alone, which is easy enough to extinguish. "All's well!" cries the centurion. Even if all is not well.

I work with students who are so thin I can wrap my thumb and index finger around their shoulders. I think again of Harry Daniels. These are twelve- and thirteen-year-old children. Children who should be eating constantly, moving constantly, and thinking constantly. Are they supposed to shut up and listen? Am I supposed to talk about nouns and verbs in the abstract? How about: "Harry is too thin!" "Society should not allow guys to get this thin!" Now go back and circle the verbs.

Why should I teach them to sit down, shut up, and listen? Because society will ask no less of them, and if they don't, they aren't going to get along well in this society.

You'd better know what you're doing, but more importantly,

you'd better be able to present yourself in an agreeable manner. The first sour face you give to your boss could cost you big time.

I politely ask students to listen to me, then, when they don't, I occasionally lose it. Today I was trying to get kids ready to go home, and everyone was bouncing around getting coats or "passing licks." A mother appears at the door and asks, "What kind of a class is this?" Before I can answer, she's walked away horrified. I lost it and start chasing kids around the room telling them to sit down. "Don't get your coats, just sit down!" Two minutes later everyone is out the door. I cool off, feeling like an ogre, and a half-dozen kids come back up the stairs and ask if they can help clean up.

My mother died on Wednesday, February 26th, after a long bout with lymphoma. My mother was one day short of turning sixty-five, and she died on her own mother's birthday.

My mother's liver shut down a few days before she died, so her doctors decided to put a small "window" in her heart to drain fluid that was backing up in her and making it hard for her to breathe.

I went to school that morning to leave a lesson plan for the week. I did this because I thought it would help keep things together for the substitute and I wanted to avoid returning to a disorganized classroom. More importantly, I wanted the kids to know what was happening. I knew if I let them know what was going on, they would rally behind me and would treat each other better. I also wanted to minimize any rumors which might start if I were gone for a week. I feared the kids would hear that I'd "transferred" or that I was sick.

I went in on Monday and told my students that I would be leaving that morning for the hospital. I said to them if all went well with the "minor" heart surgery, I would return the next day. I said that if my mother died, I would not return for a week, but that I would see them on the first day of the following week.

Many of the children told me that I should take the week off regardless, that my mother's bedside was where I should be. My students told me this in subdued voices, because they could see from my face that I was concerned.

My mother pulled through the "minor" heart surgery and I did return to work the next day. I began the day with a progress report regarding my mother's health.

The next day, Wednesday, I reported again to my students that I had seen my mother the previous night and had spoken with her. I reviewed my mother's condition with each of my four language arts classes, and then went back to my instructional program. That evening my mother died.

When I returned to work the following Wednesday, Arnetha, one of my students, presented me with a poem written by the class. It read:

We've been disobedient
so many times.
Never listening to anyone
following our own minds.

Being rude and obnoxious,
being cruel to you,
never paying attention
doing whatever we wanted to do.

Making bad impressions
on almost everyone,
especially the most important people
like Mr. Sanders and Mrs. Allen.

And now that you've lost
someone that you love,
it's time to show some respect,
to change what we've done.

We know it's hard
when a loved one dies,
to adjust to the pain
when all you can do is cry.

Especially when you've known that person
every single day of your life
and then they're gone,
just overnight.

We want to let you know that we care
and we're getting our act together.
And in the future
you can expect much better.

I got a letter from a girl in the class, telling me that four years earlier, she too, had suffered the loss of a "loved one."

Later that morning, the class presented me with a sympathy
card, signed by all of the students. Inside the card was six dollars.

23. Good Morning, Mr. Chacon

LOUANNE JOHNSON

During the last quarter of the school year, the juniors started a study unit on employment. When I asked the class for a volunteer to show me how he or she handled a job search over the phone, Raul Chacon raised his hand. I held an imaginary phone to my right ear and motioned for Raul to do the same.

"Ring-a-ding-ding," I said. "Hello, Johnson's Department Store. May I help you?"

"Do you have any jobs?" Raul asked.

"What kind of job are you looking for, sir?"

"Anything. I just need a job," Raul said. I dropped my phone.

"Is that really what you say when you call up a company to find out about employment opportunities?" I asked. He nodded.

"Usually. Sometimes I say, 'Are you hiring?'" I looked around the room.

"Is that what the rest of you guys do, too?" Everyone nodded.

"Do you get many interviews?" I asked. They all stopped nodding and shook their heads.

For the remainder of that class period, we practiced telephone etiquette. The next day, the students wrote resumés and typed them in the computer lab. We discussed interviewing techniques and communication skills. We filled out actual job applications from a variety of major corporations and local companies. After a month of practice and preparation, the kids were ready for the big test: mock interviews with personnel managers from local companies.

Six managers agreed to come to the school and conduct brief interviews with the students to help them polish their skills. On the day of the mock interviews, the students were almost delirious with anticipation. They couldn't stop talking—until the personnel managers arrived. Then they couldn't start. Some of them fell apart completely; one girl hyperventilated and had to go to the nurse's office to lie down. Two boys refused, at the last minute, to participate. One of the boys who refused was Gusmaro.

"Come on," I nudged Gusmaro with my elbow, "it's your turn."

"No way," Gusmaro insisted. "I ain't doing it."

"Why not?"

"You aren't going to be rejected," I said. "This isn't a real interview. It's practice."

"Those look like real managers to me," Gusmaro said. "Look at them suits." He glanced quickly at the man seated at the desk in front of him. The man wore a three-piece suit, as did all of the interviewers, including the women.

"That's how people dress in offices," I told Gusmaro.

"Well, they look mean," he insisted. "I ain't doing it."

I didn't press Gusmaro because I thought he'd give in when he saw the other students breezing through their interviews, but I thought wrong. Many of the kids did breeze through, but not the Hispanic boys. With the exception of Julio Lopez, who received an Average rating from his interviewer, they bombed. Their rating sheets all said the same thing: no eye contact, hostile attitude, poor articulation, sloppy posture, unwilling to talk. Raul Chacon unwilling to talk? I had a hard time imagining it.

"What happened to you?" I asked Raul. "You were great when we practiced in class." Raul shrugged and looked at the floor.

"Did you look him in the eye and shake his hand the way we practiced?"

He shook his head.

"Why not?"

"I don't know," he mumbled. "I just couldn't talk to that guy."

"Why not?" I repeated.

"I couldn't," Raul said. "I don't know why, but I just couldn't do it, Miss J."

"Did he say something mean to you?"

"No, Raul said. "He was pretty nice."

"So why didn't you talk to him?"

"He's wearing that fancy suit," Raul said.

"That's just clothes," I said. "You know better than to judge a man by his clothes." Raul kept his eyes on the floor.

"Well, he kept staring at me," Raul said.

"How else is he going to see you if he doesn't look at you?" I asked. Raul shrugged again.

"He probably thinks I'm ugly. That's why he was staring at me."

"You aren't ugly!" I said. "Where did you ever get an idea like that?"

"From the magazines," Raul said. "And catalogs and stuff. I don't look like those white guys."

"Please look at me, Raul." He looked up. I put my hand under his chin.

"Have I ever lied to you?"

"No."

"And I'm not lying now. You are not ugly. You are beautiful. You are smart and you have a great sense of humor and you are very handsome. I'm going to arrange another interview for you and I want you to shake the man's hand and look him straight in the eye. Will you do that for me?" Raul drew a deep breath and exhaled. He shook his head and looked at the floor again.

"I can't." I knew he was telling the truth. He simply couldn't do it.

"Okay," I said. "Don't worry about it. We'll practice some more in class, all right?"

"Thanks, Miss J," Raul said. He glanced at me. "I'm sorry I let you down."

"You didn't let me down," I said. "You just weren't ready."

Several weeks later, it was time for the real thing. As part of our program, we contact personnel managers of a number of local companies that hire students during the summer. Although the managers are supportive of our program and interested in hiring our students, the kids still have to arrange formal interviews and apply for available jobs in competition with the general public. One major department store called to invite student applicants for a job in the administrative office of a large warehouse. The warehouse was located on the East Side of the city and the personnel manager specifically requested applications from students who lived on the East Side.

By that time, some of the kids had already found jobs. Raul, Gusmaro, and the rest of their posse all worked together in the dining hall of a local university, busing tables and washing dishes.

"Here's your chance," I told them. "The lady who called wants a kid from the East Side for a good job. You'll get to use a computer just like the ones we have in our computer lab."

"How much does it pay?" Gusmaro said.

"Seven-fifty an hour. How much do you guys get at your jobs?"

"I only get six because I started later," Raul said.

Eight kids, including Gusmaro, Raul, and Julio, took applications for the job, but none of them applied. Every day for two weeks, they listed dozens of reasons why they hadn't gotten around to filing their applications. The personnel manager called to say that she had interviewed several students and couldn't wait any longer to hire someone. I collared Gusmaro and Raul after class and demanded an explanation. Julio came with them, but as usual, he stayed in the background, standing silently prepared if his friends needed him.

"They wouldn't of hired us, anyway," Gusmaro said.

"Why not?"

"Because we're Mexican."

"They specifically asked for a kid from the East Side," I said. "That means that they expected you to be Hispanic or black."

"They probably didn't mean it," Gusmaro said. "They just say that, but when you get there, they don't hire you."

"Why didn't you go find out?"

"I told you," he said. "I don't like rejection."

"What about you?" I asked Raul. He shrugged.

"You don't like the idea of doing anything on your own, either, do you?" I said. "You want to work at the same job with all your friends forever."

"I like working with my friends," Gusmaro said. "It's cool."

"But you can't advance in a career if you handcuff yourself to somebody else," I said. "You have to make your own way. Stand on your own."

Neither boy answered. They just looked at me. They knew that I knew their posse's motto: forever together.

"Well, if you're going to hold each other's hands," I said, "at least you could get a job where you don't have to wash dishes like a bunch of illegal aliens." It was a mean thing to say, but I was really feeling frustrated. They had worked so hard to make themselves eligible for good jobs, but they wouldn't apply for them.

Raul was waiting for me outside my room the next morning.

"I'm sorry I didn't apply for that job, Miss J," he said. "I guess we were too afraid. I'll go to the next one, I promise."

"Promise?" I asked, holding out my hand. He took my hand in a firm grip and looked me straight in the eye.

"I promise," he said. "But can I ask you something?" I nodded.

He explained that he had been reading the vocational brochures from the career center and wanted to sign up for an after-school training program in his senior year, but he couldn't decide whether to choose landscaping, auto mechanics, construction, or automated office occupations.

"What kind of job do you want to have after you graduate?" I asked.

"A good one," he said.

"What's good?"

"Where I make a lot of money."

"You can make money at a lot of jobs, but it's better if you like the work you're doing," I explained.

"But how do you know what you like until you do it?"

"Good question," I said. "Taking different classes is one way to find out. But you can narrow it down by thinking of what you like and don't like."

"I don't get you," Raul said.

"Close your eyes," I said. "And imagine yourself getting up in the morning. You eat breakfast, get into your truck, and drive out to a big company where you check the sprinklers and all of the plants and trees. In the back of the building there is a new addition and you need to decide where to put the plants and bushes and sidewalks to make it look pretty. Most of the day you're outside, working with equipment and making sure your work crew does their job, but sometimes you work indoors in an office."

Raul opened his eyes and looked at me. "I could see myself doing that," he said. "It was all right."

We did the same thing for construction and auto repair. Both of those sounded "all right," too. But after I started to describe Raul's imaginary life as an office worker, he turned his face upward and smiled dreamily, although he kept his eyes shut.

"You adjust your tie and put on your jacket before entering the main lobby," I said. "You shift your briefcase to your left hand so you can open the big glass door. As you pass the receptionist, she says, 'Good morning, Mr. Chacon,' and you say hello. In your office, you turn on your computer terminal, check your in-basket, and hang your jacket on a hanger behind the door. You get your cup and go down to the lunchroom for a cup of coffee before starting your work."

Raul's eyes flew open.

"Good morning, Mr. Chacon," he said, rolling the words out slowly, as though tasting them for flavor. He nodded. "That sounds pretty good, doesn't it?"

"It sounds wonderful," I agreed.

"And I liked it when I dressed up in that suit to eat lunch at that fancy hotel. I looked pretty good, didn't I?"

"Yes, you did."

"Mr. Chacon," he repeated. "I like that."

24. Inside the Classroom: Social Vision and Critical Pedagogy

BILL BIGELOW

There's a quote from Paulo Freire that I like: he writes that teachers should attempt to "live part of their dreams within their educational space." Teaching should be partisan, Freire believes. I agree. As a teacher I want to be an agent of transformation, with my classroom as a center of equality and democracy—an ongoing, if small, critique of the repressive social relations of the larger society. That doesn't mean holding a plebiscite on every homework assignment, or pretending I don't have any expertise. But I hope my classroom can become part of a protracted argument for the viability of a critical and participatory democracy.

This vision of teaching flies in the face of what has been and continues to be the primary function of public schooling in the United States: to reproduce a class society, where benefits and sufferings are shared incredibly unequally. As much as possible I refuse to play a part in that process.

Easier said than done. How can classroom teachers move decisively away from a model of teaching that merely reproduces and legitimizes inequality? I think Freire is on the right track when he calls for a "dialogical education." To me, this isn't just a plea for more classroom conversation. In my construction, a dialogical classroom means inviting students to critique the larger society through sharing their lives. As a teacher I help students locate their experiences socially; I involve students in probing the social factors that make and limit who they are and I try to help them reflect on who they could be.

EXAMPLES OF CRITICAL PEDAGOGY

In the Literature in U.S. History course which I co-teach in Portland, Oregon, with Linda Christensen, we use historical concepts as points of departure to explore themes in students' lives and then, in turn, use students' lives to explore history and our society today. Earlier this year, for instance, we studied the Cherokee Indian Removal through role-play. Students portrayed Indians, plantation owners, bankers, and members of the Andrew Jackson administration and saw the forces which combined to push the Cherokees west of the Mississippi against their will. Following a discussion of how and why this happened, Linda and I asked students to write about a time when they had had their rights violated. We asked students to write from inside these experiences and to recapture how they felt and what, if anything, they did about the injustice.

The aim here, of course, was not to propose a one to one correspondence between the Cherokee holocaust and students' personal experiences, but to encourage them to draw on their lives to empathize with the Cherokee. By shifting students' attention to the present, we also hoped to counter the subtext of some history classes that suggests "look how bad it was back then, thank heavens we are alive today." Finally, we wanted students to think critically about our responses to injustice, how we come to see ourselves as victims or activists.

Seated in a circle, we encouraged students to share their stories with one another in a read-around format. Before we began, we suggested they listen for what we call the "collective text"—the group portrait that emerges from the read-around. Specifically, we asked them to take notes on the kinds of rights people felt they possessed; what action they took after having their rights violated; and other common themes they noticed from the read-around. Here are a few examples: Rachel wrote on peeing in her pants because a teacher wouldn't let her go to the bathroom; Christie, about a teacher at a middle school who "leched after the girls"; Rebecca, on a teacher who enclosed her in a solitary confinement cell; Gina, who is black, on a theater worker refusing to believe that her mother, who is white, actually was her mother; Maryanne, on being sexually harassed while walking to school and her subsequent mistreatment by the school administration when she reported the incident; Clayton, on the dean's treatment when he wore an anarchy symbol on his jacket; Bobby, on convenience store clerks who watched him more closely because he is black. Those are fewer than a quarter of the stories we heard. To fracture the student/teacher dichotomy a bit, Linda and I also write each assignment, and take our turns reading.

To help students study this social text more carefully, we asked them to review their notes from the read-around and write about their discoveries. We then spent over a class period interpreting our experiences. Almost half of the instances of rights violations took place in schools. Christie said, "I thought about the school thing. The real point [of school] is to learn one concept: to be trained and obedient. That's what high school is. A diploma says this person came every day, sat in their seat. It's like going to dog school." A number of people, myself included, expressed surprise that so many of the stories involved sexual harassment. To most of the students with experience of harassment, it had always seemed a very private oppression. But hearing how common this kind of abuse is allowed young women to feel a new connection between one another—and they said so. A number of white students expressed surprise at the varieties of subtle racism black students experienced.

We talked about the character of students' resistance to rights violations. From the collective text we saw that most people did not resist at all. What little resistance occurred was individual; there was not a single instance of collective resistance. Christie complained to a counselor; Rebecca told her mother; many complained to friends. This provoked a discussion about what in their lives and, in particular, in the school system, encouraged looking for individual solutions to problems shared collectively. They identified competition for grades and positions in sought-after classes as factors. They also criticized the fake democracy of student government for discouraging activism. No one shared a single experience of schools encouraging groups of students to confront injustice. Moreover, students listed a number of ways—from advertising messages to TV sitcoms—in which people are conditioned by the larger society to think in terms of individual problems requiring individual solutions.

Students' stories were moving, sometimes poetic, and later opportunities to rewrite allowed us to help sharpen their writing skills. But we wanted to do more than just encourage students to stage a literary show-and-tell. Our broader objective was to search for social meaning in individual experience—to push students to use their stories as windows not only on their lives, but on society.

There were other objectives. We hoped that through building a collective text, our students—particularly working class and students of color—would discover that their lives are important sources of learning, no less important than the lives of the generals, the presidents, the Rockefellers and Carnegies who inhabit their textbooks. One function of the school curriculum is to celebrate the culture of the dominant and to ignore or scorn the culture of subordinate groups. The personal writing, collective texts, and discussion circles in Linda's and my classes are attempts to challenge students not to accept these judgments. And we wanted students to grasp that they can create knowledge and not simply absorb it from higher authorities.

All of this sounds a little neater than actually occurs in a classroom. Some students rebel at taking their own lives seriously. A student in one of my classes said to me recently, "Why do we have to do all this personal stuff? Can't you just give us a book or a worksheet and leave us alone?" Another student says regularly, "This isn't an English class, ya know." Part of their resistance may come from not wanting to expose painful experiences and part may come from not feeling capable as writers, but I think the biggest factor is that they simply don't feel that their lives have anything *important* to teach them. Their lives are just, well, their lives. What's important is Abraham Lincoln and Hitler. Students have internalized self-contempt from years of official neglect and denigration of their culture. When, for example, black or working-class history *is* taught, it is generally as hero worship: extolling the accomplishments of a Martin Luther King Jr. or a John L. Lewis, while ignoring the social movements that made their work possible. The message is: great people make change, you don't. So it's not surprising that some students wonder what in the world they have to learn from each other's stories.

Apart from drawing on students' own lives as sources of knowledge and insight, an alternative curriculum also needs to focus on the struggle of oppressed groups for social justice. In my history classes, for example, we study episodes of solidarity: Shay's Rebellion, the Abolition movement, and alliances between blacks and poor whites during Reconstruction. In one lesson, students role-play IWW organizers in the 1912 Lawrence, Massachusetts, textile strike as they try to overcome divisions between men and women and between workers speaking over a dozen different languages.

STUDENTS—SOCIAL RESEARCHERS ON SCHOOLS

In my experience, whether students write about inequality, resistance, or collective work, schools are *the* most prominent settings.

However, teachers and texts rarely include units that invite students to think critically about their own school lives. What is not taught is also part of the curriculum. And when schools fail to allow students to evaluate the purposes and consequences of schooling, they teach a vital lesson: Don't analyze the institutions which shape your lives; just accept whatever conditions you're handed. Immediately following our study of industrialization/immigration/unionization, Linda and I teach a unit on the history and politics of public schooling. As we move between past and present, we enlist students as social researchers, investigating their own school lives.

Linda and I begin the unit by reading an excerpt from the novel *Radcliffe*, by David Storey. In the selection, a young boy, Leonard Radcliffe, arrives at a predominately working-class British school. The teacher prods Leonard, who is from an aristocratic background, to become her reluctant know-it-all—the better to reveal to others their own ignorance. The explicit curriculum appears to concern urban geography: "Why are roofs pointed and not flat like in the Bible?" the teacher asks. She humiliates a working-class youth, Victor, by demanding he stand and listen to her harangue: "Well, come on then, Victor. Let us all hear." And as he stands mute and helpless, she chides: "Perhaps there's no reason for Victor to think at all. We already know where he's going to end up, don't we?" She points to the factory chimneys outside. "There are places waiting for him out there already." No one says a word. She finally calls on little Leonard to give the correct answer, which he does.

Students in our class readily see that these British schoolchildren are learning much more than why roofs are pointed. They are being drilled to accept their lot at the bottom of a hierarchy with a boss on top. The teacher's successful effort to humiliate Victor, while the others sit watching, undercuts any sense the students might have of their power to act in solidarity with one another. A peer is left hanging in the wind and they do nothing about it. The teacher's tacit alliance with Leonard and her abuse of Victor helps to legitimize the class inequalities outside the classroom.

We use this excerpt and the follow-up discussion as a preparatory exercise in which students research the curriculum—both explicit and "hidden"—at their own school, Jefferson, mostly African-American and predominately working class. Linda and I assign students to observe their classes as if they were attending for the first time. We ask them to notice the design of the classroom, the teaching methodology, the class content, and the grading procedures. In their logs, we ask them to reflect on the character of thinking demanded and the classroom relationships: Does the teacher promote questioning and critique? What kinds of knowledge and understandings are valued in the class? What relationships between students are encouraged?

In her log, Elan focused on sexism in the hidden curriculum:

> In both biology and government, I noticed that not only do boys get more complete explanations to questions, they get asked more questions by the teacher than girls do. In government, even though our teacher is a

feminist, boys are asked to define a word or to list the different parts of the legislative branch more often than the girls are . . . I sat in on an advanced sophomore English class that was doing research in the library. The teacher, a male, was teaching the boys how to find research on their topic, while he was finding the research himself for the girls. Now, I know chivalry isn't dead, but we are competent in finding a book.

Linda and I were pleased as we watched students begin to gain a critical distance from their own schooling experiences. Unfortunately, Elan didn't speculate much on the social outcomes of the unequal treatment she encountered, nor on what in the society produces this kind of teaching. She did offer the observation that, "boys are given more freedom in the classroom than girls, and, therefore, the boys are used to getting power before the girls."

Here's an excerpt from Connie's log:

> It always amazed me how teachers automatically assume that where you sit will determine your grade. It's funny how you can get an A in a class you don't even understand. As long as you follow the rules and play the game, you seem to get by . . . On this particular day, we happen to be taking a test on chapters 16 and 17. I've always liked classes such as algebra that you didn't have to think. You're given the facts, shown how to do it, and you do it. No questions, no theories; it's the solid, correct way to do it.

We asked students to reflect on who in our society they thought benefitted from the methods of education to which they were subjected. Connie wrote:

> I think that not only is it the teacher, but more importantly, it's the system. They purposely teach you using the "boring method." Just accept what they tell you; learn it and go on; no questions asked. It seems to me that the rich, powerful people benefit from it, because we don't want to think; we're kept ignorant, keeping them rich.

Connie's hunch that her classes benefit the rich and powerful is obviously incomplete. But it does put her on the road to understanding that the degrading character of her education is not simply accidental. She's positioned to explore the myriad ways schooling is shaped by the imperatives of a capitalist economy. And instead of being just more of the "boring method," as Connie puts it, this social and historical study would be a personal search for her, rooted in her desire to understand the nature of her *own* school struggle.

In class, students struggled through a several-page excerpt form *Schooling in Capitalist America* by Sam Bowles and Herb Gintis. They read Bowles and Gintis' assertion that: ". . . major aspects of educational organization replicate the relationships of dominancy and subordinancy in the economic sphere. The correspondence between the social relation of schooling and work accounts for the ability of the educational system to produce an amenable and fragmented labor force. The experience of schooling, and not merely the content of formal learning, is central to this process." If Bowles and Gintis are right, we should expect to find different hidden curricula at schools enrolling students of different social classes. We wanted our students to test this notion for themselves. A friend, who teaches at a suburban high school south of Portland serving a relatively wealthy community, enlisted volunteers in her classes to host our students for a day. My students logged comparisons of Jefferson and the elite school I'll call Ridgewood. Trisa wrote:

> Now, we're both supposed to be publicly funded, equally funded, but
> not so. Jefferson, the average class size is 20–25 students; at Ridgewood—
> 15. Jefferson's cafeteria food is half-cooked, stale and processed.
> Ridgewood—fresh food, wide variety, and no mile-long lines to wait in.
> Students are allowed to eat anywhere in the building as well as outside,
> and wear hats and listen to walkmen (both rule violations at Jefferson).

About teachers' attitudes at Ridgewood, Trisa noted: "Someone said, 'We don't ask if you're going to college, but what college are you going to?'"

KNOWLEDGE CAN CREATE ANGER

In general, I was disappointed that students' observations tended to be more on atmosphere than on classroom dynamics. Still, what they noticed seemed to confirm that their own school, serving a black and working-class community, was a more rule-governed, closely supervised environment. The experience added evidence to the Bowles and Gintis contention that my students were being trained to occupy lower positions in the occupational hierarchy.

Students were excited by this sociological detective work. But intuitively, they were uneasy with the determinism of Bowles and Gintis' correspondence theory. It wasn't enough to discover that the relations of schooling mirrored the relations of work. They demanded to know exactly who designed a curriculum that taught them subservience. Was there a committee somewhere, sitting around plotting to keep them poor and passive? "We're always saying 'they' want us to do this, and 'they' want us to do that," one student said angrily. "Who is this 'they'?" Students wanted villains with faces and we were urging that they find systemic explanations.

Omar's anger exploded after one discussion. He picked up his desk and threw it against the wall, yelling: "How much more of this shit do I have to put up with?" This "shit" was his entire educational experience, and while the outburst was not directed at our class in particular—thank heavens—we understood our culpability for his frustrations.

We had made two important and related errors in our teaching. Implicitly, our search had encouraged students to see themselves as victims—powerless little cogs in a machine daily reproducing the inequities of the larger society. Though the correspondence theory was an analytical framework with a greater power to interpret their school lives than any other they had encountered, ultimately it was a model suggesting endless oppression and hopelessness. If schooling is always responsive to the needs of capitalism, then what point did our search have? Our observations seemed merely to underscore students' powerlessness.

The major problem was that although our class did discuss students' resistance, we did so anecdotally and unsystematically, and thereby deprived students of the opportunity to question their own roles in maintaining the status quo. The effect of this omission, entirely unintentional on our part, was to deny students the chance to see schools as sites of struggle and social change— places where they could have a role in determining the character of their own education. Unwittingly, the realizations students were drawing from our study of school fueled a worldview rooted in cynicism; they might learn about the nature and causes for their subordination, but they could have no role in resisting it.

Still stinging from my own pedagogical carelessness, I've made efforts this year to draw students into a dialogue about the dynamics of power and resistance. One of the most effective means to carry on this dialogue is metaphorically, through role-play and simulation.

In one exercise called the Organic Goodie Simulation, I create a three-tiered society: half the class members are workers, half unemployed. I'm the third tier: the owner of a machine that produces organic goodies.* I tell students that we will be in this classroom for the rest of our lives and that the machine produces the only sustenance. Workers can buy adequate goodies with their wages, but the unemployed will slowly starve to death on their meager dole of welfare-goodies. Everything proceeds smoothly until I begin to drive wages down by offering jobs to the unemployed for slightly less than the workers earn. It's an auction, with jobs going to the lowest bidder. Eventually, all classes organize some kind of opposition, and usually try to take away my machine. One year, a group of students arrested me, took me to a jail in the corner of the room, put a squirt gun to my head and threatened to "kill" me if I said another word. But this year, before students took over the machine, I backed off, called a meeting to which only my workers were invited, raised their wages and stressed to them how important it was that we stick together to resist the jealous unemployed people who wanted to drag all of us into the welfare hole that they were in. Some workers defected to the unemployed, some vigorously defended my right to manage the machine, but most bought my plea that we had to talk it out and reach unanimous agreement before any changes could be made. For an hour

* See Bill Bigelow and Norm Diamond, "The Power in Our Hands: A Curriculum on the History of Work and Workers in the United States," *Monthly Review*, 1988.

and a half they argued among themselves, egged on by me, without taking any effective action.

The simulation provided a common metaphor from which students could examine firsthand the issue we had not adequately addressed the previous year: to what extent are we complicit in our own oppression? Before we began our follow-up discussion, I asked students to write on who or what was to blame for the conflict and disruption of the previous day. In the discussion some students singled me out as the culprit. Stefani said, "I thought Bill was evil. I didn't know what he wanted." Rebecca concurred: "I don't agree with people who say Bill was not the root of the problem. Bill was management, and he made workers feel insecure that the unemployed were trying to take their jobs." Others agreed with Rebecca that it was a divisive structure that had been created, but saw how their own responses to that structure perpetuated their divisions and poverty. Christie said: "We were so divided that nothing got decided. It kept going back and forth. Our discouragement was the root of the problem." A number of people saw how their own attitudes kept them from acting decisively. Mira said: "I think that there was this large fear: we have to follow the law. And Sonia kept saying we weren't supposed to take over the machine. But if the law and property hurt people, why should we go along with it?" Gina said: "I think Bill looked like the problem, but underneath it all was us. Look at when Bill hired unemployed and fired some workers. I was doin' it too. We can say it's a role-play, but you have to look at how everything ended up feeling and learn something about ourselves, about how we handled it."

From our discussion students could see firsthand that their make-believe misery was indeed caused by the social structure: the number of jobs was held artificially low; workers and unemployed were pitted against each other for scarce goodies. As the owner I tried every trick I knew to drive wedges between workers and unemployed. By analyzing the experience, however, students could see that the system only worked because they let it work—they were much more than victims of my greed: they were my accomplices.

KNOWLEDGE DOES NOT ENSURE EMPOWERMENT

I should hurry to add—and emphasize—that it is not inherently empowering to understand one's own complicity in oppression. I think it's a start—because this understanding suggests that we can do something about it. But a critical pedagogy needs to do a lot more: it should highlight times, past and present, when people built alliances to challenge injustice. Students also need to encounter real live individuals and organizations active in working for a more egalitarian society; students need to be encouraged to see themselves as capable of joining together with others, in and out of school, to make needed changes. All of these are mandatory components of the curriculum. The danger of students becoming terribly cynical as they come to understand the enormity of injustice in this society and in the world is just too great. They have to know that it is possible—even joyous, if I dare say so—to work toward a more humane society.

At the outset I said that all teaching should be partisan. In fact, I think all teaching *is* partisan. Whether or not we want to be, all teachers are political agents because we help shape students' understandings of the larger society. That's why it's so important for teachers to be clear about our social visions. Toward what kind of society are we aiming? Unless teachers answer this question with clarity, we are reduced to performing as technicians, unwittingly participating in a political project with no comprehension of its objectives or consequences. Hence, teachers who claim "no politics" are inherently authoritarian because their pedagogical choices act upon students, but students are denied a structured opportunity to critique or act upon their teachers' choices. Nor are students equipped to reflect upon the effectiveness of whatever resistance they may put up.

For a number of reasons, I don't think our classrooms can ever be exact models of the kind of participatory democracy we would like to have characterize the larger society. If teachers' only power was to grade students, that would be sufficient to sabotage classroom democracy. However, as I've suggested, classrooms can offer students experiences and understandings which counter, and critique, the lack of democracy in the rest of their lives. The character of student interactions in the classroom can offer a glimpse of certain features of an egalitarian society. And we can begin to encourage students to learn the analytic and strategic skills to help bring this new society into existence. As I indicated, by creating a collective text of student experience we can offer students practice in understanding personal problems in their social contexts. Instead of resorting to consumption, despair, or other forms of self-abuse, they can ask, "Why?" and "What can I do about it?" While schools will never be the sole arena of social change, they are sites where students can begin to become the subjects of their lives.

Afterword:
Organizing and Teaching

- PAT -

Neesie and I attended the same high school, Whitney Young on the Near West Side, one of the top public high schools in Chicago. It is a magnet school where students are granted admission based upon their academic performance, attendance, and race. The school would like to maintain diversity, so they accept a certain number of African-American females, African-American males, white females, white males, Latino males, and on and on. Like most magnet schools in big cities, competition amongst minority students is high. African-American students from all over Chicago compete to gain admission into one of the few high schools that work, so needless to say, only Neesie, myself, and four other friends from our neighborhood, Cabrini-Green, attended this school during my entire four years. Due to white flight from large cities and public schools, there aren't many of them left in the system, and so whites fare better when it comes to gaining admission into magnet schools. Our school is one of the few integrated high schools in the city, and boasts the best graduation rate and highest standardized test scores for a public school.

One semester, Neesie and I found ourselves in a history class taught by Ms. Lisbon. One of her assignments over the course of the semester was a written and oral research project on the communities we lived in. During this time, in a very close race, Mayor Jane Byrne was running for re-election. There had been a recent rash of murders in our neighborhood, and, as a political ploy, the mayor moved briefly into one of the public housing apartments to dramatize the need to stop the senseless bloodshed. Cabrini consists of rowhouse apartments, and high-rises which range from seven to twenty stories high. My family lived in the rowhouses and

Neesie's family lived in the high-rises. Mayor Byrne moved into a high-rise, fully equipped with security guards and a limousine. The building that housed her "newly renovated" apartment was more secure than Fort Knox. This slap in the face was too much for residents who had lived in Cabrini for years in apartments in desperate need of repair, with police routinely treating all like criminals. No one ever knew if Jane Byrne spent one night in the projects and, of course, she never gave up her posh apartment on the Lakefront during her brief stay in our neighborhood. Nonetheless, our neighborhood was blasted on the news every night, night after night, because of this stunt. Unfortunately for us, shortly after this time, Ms. Lisbon assigned our community projects.

Neesie and I were terrified. She cornered me after class and asked, "Pat, what are you going to do? You won't tell them we live in Cabrini-Green, will you? I mean, with all the negative stuff that's being said on the news about us, I don't want them to know." In this integrated environment, we knew it wasn't cool to come from the projects. Our neighborhood elementary school was comprised of students just like us and this was our first experience in a racially and economically mixed setting. Most of the students at the school were from middle- or upper-class backgrounds and seemed fabulously rich to us. Our circle of friends knew where we lived, but other students assumed we all came from similar backgrounds.

The next day, Neesie approached me with an idea. Technically speaking, our community was called the "Near North Side" and consisted of many neighborhoods. The Near North Side was interesting because it was made up of neighborhoods that were extremely wealthy and depressingly poor. Our community encompassed the affluent Gold Coast (home of Chicago's Magnificent Mile and Mayor Byrne) and Cabrini-Green, with its high unemployment rate and a school drop-out rate of over sixty-five percent (and home to Mayor Byrne!). The Water Tower and Michigan Avenue's shopping district is a few minutes' walk away from where I grew up. Neesie decided we could tell our classmates we lived in Atrium Village. Atrium Village was a new, mixed-income development that had just been built and was located five minutes away from where we lived. I was torn between telling the truth and being ostracized, and telling a lie and feeling ashamed.

I went home and immediately began to work on the research project. I was intrigued by Neesie's idea to wrap ourselves up with our wealthy neighbors. For years, I experienced old ladies clutching their purses as I walked through those wealthy neighborhoods to go to the park or beach, and long stares from patrons of the nice grocery store as we hauled food by the shopping cart seven blocks away to our apartment. It was clear that we lived in two different worlds. I was surprised when I found out Italian immigrants were the first to inhabit Cabrini-Green. I had believed that only black people ever lived in public housing projects.

That night, I shared my apprehensions about the project with my mom and I asked her for advice. I remember the look in her eyes as she calmly said, "I know you will do the right thing. I believe in you and whatever decision you make will be a good one." Was that it?, I thought. I desperately wanted and needed my mother to tell me it was okay to tell my fellow students I lived in Atrium Village. She did not.

As weeks went by, I still didn't know what to do about my oral presentation. And then it hit me. Maybe there was a personal lesson to be learned that I had not thought about. After all, I was a good student who had the respect of my peers and teachers. This might be an opportunity to educate everyone on life in the projects from a realistic viewpoint, not Jane Byrne style. I began to figure out the right thing to do. I told Neesie about my intentions and she looked at me as if I had sold her out. "You won't tell them about me, will you?" she asked. I told her I wouldn't, but I encouraged her to tell the truth too.

My turn to present my project came. Doing the right thing was scary and lonely. I was very nervous as I stood before the class and told them all about my community, the North Side, and then about my neighborhood, the infamous Cabrini-Green. Of course, my classmates were shocked because I didn't fit the "stereotype." I told them how most of my friends in the neighborhood were just like me. Even though our neighborhood had a lot of problems, only a minority of Cabrini's residents were involved in illegal activities. I shared how my family moved to the neighborhood when I was a year old after my parents divorced. Most of my neighbors, like us, found themselves in public housing because they were out of work and had no other place to go. I talked about the black migration from the South (which my mom was part of) and how disappointed blacks were to find the promised land of milk and honey was not that much better than the segregated South they fled from. I told them how I felt about seeing my neighborhood raped by politicians and then abandoned. I pointed out that the honorable Jane Byrne moved out after a couple of months of bogus publicity, and the rest of the city soon forgot about Cabrini-Green and its residents. My classmates were extremely attentive and after my presentation there were lots of questions and everyone clapped for me. After the clapping subsided, I let them know I wasn't an exception. Yes, the drop-out rate was atrocious and, yes, gangs and drugs are prevalent, but I had several friends just like me, just like them, who were doing well in school. Unfortunately, we were seriously lacking resources and those making the decisions were not inclusive. Residents were almost never involved in setting policy for our neighborhood. This, in my mind, was part of the problem.

I did a great job. Ms. Lisbon told me how much she appreciated my forthrightness and honesty and thanked me. I later learned I received the highest grade for my thorough project.

The forty-minute bus ride home seemed longer than usual that afternoon. I couldn't wait to share my success with my mom. I knew that she had planted the seed for my success, and that she would have been hurt and disappointed if I had gone to school that day and lied. My mother was very proud of me and cooked a special dinner in my honor that evening.

Although it's been many years since I was assigned that project, that afternoon in a classroom at Whitney Young, I learned one of the most important lessons in my life. Since I spoke their language and was "socially acceptable," I had the power to educate and enlighten my peers and teacher about the plight of growing up poor and black in "this America.". From that point on, I knew it was important for me to share who I was as often as possible in relevant situations, if for no other reason than to help people understand from a firsthand account. The narrow view of who I was and where I came from had been defined by other people who thought I was worthless and vicious. In Derrick Bell's *Faces At The Bottom of The Well,* he writes:

> It is no accident that white writers have dominated the recording of race relations in this country: they are considered the more objective commentators on racial issues. For example, the litigation leading up to the Court's decision in Brown v. Board of Education has been well documented by Richard Kluger's *Simple Justice*—as the life and work of Dr. Martin Luther King Jr., by David Garrow and Taylor Branch, among other white writers, whose work covers the protest aspects of the civil rights movement. Black writers who have covered similar ground, however, have not received the attention or the rewards of their white colleagues. The writer Gloria Joseph summarizes the problem as, having commended as exemplary a white writer's essay on feminism and racism, she then acknowledges that the white writer "reiterates much that has been voiced by black female writers, but the acclaim given her article shows again that it takes whiteness to give even blackness validity." The black writer and poet bell hooks articulates the frustration resulting from this phenomenon when she complains: "We produce cultural criticism in the context of white supremacy. At times, even the most progressive and well-meaning white folks, who are friends and allies, may not understand why a black writer has to say something a certain way, or why we may not want to explain what has been said as though the first people we must always be addressing are privileged white readers."

Neesie's lesson, on the other hand, was one of shame and guilt. If you missed your first presentation, your grade was automatically lowered one letter. Neesie failed to show up for her presentation and she missed her reassigned make-up presentation. She received a zero for the project and an "F" for the quarter. She was absent the day I gave my presentation and even though I told her how well it went, I was unable to convince her to do her project. There was no investigation or interest by Ms. Lisbon of why Neesie failed to do her assignment. Good teachers establish a safe learning environment where differences are accepted and appreciated; a place where students learn from one another and know their contributions and experiences are valid and worthwhile. Ms. Lisbon missed an opportunity.

Reading an article in one of the major papers in Chicago about the recent takeover of the Chicago Housing Authority by HUD, my old neighborhood was described by a white writer as a place where "the poorest of Chicago's poor live." My neighborhood and its residents are so much more than that. It was here that I learned the importance of hard work and responsibility. It was here that I experienced my first kiss on the stairway of our cramped three-bedroom rowhouse apartment. It was here that I developed life-long friends who are there for me through thick and thin. It was here that my alcoholic neighbor of sixteen years gave me a card telling me how proud she was of me—with twenty-five dollars in it—before I went away to school. It was here that my mom prayed for my safe arrival home, when after being the first in my family to receive a driver's license, I insisted on renting a car and driving myself the three hours from college to Chicago. It was here that I called home.

As I continue to grow and develop, my childhood experiences in Cabrini-Green are at the core of my very being. I am constantly defining and shaping who I am and what I want to contribute to this world so those after me will know I was here. I am also helping those around me redefine for themselves who they are, in their own words, in their own way. While I acknowledge and embrace my childhood in public housing, I resist all labels that relegate me as the "Cabrini-Green poster girl." I am a daughter, sister, Christian, mother to my twin nieces, lover, friend, aunt, cousin, advocate, and educator. I am African-American, beautiful, proud, strong, weak, courageous, afraid, ambitious, happy, outraged, and blessed.

This past year, I was visiting my sisters on a hot summer day when I decided to go to the store to purchase some ice cream and cones for all my younger nieces and nephews. My great nephews, Ernie (a three year old) and Anthony (a five year old), accompanied me to the grocery store my family shopped at when I was a child.

Once in the store, I saw lots of odds and ends that I needed and began to pick up more items than I had originally planned. While standing in the checkout line, I realized I didn't have much cash on me so I frantically added up the total of my groceries in my head. I told the boys I might not have enough money to get everything and we would probably have to put a few items back. Anthony, with a huge grin on his face, said, "Auntie Pat, I have some money. My mom gave me a dollar the other day and I saved it. I'll give it to you and we'll have enough." He anxiously reached down, pulled off his shoe where his treasure was hidden and announced loudly, "Here's a dollar in food stamps. Now we have enough money." I anxiously and hurriedly told Anthony to put his money away as I glanced around me to see if other patrons in he store noticed our little exchange. A flood of old emotions hit me like a ton of bricks. I remembered coming to this grocery store as a kid and feeling humiliated. The checkout clerk would automatically assume I was paying with government food stamps. She would say, "Stamps, right?" On several occasions, we paid with cash because food stamps did not last through the end of the month. I always felt good when I proved her wrong and countered with, "No, I have cash." More times than I care to remember, I paid with food stamps and suffered through the scorn of the checkout clerk and the store's mostly middle-class patrons. Anthony didn't know that humiliation yet. I looked at his innocent and puzzled face, gave him a big hug and said, "I think we have enough money. You can save yours till next time, honey."

On a recent visit to the Water Tower Place, an upscale shopping mall on Chicago's Magnificent Mile, I saw an older white woman whom I met years ago shortly after graduating from college. She was the sales lady at an exclusive department store. We became acquainted during a storewide sale over eight years ago. Her name was Marge and she was especially helpful as I tried on outfit after outfit. She mentioned her recent retirement and informed me that she had been with the store for six months. Marge and her husband lived down the street in a condominium.

After much contemplation, I finally decided to purchase three out-fits. Marge rang them up and then I discovered they didn't accept Visa. Marge suggested I apply for their department store credit card since she could process my application quickly on the spot. As a recent college graduate with a new job, I was revelling in my new found freedom to obtain credit and decided to take her up on the offer. She proceeded to ask all the pertinent questions for an instant credit card, but when I gave her my address and zip code, she turned into Dr. Jekyll and Mr. Hyde. Marge gathered from the information I gave that I lived in Cabrini-Green. What made this clear to me was the tone of her voice, her shocked facial expression, and the insensitive comments, "We should stay with our own kind" and "There goes the neighborhood" which she mumbled under her breath.

I was stunned and hurt by this change in demeanor and it took me a moment to collect my thoughts and respond. I asked if there was something wrong and she answered "no," without looking me in the eyes. I was faced with a huge moral dilemma. If I walked out of the store, I would give her the satisfaction of rejecting me since she did not think I belonged there anyway. If I completed the transaction, I would suffer a more humiliating experience. I decided to stay. After the transaction was complete, I took my bag of new merchandise and reminded Marge that my money was as good as anyone else's. Obviously, I met the requirements for receiving credit and the department store was not "giving" me any-thing because of their ridiculously high interest rate. I suggested she look for another place of employment since she had problems serving all of the store's patrons and then walked away.

Over the next several weeks, I could not get this incident out of my head and I never wore my new clothes. They remained in the shopping bag with their price tags and tissue paper folded neatly around them. I went back to the store, returned everything and went to the management office where I detailed what happened. The manager on duty apologized and said he would handle the matter and thanked me for reporting the incident.

Seeing Marge in the mezzanine of the Water Tower Place and

visiting the grocery store both conjured up memories I hadn't thought about in a long time. Unknowingly, these separate but similar experiences have been buried for many years. Poverty's deepest wounds are those inflicted upon the human spirit. If we would dare to achieve the nobility of our purpose, we must teach with a sensitivity to the wounds of our pupils.

After graduating from high-school, I received a card from Mark addressed to "The Pat Ford." When I graduated from college, I received a card from Mark addressed to "The Pat Ford." When I was offered and accepted a full time position as Academic Director at c.y.c.l.e., I received a note of congratulations from Mark. It, too, was addressed to "The Pat Ford." On birthdays, at the completion of my master's degree, and during other moments of personal success and challenge, Mark always penned special notes of affirmation. They were always uniquely distinguished and addressed to "The Pat Ford."

I remember the first time I saw "The Pat Ford" and how special it made me feel. Somehow, these small but simple words validated my significance; they validated who I was.

Several years ago, Mark died from a sudden heart attack. I was among a thousand others who gathered at the memorial service to celebrate Mark's life. As I quietly sat and remembered Mark, I was profoundly impacted by his special ability to make others feel special. We first met when I was thirteen and he was forty-something. I came from a family of seven and he was married with four children. Mark was a teacher, preacher, and founder of several not-for-profit organizations that served young people and their families, including c.y.c.l.e. I began working at c.y.c.l.e. the summer prior to starting high school. Mark always greeted everyone with a twinkle in his eye and a firm handshake. His genuine interest in our lives connected with me and the other high school students who also worked at c.y.c.l.e. Through the years, Mark and I had managed to keep in touch.

During the ceremony, people were allowed a brief opportunity to approach a microphone and say a few words about Mark and what he meant to them. One by one, people from all walks of life recounted stories of how Mark had especially touched their lives. Blacks and whites, young and old, rich and poor, illiterate and educated, recovering alcoholics, students, the jobless and urban professionals—all were touched by Mark. Several people spoke of receiving special notes from Mark over the years. Many people shared how they were deeply impacted by Mark's special ability to craft notes of affirmation that made them feel especially valuable as people. After several stories about Mark's charming notes, each new story brought on the eruption of a contagious chuckle from the audience. We had all supposed that we were Mark's favorite.

I miss my friend. He possessed the rare capacity to add meaning and value to people's search for significance. I will long cherish the many lessons I've gleaned from his unique style of deliberate and intentional relationship building. He built connections with people that resulted in their being indelibly marked by his intentionally caring way.

I'm often regarded by friends and acquaintances as someone who has a good recall of names and faces. It is something that I work at rather diligently. I share myself in personal ways in an effort to let those around me know who and what I value. If this has added significance to peoples' lives, I owe this to my friend's credit. I guess it's contagious.

- BILL -

In the mid 1960s I became an organizer for the East Side Community Union in the Lakeview section of Cleveland, Ohio. The Community Union was an extension of the Southern civil rights movement into the North—a grassroots effort to organize disenfranchised and marginalized citizens of the ghetto into a powerful force capable of effectively fighting for their own needs and aspirations. Our buttons read "Let the People Decide," and "Build an Interracial Movement of the Poor." The other organizers and I believed then that legitimate and just social change should be led by those who had been pushed down and locked out, and that struggling in the interest of the most oppressed people in society held the key to a fundamental transformation that would ultimately benefit all people. We saw our political work as also ethical work—organizing and righteousness. I was twenty years old.

Our first job was to become part of the community, to listen hard to what people told us, to be respectful neighbors. We knocked on doors, talked around kitchen tables, hung out on stoops, and went to barbeques in the park. We were identifiable outsiders, of course, and we lived here by choice and with a larger purpose, but we were mindful of the fact that our agenda meant nothing unless it could be realized in light of the particular agendas of the people of Lakeview. We knew, too, that we did not want to build a "career" here, that the point of our work was to somehow, as we said at the time, "organize ourselves out of a job." We could perhaps be catalysts for change, but we could never substitute for indigenous, community leadership. We wanted to create organizations of, by, and for the poor.

I remember the day we knocked on Dolores Hill's door. "Oh, you're the civil rights kids from down the block," she exclaimed with a big welcoming smile. "I've been waiting for you. Come on in." We talked into the night about kids, welfare, schools, crime, dope, rent, gangs. It was the beginning of a beautiful friendship.

Dolores Hill was a natural leader, widely known and deeply respected. Perceptive, articulate, hard-working, honest, and tough, she had grown up on the block and was now raising her own children here. Active in her church and PTA, she was a person others looked to for guidance and help. When a child was hit by a car on Lakeview Avenue, it was Dolores Hill who called a meeting in her living room to press the city to install a stoplight; when a back-to-school welfare allowance was cut, Dolores Hill organized the protest; when a rat bit a youngster while she slept in her apartment, Dolores Hill thought up the rather dramatic tactic of taking a few rats with us downtown to the protest picket line, as well as the memorable accompanying slogan, "Get the rats out of Lakeview and City Hall." She was the first president of the Community Union.

Mrs. Hill opened meetings with a prayer. We would invariably sing a few songs—"Will the Circle Be Unbroken?" "This Little Light of Mine," "Oh Freedom!" Singing brought us together as a group of people, helped remind us of our common purpose, and made us all feel a little stronger. When Dolores Hill began to set the agenda, she would usually interject her own words of wisdom as introduction and frame: "Tonight we'll be talking about welfare rights. Now remember, just because you're poor and on welfare doesn't mean you're not a citizen, and citizens have rights"; or, "Now we'll move on to figuring out about starting a Children's Community preschool. Our children are poor, true, but that doesn't mean they don't have fine minds. We have to think about how to stimulate those minds."

Within a couple of years the East Side Community Union had become a vital part of the neighborhood. There was a large, dynamic welfare rights project affiliated with a national organization; there was a housing and rent strike committee organizing building by building, demanding fair rents and reasonable upkeep and repairs; there was a community health project led by two young doctors; there was a storefront office where people could drop in for coffee and conversation; and there was a preschool operating out of a church basement. All of these projects were built on the energy and intelligence of the people of Lakeview— energy and intelligence the society had largely ignored, locked up, and kept down. Dolores Hill never missed an opportunity to underline the point: "I'm poor because I haven't got any money. I'm not mentally ill! I'm not lazy! I'm not stupid!"

The Community Union lived for only a few years. It was founded shortly after Reverend Bruce Klinger was run over by an earth-mover and killed during a sit-in at the Lakeview Avenue construction site of what would become another segregated and marginalized school. It was gone by the time Ahmed Evans and a group of young nationalists engaged in a deadly shoot-out with the Cleveland police in a Lakeview Avenue apartment. In between there was struggle, hope, possibility, occasional heroism, and perhaps the most loving attempt we will ever see to change all that is glaringly wrong in our society.

In the midst of our efforts and in what some have called a cynical response to the massive upheaval among African-Americans, agents of government-sponsored poverty programs began to appear. Their first efforts involved a "community needs assessment" in which they surveyed neighborhood people in an attempt to define problems and craft solutions. They used a "scientifically" developed instrument, a questionnaire that could be easily quantified and rated. Instead of searching for the strengths and capacities in the community, they looked exclusively at deficiencies; instead of focusing on problems as shared and social, they probed individual deficits; instead of uncovering root causes and building focused strategies and tactics to bring about change, they stopped short of collective action. In brief, while they learned and applied the rhetoric of the civil rights movement, they shared none of its spirit or larger ethical and political purposes. Their approach was narrow, myopic, and certain to fail.

Dolores Hill, in the eyes of the poverty program workers, was a vast collection of ills. She had dropped out of high school, become pregnant at nineteen, and was a single mother with three young children, one of whom needed expensive glasses. She had been arrested once as a teenager for shoplifting, and had hung out at that time with a group of Lakeview Avenue youngsters who called themselves the Street Demons. Now she was on welfare, and she occasionally worked cleaning white people's houses while her oldest boy watched the children. She also took cash from the children's father, a long-distance truck driver who sometimes spent the night at her apartment. In other words Dolores Hill, by their account, represented the whole litany of behaviors that add up to a "culture of poverty" or a "tangle of pathologies": welfare cheat, gang member, criminal, unwed mother, neglectful parent, pregnant teen, high school drop-out, and so on. They were fairly drooling over her.

This kind of portrait was rather easily sketched of many people in Lakeview. It is, of course, a false picture—incomplete, negative, pretentious, self-fulfilling. It fails to see human life as embedded, dynamic, complex, and contradictory—powered by chance as well as choice, directed by mind and meaning as much as punishment and reward. It highlights certain isolated incidents in a life at the expense of other incidents. It attributes explanatory power to those incidents, a procedure that would never be allowed if the subjects were white and well-off. I (and many others I know and have known) could be tagged and stuck with several of these labels depending on how the observer looked and where the action was stopped—let's see . . . gang member, criminal, drug involved, drop-out. But I would never be tarred as representing a "culture of poverty"—the privileges of race and background that accrue to me by accident and chance.

The pathology portrait of the poor conveniently lumps those few selected items and incidents together to fit a preconceived, stereotyped view. Embraced by conservatives and liberals alike, this facile view assumes that the existing social system and structure is fundamentally fine, any problems related to race and class are relics of the past, and anyone should be able to do well now unless plagued by some complex, difficult to change, *internal* psychocultural effects. In other words "we've done too much already" (conservatives) or "we've done as much as we can" (liberals) and we'll all hope for *"those people"* to get it together or somehow disappear.

Not surprisingly, the programs proposed as a result of this kind of shoddy, suspect analysis tend to be unhelpful at best, often debilitating or even harmful. They offer services rather than solidarity. They turn people into clients rather than assisting them to become agents. They perpetuate dangerous generalities and degrading stereotypes about individuals, and, most important, they fail to identify or uncover any underlying structural causes that might generate the problems in the first place—they find no enemies except those posited, presumed traits within poor people themselves.

In those years I was both an organizer and a teacher—roles I found complementary and analogous. Whether knocking on doors or teaching a class, I began with an attempt to see the person, to hear him or her, to understand what she was going through. Each vocation is rooted, after all, in relationship and an abiding faith in the human capacity to grow and learn—a facility that is natural, inherent, and intense. Each is built upon a belief that all people— kids, parents, teachers, citizens—bring an intelligence with them to the school or the community meeting, and that intelligence is the starting point for action and further learning. These are basic democratic values, values that we fought for then, and are still fighting for now. To talk of irreversibility or the irredeemable, to talk of bell curves and absolute deficiencies, to talk of hopelessness is to raise bells of alarm in every fiber of an organizer's or a teacher's being.

I taught at the Children's Community, our church basement preschool, and I worked with Head Start, one of the few truly hopeful programs emerging from the War on Poverty. Attacked by conservatives at its inception as a communist plot, the socializing of child-rearing, and a frontal assault on family values, Head Start has become sanctified as a symbol of doing something good for the poor (even as it is constantly and quietly eroded, menaced, and cut back). But it is worth remembering that liberals justified Head Start as a program that would create a "level playing field" for youngsters, without questioning the meritocratic and hierarchic realities of schools and society, and that once again the poor were blamed for their situations. The first brochures explaining Head Start to parents and staff described the poor as living in "islands of nothingness." It was from this nothingness that children were to be lifted up and brought into the "human family." This is not policy that loves or supports families or parents or children. It is not policy that understands or builds upon strengths. Rather this kind of policy makes the cost of participation acceptance of degrading and self-denying generalizations.

Like the organizer, the fundamental message of the teacher is this: you can change your life. Whoever you are, wherever you've been, whatever you've done, the teacher invites you to a second chance, another round, perhaps a different conclusion. The teacher posits possibility, openness, and alternative; the teacher points to what could be, but is not yet. The teacher beckons you to change your path, and so she has but one basic rule, which is to reach.

But of course the teacher can only create a context, set a stage, open a curtain. The teacher's task is excruciatingly complex precisely because it is idiosyncratic and improvisational—as inexact as a person's mind or a human heart, as unique and inventive as a friendship or falling in love. The teacher's work is all about background, environment, setting, surround, position, situation, connection. And relationship. It is about having one eye on the students before you—three-dimensional, complex, trembling, and real—and one eye on the world we share—dynamic, complex, in need of repair. As Martin Heidegger said, teaching is tougher than learning in one respect: teaching requires the teacher to *let learn*. Learning requires action, choice, and assent from the student. Teaching, then, is undertaken with hope, but without guarantees. Teaching, like organizing, is an act of faith.

- PAT -

Freddie was a first-grade student I met while student teaching at an elementary school years ago. Ms. Howard, my cooperating teacher, was an African-American woman in her mid-forties. Even though Ms. Howard and I spoke on the phone to introduce ourselves and establish a date to meet, we each assumed the other was white, and we had a good laugh when we finally met. Ms. Howard had never met an African-American student teacher from my predominantly white university, and I never had the fortune of working with one of the few African-American teachers in the system.

Ms. Howard was a traditional teacher. Her primary method for reading instruction was phonics. There were daily dictation assignments, weekly spelling tests, biweekly timed math tests, daily reading selections from a basal text, and weekly story hour sessions. Students either read the daily selection silently at their seats, or read round-robin as a class. Either way, questions from Ms. Howard about the reading selection would follow.

The classroom consisted of twenty-five students; ten African-Americans, ten whites, three Latinos, and two Asians. Immediately, I noticed an African-American boy who was slightly larger than his classmates and a bit unkempt, clothed in an outfit three sizes too big, sitting at his desk staring idly out the window as Ms. Howard gave instructions. His name was Freddie. I soon learned that he was infamous for his behavior during daily recess time. Negative reports on Freddie's lack of self-control from teachers assigned to recess were a regular phenomenon. Freddie was the first to be blamed by his fellow classmates in any altercation whether guilty or not, and he returned their scorn with his fists if someone accidentally stepped on his foot or bumped him while getting in line. Freddie slept most of the day or gazed idly out of the window. As I was recording grades in Ms. Howard's record book, I noticed Freddie had straight F's. When I asked Ms. Howard what the story was with Freddie, she quickly told me while rolling her eyes, "Freddie is from the 'valley', and he is repeating first grade. I know he isn't learning much, but just to have him sitting quietly is accomplishment enough. The students and I have learned to ignore Freddie and he seems as happy with this arrangement as the rest of us."

The "valley" was the term used for the poor, African-American community in town, and saying he was from the "valley" was supposed to explain it all. My heart immediately went out to Freddie, for I was a "valley girl" too. My neighborhood in Chicago, Cabrini-Green, had a national reputation.

For that entire first week, I watched Ms. Howard ignore Freddie. By Friday, I felt I could no longer contain myself. After students were dismissed, I confronted my cooperating teacher. "How could you show total disregard for a little boy by acting as if he was invisible?" I said. "And what about your obligation as an African-American teacher to help the Freddies of this world? I long ago learned that not all African-Americans share the same experiences, but shouldn't we, of all people, empathize with our less fortunate brothers and sisters?"

I now know that victims of racism can be racists. I had come to college because I thought it would equip me with the ammunition I needed to further the fight against poverty and inequity. After four years of disillusionment, my last shred of hope was unraveling before me. I knew that Ms. Howard would be responsible for the grade I received, but I had to speak out, and I did. Although a bit taken aback, Ms. Howard managed to respond somewhat cynically, "Freddie is now your project. Let's see what you can do with him and the other twenty-four students in this classroom." Our initially hopeful relationship was in jeopardy. I left that Friday afternoon depressed.

To her credit, Ms. Howard phoned me over the weekend to call a truce. We talked a lot about my experiences with children in Chicago and about our lives. Ms. Howard was divorced and raising two teenage sons alone. She was originally from a small southern town, and had moved north right after she married her husband. Her eldest son was a freshman at a nearby state university and she was helping him raise his one-and-a-half-year-old daughter. The child's mother was forced by her parents to give the child up for adoption and Ms. Howard's son wanted desperately to be a part of his daughter's life. He presented his mom with the plan. Ms. Howard, having raised her sons alone, agreed to take care of the little girl as long as he continued his education. This arrangement also gave the young mother of the child the opportunity to be involved in her daughter's life. Ms. Howard's son worked in addition to being a full-time student, and came home every weekend to participate in raising his daughter.

I discussed my family's background with Ms. Howard. I had recently been informed by my mom that my youngest brother dropped out of high school despite her desperate appeals. For most of his elementary-school life, my little brother was, like Freddie, invisible. He was quiet and shy and always behind in school. He wasn't a discipline problem, but because he learned at a different pace from the rest of his classmates, he became a burden for his teachers. His teachers, over the years, took the easy way out. They ignored him. Like Ralph Ellison's "invisible man," my brother could have written, "I am invisible, understand, simply because others refuse to see me." My brother, Freddie, and countless other African-American children are ignored every day in large, urban school settings. Now at the age of seventeen, my brother had had enough.

Ms. Howard and I apologized to one another for last Friday's debacle and started to discuss a strategy for Freddie. l was determined to "see" Freddie.

Over the next several months, I developed a relationship with Freddie. I learned that his favorite food was fried chicken and that he hated green beans. I learned Freddie sucked his thumb at night and had a knack for telling stories and jokes. I learned about his hobbies and interests, and how he spent his time after school. I started writing Freddie's stories down while he dictated, and then we produced books that he illustrated. We started a vocabulary list based upon these stories and this became the week's spelling lesson. I combined these methods with phonics, which was the reading instructional method adopted by the school. Over a period of time, Freddie began writing and reading his own stories and jokes. One week, during story hour, I stepped out on faith and asked him to read one of his stories aloud during story hour. Although a bit hesitant, Freddie conceded. His classmates and Ms. Howard were amazed! Freddie could actually read, and he had a sense of humor, too. His books of stories and jokes became favorites of the class. Freddie's triumphant smile was all I needed to confirm that the weeks of cajoling, frustration, and patience had paid off.

I was now on to my next challenge. I desperately wanted to meet Freddie's mother. While I knew the teacher/parent partnership was important, it was nonexistent between Ms. Howard and Freddie's mother. Ms. Howard hinted that I was undertaking an impossible feat, since the family's phone service was almost always disconnected and his mother never responded to notes she sent home with Freddie. Although his mother attended one parent/teacher conference, Ms. Howard decided that she, just like most single welfare mothers, didn't care about Freddie.

I, on the other hand, firmly believe most parents, even those addicted to drugs, want their children to do well, just as I believe that most teachers go into the field of education for all of the right reasons. While not excusing or condoning every behavior, I know many single moms in my neighborhood have a hard time negotiating life. Stretching a welfare check to put food on the table daily and raising children consumes a lot of energy and time. And no, after twenty-one years of living in public housing, I have never met a "welfare queen." And what about those single mothers sitting at home all day watching soap operas and talk shows while our hard-earned tax dollars pay for their shiftlessness? I've never seen it—not like that. The huge number of women raising families on limited, fixed incomes is indicative of larger social issues and problems. Love, safety, food, and shelter are basic needs for all humans. Some women I know are mothers out of ignorance, some seeking love. Too many have given up hope altogether. Adults with unmet needs raise needy children. Combine this with racism, class hierarchies, unemployment, physical isolation (most public housing complexes and poor neighborhoods are islands of oppression and deprivation), and a lack of resources and opportunities, and you get a state of despair that is pervasive and often overwhelming.

I sent a note home asking Freddie's mother to come for a conference at her convenience one day after school. After two days with no response, I sent home another note. No response. Freddie then informed me of his mom's need to pick up his younger sister from preschool every afternoon. On the third note, I asked if I could meet her at her home one evening if it was more convenient. I also noted how excited I was to share Freddie's progress over the last several weeks with her. The following day, I received a response with a scribbled date and time.

When we met at their small, tidy apartment full of second-hand furniture, it was obvious Freddie's young mother loved her children. As I listened to her tell me stories about the disrespectful, contemptuous treatment she received from the school by teachers and administrators, it all sounded too familiar: teachers blaming parents for their children's failure, and parents blaming teachers. Freddie's mom, like countless other parents who are poor and black, felt she was talked down to and only called by the school to hear one negative report after another. She was happily surprised I wanted to meet with her to talk about his success at school, since it was the first time a teacher had something good to say about her son. We swapped strategies on how to get Freddie to follow through on his homework, and I gave her ideas of how to use household materials to help Freddie bolster his addition and subtraction abilities. Even though she was convinced that other students "picked on" Freddie, and in some instances this was true, I solicited her help in coming up with ways to help Freddie control his temper. I loaned her some books and asked her to listen to Freddie read, and to read to him every night. I also suggested he read to his younger sister. She agreed. Two weeks later, I received a note requesting more books and an invitation for dinner. After I accepted the invitation, she wanted to know if I liked fried chicken.

My success with Freddie was not miraculous. Progress was sometimes slow, tedious, and draining, but teachers must invest in the lives of their Freddies. I have heard many teachers complain over the years, "I am not a social worker. I can't fix all their problems. It's my job to teach my students some skills and if they can't grasp the concepts, it's their problem." Marian Wright Edelman counters with this challenge: "How many potential Colin Powells, Bill Cosbys, Alice Walkers, Condoleeza Rices, Sally Rides, Gloria Steinems, Barbara McClintocks, Wilma Mankillers, Daniel Inouyes, Henry Cisneroses, and Cesar Chávezes will our nation waste before it wakes up and recognizes that its ability to compete and lead in the new century is as inextricably intertwined with its poor nonwhite children as with its white privileged ones, with its girls as well as its boys? Every one of our shrinking pool of children should be seen as a blessing rather than a burden: as potential leaders and workers rather than as problems. We tend to get what we expect and seek."

How do we help each teacher envision a future for his or her students that is not pathological? How do we counter society's indifference toward poor children of color? This is a monumental task, a teacher's task. Teachers must believe their students can experience a future that is full of hope, promise, and potential, or they should, quite simply, not teach our children.

This past spring, Terry B., a thirty-one-year-old African-American male, was gunned down while pumping gas at the Amoco station near Cabrini-Green. Terry was a known gang leader and high school drop-out. Routinely, he shot at other rival gang members while protecting his gang and drug turf. As a consequence, he was often shot at by others. Another African-American male accousted Terry while he was pumping gas and shot him at twice close range in the head. Terry died immediately. The police arrived, but, because he was already dead, they had to wait for a paddy wagon, commonly referred to as the "meat truck" to pick up his body. His slain body lay for over two hours before the paddy wagon showed up as his family and onlookers stood by in horror. Within the half hour, the bloody spot where this young man's body once laid was hosed down and washed clean. The yellow police tape was removed and business went on as usual at the gas station.

Terry, like many other African-American males, was on a path that led to destruction. Regretably, he was a benefactor of a school system that places little value on the education of African American boys. Our society prefers to build more prisons before funds are allocated to educate children of color in an equitable fashion. Over seventy percent of young men who are incarcerated are high school drop-outs. This correlation shows us the huge price we pay in the end for not investing in young lives up front. Unfortunately, scenes like the one above are commonplace in most economically disadvantaged neighborhoods. Ironically, Terry B. was the first boy I slow danced with in the seventh grade to the song, "Always and Forever" by Heatwave.

Many teachers know what it means to teach against the grain, against oppression, opposition, and obstinacy. Against a history of evil. Against glib, commonsense assumptions. I remember reading Frederick Douglass' account of his master exploding in anger when he discovered that his wife had taught the young Douglass to read: "It will unfit him to he a slave."

Education lives an excruciating paradox precisely because of its association with and location in schools. Education is about opening doors, opening minds, opening possibilities. School is too often about sorting and punishing, grading and ranking and certifying. Education should be unconditional—asking nothing in return. School demands obedience and conformity as a precondition to attendance. Education is surprising and unruly and disorderly, while the first and fundamental law of school is to follow orders. A real educator unleashes the unpredictable, while a defeated schoolteacher starts with an unhealthy obsession with classroom management.

In teaching, as in organizing, you need to be intensely aware of what you value, what you honor, what you stand for. Otherwise you will become the person you now despise. Even with this awareness, the machinery of schooling will work on you like water on rock—it will wear you down, shape you and smooth you. Soon, if you're not careful, your life will begin to make a mockery of your values. Resisting this fate involves conscious struggle, an attempt to find allies among the students, the parents, the teachers, and the citizenry. It requires collective action. It requires wedding your consciousness to your conduct, and it involves taking responsibility for yourself, your work, the world you see and can understand. Mikhail Bakhtin sums up this idea:

> What is it that guarantees the internal connection between the elements of personality? Only the unity of responsibility. For what I have experienced and understood, . . . I answer with my life.

An essential challenge to city teachers is this: Can we make education take root and bloom on the hard surfaces of urban schools? That is the job. Accept nothing less.

To be a successful city teacher you need to commit to a lifetime of learning, growing, developing, moving. You need to commit to staying wide awake and aware. You should research the city, certainly, to keep discovering its possibilities, and you should, as well, study culture, art, architecture, history, music, geography, math, physics, literature, sociology, urban planning, and much else. In this search, city kids and city parents will be your most persistent allies if you will invite them in. We offer here not a definitive list, but an invitation to a few books, a few films, a few works of imagination that have opened us to things as they are, and things as they might be but are not yet. These could be worthwhile to you, to a teacher's study group, or to a class of youngsters involved in their own quests.

City Kids

Ellen A. Brantlinger, Susan M. Klein and Samuel L. Guskin. *Fighting for Darla*. New York: Teachers College Press, 1994.

Ben Carson. *Gifted Hands*. MI: Zondervan Books, 1990.

Jay Dand, ed. *Growing Up Black*. New York: Avon Books, 1968.

Lisa Delpit. *Other People's Children*. New York: The New Press, 1995.

Mary Frosch, ed. *Coming of Age in America*. New York: The New Press, 1994.

Janice E. Hales-Benson. *Black Children, Their Roots, Culture, and Learning Styles*. Baltimore: Johns-Hopkins University Press, 1986.

Phillip Hoose. *It's Our World Too*. Boston: Little, Brown & Co., 1993.

Ben Joravsky. *Hoop Dreams*. Atlanta: Turner Publishing, Inc., 1995.

Susanna Kaysen. *Girl, Interrupted*. New York: Vintage Books, 1993.

Herbert Kohl. *Golden Boy as Anthony Cool*. New York: Dial, 1972.

Alex Kotlowitz. *There Are No Children Here*. New York: Doubleday, 1991.

Sylvester Monroe and Peter Goldman. *Brothers*. New York: Newsweek, 1988.

Shooting Back from the Reservation: A Photographic View of Life by Native American Youth selected by Jim Hubbard. New York: The New Press, 1994.

Women's Action Coalition. *WAC Stats: The Facts About Women*. New York: The New Press, 1993.

Malcolm X and Alex Haley. *The Autobiography of Malcolm X*. New York: Ballantine, 1973.

Marge Tye Zuba. *Wish I Could've Told You: Portraits of Teenagers Almost Dropping Out*. DeKalb, IL: LEPS Press, 1995.

City Issues

At Home in Our Schools. Oakland, CA: Developmental Studies Center, 1994.

James A. Banks. *Multiethnic Education*. Boston: Allyn & Bacon, 1994.

Derrick Bell. *Faces at the Bottom of the Well*. New York: Basic Books, 1992.

Rita S. Brause. *Enduring Schools*. Washington, DC: The Falmer Press, 1992.

James Comer. *Maggie's American Dream*. New York: New American Library, 1988.

James Comer. *School Power*. New York: Free Press, 1980.

Harriet K. Cuffaro. *Experimenting with the World*. New York: Teachers College Press, 1995.

Louise Derman-Sparks. *Anti-Bias Curriculum*.

Marian Wright Edelman. *The Measure of Our Success: A Letter to My Children and Yours*. Boston: Beacon Press, 1992.

Kieran Egan and Dan Nadane. *Imagination and Education*. New York: Teachers College Press, 1988.

Kieran Egan. *Teaching as Story Telling*. Chicago: University of Chicago Press, 1986.

Michelle Fine, ed. *Chartering Urban School Reform.* New York: Teachers College Press, 1994.

Michelle Fine. *Framing Dropouts.* New York: SUNY, 1991.

Norm Fruchter, Anne Galleta and J. Lynne White. *New Directions in Parent Involvement.* Washington, DC: Academy for Educational Development, 1992.

Nikki Giovanni. *Racism 101.* New York: W. Morrow & Co., 1994.

Andrew Hacker. *Two Nations: Black and White, Separate, Hostile, Unequal.* New York: Charles Scribner's Sons, 1992.

Linda Darling Hammond. *Authentic Assessment in Action.* New York: Teachers College Press, 1995.

Shirley Brice Heath and Milbrey W. McLaughlin, eds. *Identity and Inner-City Youth.* New York: Teachers College Press, 1993.

Don Hellison. *Teaching Responsibility Through Physical Activity.* Champaign, IL: Human Kinetics, 1995.

Hinojosa, Maria. *Crews: Gang Members Talk to Maria Hinojosa.* San Diego: Harcourt Brace & Co., 1994.

bell hooks. *Art on My Mind: Visual Politics.* New York: The New Press, 1995.

bell hooks. *Black Looks: Race & Representation.* Boston: South End Press, 1992.

bell hooks. *Teaching to Transgress.* New York: Routledge, 1994.

Lisa Jones. *Bulletproof Diva.* New York: Doubleday, 1994.

Herbert Kohl. *I Won't Learn From You.* New York: The New Press, 1994.

Jonathan Kozol. *Savage Inequalities.* New York: Crown Publishers, 1991.

Jawanza Kunjufu. *Countering the Conspiracy to Destroy Black Boys.* Chicago: African American Images, 1985.

Mary O. Lewis. *Herstory: Black Female Rites of Passage.* Chicago: African American Images, 1988.

Sara Lawrence Lightfoot. *The Good High School.* New York: Basic Books, Inc., 1985.

Sara Lawrence Lightfoot. *Worlds Apart.* New York: Basic Books, Inc., 1978.

Douglas S. Massey and Nancy A. Denton. *American Apartheid.* Cambridge, MA: Harvard University Press, 1993.

Peter McLaren. *Schooling as Ritual Performance.* New York: Routledge, 1986.

Milbrey McLaughlin, Merita Irby, and Juliet Langman. *Urban Sanctuaries.* San Francisco: Jossey-Bass, Inc., 1994.

Milton Meltzer. *Cheap Raw Material: How Our Youngest Workers Are Exploited and Abused.* New York: Viking, 1994.

Gary Paul Nabhan and Stephen Trimble. *The Geography of Childhood.* Boston: Beacon Press, 1994.

Nel Noddings. *Educating for Intelligent Belief or Unbelief.* New York: Teachers College Press, 1993.

Vito Perrone. *Working Papers: Reflections on Teachers, Schools and Communities.* New York: Teachers College Press, 1989.

Frank Pignatelli and Susanna W. Pflaum. *Celebrating Diverse Voices.* Newbury Park, CA: Corwin Press, 1993.

Frank Pignatelli and Susanna W. Pflaum, eds. *Experiencing Diversity, Toward Educational Equity.* Thousand Oaks, CA: Corwin Press, 1994.

Rethinking our Classrooms: Teaching for Equity and Justice, a special edition of *Rethinking Schools,* 1994.

Mara Sapon-Shevin. *Playing Favorites.* Albany: SUNY Press, 1994.

Jonathan G. Silin. *Sex, Death and the Education of Children.* New York: Teachers College Press, 1994.

Christine E. Sleeter and Carl A. Grant. *Making Choices for Multicultural Education.* New York: Macmillan, 1994.

J. David Smith. *Pieces of Purgatory: Mental Retardation, In and Out of Institutions.* Pacific Grove, CA: Brooks/Cole Publishing Co., 1995.

Joel Spring. *The Sorting Machine Revisited.* New York: Longman, 1989.

Cornel West. *Race Matters.* New York: Vintage, 1993.

Patricia J. Williams. *The Alchemy of Race and Rights.* Cambridge, MA: Harvard University Press, 1991.

City Teachers

Cynthia Stokes Brown, ed. *Ready from Within: Septima Clark and the Civil Rights Movement*. Navarro, CA: Wild Trees Press, 1986.

Kathleen Casey. *I Answer with my Life*. New York: Routledge, 1993.

Paulo Freire. *Pedagogy of the City*. New York: Continuum, 1993.

John Taylor Gatto. *Dumbing Us Down*. Philadelphia: New Society Publishers, 1992.

James Herndon. *Notes From a School Teacher*. New York: Simon & Schuster, 1985.

bell hooks. *Teaching to Transgress*. New York: Routledge, 1994.

Myles Horton and Paulo Freire. *We Make the Road by Walking*. Philadelphia: Temple University Press, 1990.

Pamela Bolotin Joseph and Gail E. Burnaford, eds. *Images of Schoolteachers in Twentieth-Century America*. New York: St. Martin's Press, 1994.

Phillip Lopate. *Being with Children*. New York: Poseidon Press, 1975.

Deborah Meier. *The Power of Their Ideas*. Boston: Beacon Press, 1995.

Ned O'Gorman. *The Storefront*. New York: Harper & Row, 1970.

Susan Ohanian. *Who's in Charge: A Teacher Speaks Her Mind*. Portsmouth: Boynton/Cook, 1995.

Vito Perrone. *A Letter to Teachers*. San Francisco: Jossey-Bass Publishers, 1991.

Mike Rose. *Possible Lives*. New York: Houghton Mifflin, 1995.

Deborah Stern. *Teaching English So it Matters*. Thousand Oaks, CA: Corwin Press, 1995.

Patricia A. Wasley. *Stirring the Chalkdust*. New York: Teachers College Press, 1994.

Howard Zinn. *You Can't be Neutral on a Moving Train*. Boston: Beacon Press, 1994.

Mixed Media

Sandra Cisneros. *The House on Mango Street*. New York: Knopf, 1994.

Toni Morrison. *Jazz*. New York: Knopf, 1992.

Anna Deavere Smith. *Fires in the Mirror*. New York: Avalon/Doubleday, 1993.

Amy Tan. *The Kitchen God's Wife*. New York: G. P. Putnam's Sons, 1991.

Films/Movies

Boyz 'N the Hood. John Singleton, 1991.

Do The Right Thing. Spike Lee, 1989.

Higher Learning. John Singleton, 1995.

Hoop Dreams. Steve James, 1994.

Kids. Larry Kramer, 1995.

Laurel Avenue. Carl Franklin, 1993.

Lean On Me. John Avildsen, 1989.

Malcolm X. Spike Lee, 1992.

Menace II Society. The Hughes Brothers, 1993.

Stand and Deliver. Ramon Menendez, 1988.

Taxi Driver. Martin Scorsese, 1976.

JAMES BALDWIN was a renowned novelist and a searing essayist. Born the son of a Harlem minister, he was an astute observer and incisive critic of the American scene.

BILL BIGELOW teaches high school history in Portland, Oregon and is an associate at *Rethinking Schools*.

LYNN CHERKASKY-DAVIS is the founder and lead teacher at the Foundations School, an innovative Chicago public school.

CONSTANCE CLAYTON is a school reform activist and former superintendent of Philadelphia public schools.

LISA DELPIT is a professor at Georgia State University and winner of a MacArthur Fellowship. Her writings, including the award-winning book *Other People's Children,* have sparked a wide and deep struggle among progressive educators.

MARTIN HABERMAN is Professor of Education at the University of Wisconsin at Milwaukee.

LOUANNE JOHNSON is the author of *My Posse Don't Do Homework.*

JUNE JORDAN is an essayist, critic, novelist, playwright, and poet. She writes of rage and love, and the ways the two must feed each other.

GLORIA LADSON-BILLINGS is an associate professor of education at the University of Wisconsin at Madison. She is the author of *The Dreamkeepers.*

LEWIS H. LAPHAM is the editor of *Harper's.*

AUDRE LORDE was a poet, political activist, feminist, and spiritual mother of the modern lesbian movement. *ZAMI,* the title of her autobiography, is a Carriacou name for women who work together as friends and lovers.

DEBORAH MEIER is the founder of Central Park East and the movement to create innovative small public schools in New York. A MacArthur Fellow, she is president of the Center for Collaborative Education.

NELSON PEERY was a hobo and itinerant laborer. He became a revolutionary as a U.S. soldier during World War II. He credits Meridel Le Seur with teaching him to write.

BOB PETERSON is a founding editor of *Rethinking Schools* newspaper and teaches fifth grade at La Escuela Fratney in Milwaukee, Wisconsin. He is cochair of the National Coalition of Education Activists, and Wisconsin Teacher of the Year for 1995.

JAY REHAK is a songwriter, father, and social activist who teaches English at Whitney Young High School in Chicago.

LUIS RODRIGUEZ is an award-winning poet and writer. Once a convicted felon, arsonist, robber, and drug addict, Rodriguez is currently working on a book of essays, a short story collection, and a screenplay.

YOLANDA SIMMONS and **PAT BEARDEN** are both Chicago public school teachers who happen to be twins.

SAM SMITH is editor of *The Progressive Review* and writes extensively on urban issues. He was a cofounder of the Washington D.C. statehood movement, and is author of *Shadows of Hope: A Freethinker's Guide to Politics in the Time of Clinton* (Indiana University Press).

DEBORAH STERN is a high school teacher and school reform activist in Chicago, author of *Teaching English So It Matters* (Corwin Press).

RITA TENORIO, a former Teacher of the Year in Wisconsin, is program implementor at La Escuela Fratney in Milwaukee, Wisconsin. She is a founding editor of *Rethinking Schools* newspaper.

WILLIAM UPSKI WIMSATT is a writer, graffiti artist, participant in and documenter of the hip-hop scene.